Adobe® Premiere®
Elements 11

CLASSROOM IN A BOOK®

The official training workbook from Adobe Systems

DVD-ROM Included for Windows and Mac OS

Adobe Press books are published by Peachpit, a division of Pearson Education located in Berkeley, California. For the latest on Adobe Press books, go to www.adobepress.com. To report errors, please send a note to errata@peachpit.com. For information on getting permission for reprints and excerpts, contact permissions@peachpit.com.

Writer: Jan Ozer
Editor: Connie Jeung-Mills
Development Editor: Stephen Nathans-Kelly
Copyeditor: Anne Marie Walker
Production Editors: Katerina Malone, Cory Borman
Keystroker: John Cruise
Compositor: David Van Ness
Indexer: Jack Lewis
Cover design: Eddie Yuen
Interior design: Mimi Heft

Printed and bound in the United States of America

ISBN-13:   978-0-321-88372-8
ISBN-10:   0-321-88372-1

9 8 7 6 5 4 3 2 1

WHAT'S ON THE DISC

Here is an overview of the contents of the Classroom in a Book disc

The *Adobe Premiere Elements 11 Classroom in a Book* disc includes the lesson files that you'll need to complete the exercises in this book, as well as other content to help you learn more about Adobe Premiere Elements 11 and use it with greater efficiency and ease. The diagram below represents the contents of the disc, which should help you locate the files you need.

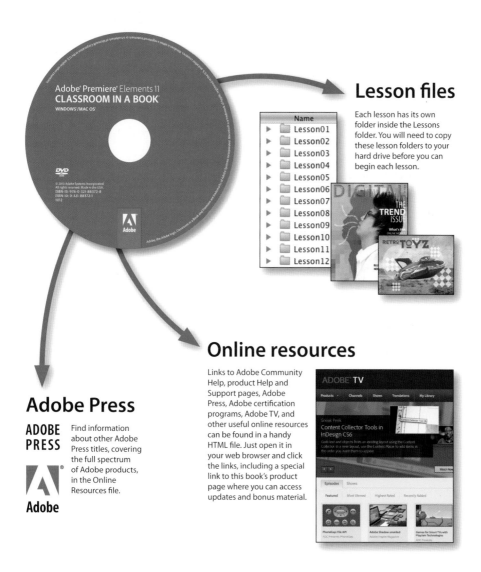

Lesson files

Each lesson has its own folder inside the Lessons folder. You will need to copy these lesson folders to your hard drive before you can begin each lesson.

Online resources

Links to Adobe Community Help, product Help and Support pages, Adobe Press, Adobe certification programs, Adobe TV, and other useful online resources can be found in a handy HTML file. Just open it in your web browser and click the links, including a special link to this book's product page where you can access updates and bonus material.

Adobe Press

ADOBE PRESS

Find information about other Adobe Press titles, covering the full spectrum of Adobe products, in the Online Resources file.

CONTENTS

GETTING STARTED

Adobe® Premiere® Elements 11 delivers video editing tools that balance power and versatility with ease of use. Adobe Premiere Elements 11 is ideal for home users, hobbyists, business users, and professional videographers—anyone who wants to produce high-quality movies and DVDs.

If you've used earlier versions of Adobe Premiere Elements, you'll find that this Classroom in a Book covers the updated interface that Adobe Systems introduced in this version, plus new advanced skills and features. If you're new to Adobe Premiere Elements, you'll learn the fundamental concepts and techniques that will help you master this application.

About Classroom in a Book

Adobe Premiere Elements 11 Classroom in a Book is part of the official training series for Adobe graphics and publishing software developed by Adobe product experts. Most lessons in this book include self-paced projects that give you hands-on experience using Adobe Premiere Elements 11.

Adobe Premiere Elements 11 Classroom in a Book includes a DVD attached to the inside back cover. On the DVD, you'll find all the files used for the lessons in this book. You will almost certainly get the most benefit from working on the lessons in the order in which they occur in the book.

As an overview, in the first two lessons, you'll learn your way around Adobe Premiere Elements' and the Adobe Organizer's interfaces, how to set up a project in Adobe Premiere Elements, and how to customize critical preferences.

In Lesson 3, you'll learn how to capture and otherwise import video into Adobe Premiere Elements. Starting with Lesson 4 and continuing through Lesson 12, you'll open projects on the DVD or create your own from contents on the disc, and learn how to convert your raw, captured clips into a polished movie.

Note that the project files had to be created separately for Mac and Windows computers, and were created using pre-release software and content. For this reason, there may be some minor differences between the screens in the book and what you might see onscreen when you're using Adobe Premiere Elements. Inside the book, we tried to identify the most likely places for this to happen but want to apologize in advance for any differences or inconvenience.

Prerequisites

Before you begin working on the lessons in this book, make sure that you and your computer are ready.

Requirements for your computer

You'll need a maximum of about 4.3 gigabytes (GB) of free space on your hard drive for the lesson files and the work files you'll create. For some lessons, you'll need to have 2 GB of RAM installed on your computer. Note that the lessons assume that you have installed all templates and associated content available with the DVD version of Adobe Premiere Elements 11 and via download. If you see a template that's not installed on your computer, you should be able to simply choose another template and continue with the lesson.

Required skills

The lessons in this *Adobe Premiere Elements 11 Classroom in a Book* assume that you have a working knowledge of your computer and its operating system. This book does not teach the most basic and generic computer skills. If you can answer *yes* to the following questions, you're probably well qualified to start working on the projects in these lessons:

- Do you know how to use the Microsoft Windows Start button and the Windows task bar? On the Mac, do you know how to run applications from the Dock or in the Applications folder? In both operating systems, can you open menus and submenus, and choose items from those menus?

- Do you know how to use My Computer, Windows Explorer, Finder, and/or a browser—such as Chrome, Firefox, Internet Explorer, or Safari—to find items stored in folders on your computer, or to browse the Internet?

- Are you comfortable using the mouse to move the pointer, select items, drag, and deselect? Have you used context menus, which open when you right-click items in Windows or Mac OS, or Control-click items on the Mac if you're working with a single-button mouse?

- When you have two or more open applications, do you know how to switch from one to another? Do you know how to switch to the Windows or Macintosh desktop?

- Do you know how to open, close, and minimize individual windows? Can you move them to different locations on your screen? Can you resize a window by dragging?

- Can you scroll (vertically and horizontally) within a window to see contents that may not be visible in the displayed area?

- Are you familiar with the menus across the top of an application and how to use those menus?

- Have you used dialogs (special windows in the interface that display information), such as the Print dialog? Do you know how to click arrow icons to open a menu within a dialog?

- Can you open, save, and close a file? Are you familiar with word-processing tasks, such as typing, selecting words, backspacing, deleting, copying, pasting, and changing text?

- Do you know how to open and find information in Microsoft Windows or Apple Macintosh Help?

If there are gaps in your mastery of these skills, see the documentation for your operating system. Or, ask a computer-savvy friend or instructor for help.

Installing Adobe Premiere Elements 11

Adobe Premiere Elements 11 software (sold separately) is intended for installation on a computer running Windows XP, Windows Vista, or Windows 7, or Mac OS 10.5x or later. For system requirements and complete instructions on installing the software, see the Adobe Premiere Elements 11 application DVD and documentation. To get the most from the projects in this book, you should install all the templates included with the software. Otherwise, you may notice "missing file" error messages.

Copying the Classroom in a Book files

The DVD attached to the inside back cover of this book includes a Lessons folder containing all the electronic files for the lessons in this book. Follow the instructions to copy the files from the DVD, and then keep all the lesson files on your computer until after you have finished all the lessons.

Copying the lesson files from the DVD

1 Insert the *Adobe Premiere Elements 11 Classroom in a Book* DVD into your DVD-ROM drive. Open the DVD in My Computer or Windows Explorer (Windows), or in the Finder (Mac OS).

2 Locate the Lessons folder on the DVD and copy it to any convenient folder on your computer. Just remember where you copied it, because you'll be opening the lesson files frequently throughout the book. In the Lessons folder, you'll find individual folders containing project files needed for the completion of each lesson.

3 When your computer finishes copying the Lessons folder (which could take several minutes), remove the DVD from your DVD-ROM drive, and store it in a safe place for future use.

Additional resources

Adobe Premiere Elements 11 Classroom in a Book is not meant to replace documentation that comes with the program or to be a comprehensive reference for every feature. Only the commands and options used in the lessons are explained in this book. For comprehensive information about program features and tutorials, please refer to these resources.

Adobe Community Help: Community Help brings together active Adobe product users, Adobe product team members, authors, and experts to give you the most useful, relevant, and up-to-date information about Adobe products.

To access Community Help: To invoke Help, press F1 or choose Help > Premiere Elements Help.

Adobe content is updated based on community feedback and contributions. You can add comments to both content and forums, including links to web content. Find out how to contribute at www.adobe.com/community/publishing/download.html.

See community.adobe.com/help/profile/faq.html for answers to frequently asked questions about Community Help.

Adobe Premiere Elements 11 Help and Support: Point your browser to www.adobe.com/support/premiereelements where you can find and browse Help and Support content on adobe.com.

Adobe Forums: forums.adobe.com lets you tap into peer-to-peer discussions and questions and answers on Adobe products.

Adobe TV: tv.adobe.com is an online video resource for expert instruction and inspiration about Adobe products, including a How To channel to get you started with your product.

Adobe Design Center: www.adobe.com/designcenter offers thoughtful articles on design and design issues, a gallery showcasing the work of top-notch designers, tutorials, and more.

Adobe Developer Connection: www.adobe.com/devnet is your source for technical articles, code samples, and how-to videos that cover Adobe developer products and technologies.

Resources for educators: www.adobe.com/education offers a treasure trove of information for instructors who teach classes on Adobe software. Find solutions for education at all levels, including free curricula that use an integrated approach to teaching Adobe software and can be used to prepare for the Adobe Certified Associate exams.

Also check out these useful links:

Adobe Marketplace & Exchange: www.adobe.com/cfusion/exchange is a central resource for finding tools, services, extensions, code samples, and more to supplement and extend your Adobe products.

Adobe Premiere Elements 11 product home page: www.adobe.com/products/premiereel.

Adobe Labs: http://labs.adobe.com gives you access to early builds of cutting-edge technology, as well as forums where you can interact with the Adobe development teams building that technology and other like-minded members of the community.

Free trial versions of Adobe Photoshop Elements 11 and Adobe Premiere Elements 11: The trial version of the software is fully functional and offers every feature of the product for you to test-drive (does not include Plus membership). To download your free trial version, browse to http://adobe.ly/NBGbfD.

1 THE WORLD OF DIGITAL VIDEO

Lesson overview

This lesson describes how you'll use Adobe Premiere Elements 11 to produce movies and introduces you to the key views, windows, tools, and adjustments within the application. If you're new to Adobe Premiere Elements, you'll find this information useful, but even experienced Adobe Premiere Elements users should invest time reading this lesson, because the interface and workflow have changed dramatically from previous versions.

This lesson will introduce the following concepts:

- The Quick and Expert views, and key similarities and differences between them
- The various windows and panels in the Adobe Premiere Elements interface
- The functions in the Action bar
- Adobe Premiere Elements' key tools
- What's new in Adobe Premiere Elements 11

 This lesson will take approximately 45 minutes.

Adobe Premiere Elements in Quick view.

How Adobe Premiere Elements fits into video production

Video producers are a diverse group, and each uses Adobe Premiere Elements differently. At a high level, however, all producers will use Adobe Premiere Elements to import and organize footage (video, stills, and audio)—whether from a camcorder, digital camera, or other source—and then edit the clips into a cohesive movie. If you have Adobe Premiere Elements and Adobe Photoshop Elements, you have an extraordinarily flexible and well-featured platform for projects combining still images and video.

From a video perspective, such editing will include trimming away unwanted sections of your source clips, correcting exposure and adjusting color as needed, and then applying transitions and special effects as well as adding titles. On the audio front, perhaps you'll add narration to your productions or a background music track. When your movie is complete, you might create menus for recording to DVD and/or Blu-ray Discs, and then output the movie for sharing with others via disc (such as DVD or Blu-ray) and/or web or file-based output.

Adobe Premiere Elements facilitates this workflow using a new interface with two views, Quick and Expert. Quick view aggregates basic features that hobbyists use frequently to quickly edit video footage and share it with others. It's a great workspace for dipping your toe in the video editing waters and learning the basics.

Expert view provides advanced features and tools that professionals can use to accomplish intricate video editing tasks. Although the basic look and feel and workflows are very similar, Expert view contains more editing effects and more functionality.

The view you choose to use will depend on your experience level with Adobe Premiere Elements and the complexity of your projects. For simple projects, even expert users may choose to use Quick view for its streamlined interface. In contrast, there are some functions, like greenscreen and picture-in-picture effects, that can be accomplished only in Expert view.

Enough talking about it; let's start Adobe Premiere Elements, load some video files, and have a look.

The Adobe Premiere Elements workspace

When you launch Adobe Premiere Elements, a Welcome screen appears. From here, you can open the Organizer or the Video Editor. The Organizer is a great place to start many projects, particularly if you've already captured the source video footage to your hard drive. It offers excellent tagging and search tools, the ability to view all your media in one place irrespective of its actual location on your hard drive, and the ability to easily share and archive your collections of video and still images. If you also own Adobe Photoshop Elements, you'll share the same Organizer, so you can access all your content from either Adobe Premiere Elements or Adobe Photoshop Elements. In addition, you can launch a range of activities and workflows from either application within one common content database.

Note: The screen that you see may be slightly different than this if you haven't run Adobe Premiere Elements before, but the major buttons and operations will be identical.

Let's load some video files to see how starting projects in the Organizer works. Specifically, let's load the video files from the Lesson01 folder that you copied to your hard drive from the DVD.

1 Start Adobe Premiere Elements and click the Organizer button (not the Video Editor button) in the Welcome screen. The Organizer opens. If this is the first time you've worked with Adobe Premiere Elements or the Organizer, it will be empty and may ask you to identify folders where your media is located. If you've worked with it previously, it will contain other content that you've used before.

2 In the Organizer, choose File > Get Photos and Videos > From Files and Folders. The Get Photos and Videos from Files and Folders dialog opens.

3 Navigate to your Lesson01 folder.

● **Note:** The Organizer can import video footage directly from all camcorders except for tape-based camcorders, like DV and HDV, and analog camcorders. Footage from these devices must be captured before importing the video into the Organizer. For this reason, if your project involves video from DV, HDV, or analog camcorders that you previously haven't captured to your hard drive, you should start your projects by clicking New Projects in the Welcome screen, as shown in "Setting up a new project" in Lesson 2. Otherwise, if you're working with footage from any camcorder or digital camera that stores video onto a hard drive, DVD, SD-card based media, or similar nontape-based storage, you can input that footage directly from the Organizer.

4 Select all files with a .mp4 extension.

5 On the bottom right of the Get Photos and Videos from Files and Folders dialog, click Get Media. The Organizer loads the video into the Browser pane. If this is the first time you've used the Organizer, you may get a status message stating that the only items in the main window are those you just imported. Click OK to close the message; do not click Show All, which displays the entire Catalog.

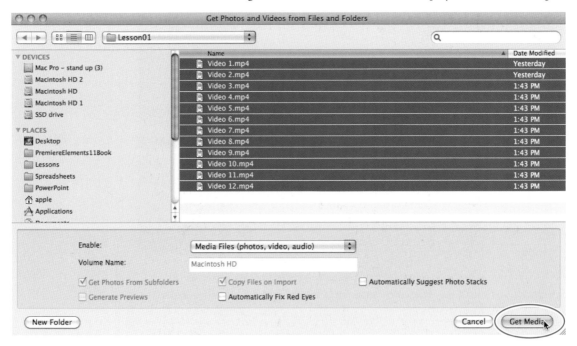

Working in the Organizer

In the Organizer, the main work area is the Browser pane where you can find, sort, and organize your video, audio, photos, and other media files. You'll learn these operations in Lesson 4; for now, here are a couple of highlights. To make sure your Organizer looks the same as the figure, do the following:

* In the Organizer menu, choose View > Media Types. Make sure photos, video, and audio are all selected.

* Choose View > Details, View > File Names, and View > Grid Lines to show these elements.

* In the Sort By list box on top of the Organizer's media browser, make sure Oldest is selected.

● **Note:** The presentation of content in the Organizer is determined by the creation date of the content, which unfortunately may change when the DVD is created. For this reason, don't be surprised if the order of content in the Organizer and the dates thereof differ between what you see in the figure and what you see in your application. Either way it won't affect this exercise.

If you click the Tags/Info icon on the lower right, you open the Keyword Tags panel, where you can apply tags to your videos to help organize them. You can also right-click any clip in the Browser pane window and run the Auto-Analyzer, which applies Smart Tags to the clips. Smart Tags assist in multiple activities, including creating InstantMovies (Lesson 4) and directing Smart Trimming (Lesson 5) and SmartFix (Lesson 6). To run the Auto-Analyzer function, select a clip or clips, right-click, and choose Run Auto-Analyzer.

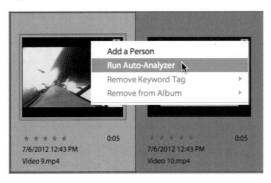

In addition, if you click Create on the upper right, the Create panel opens. In this panel you can start a number of types of projects, including InstantMovies and DVDs with menus, as well as a host of photo-related projects. If you click Share to open the Share panel, you can upload video to YouTube or to a mobile phone. And if you click the Editor drop-down list at the bottom of the Organizer, you can send all selected videos to Adobe Premiere Elements for editing. Let's do that to start your tour of the Adobe Premiere Elements workspace.

1 Press Ctrl+A (Windows) or Command+A (Mac OS) to select all videos currently in the Organizer (only those videos that you just imported should be displayed).

2 In the Tools panel on the bottom of the Organizer, click the down triangle next to the Editor icon, and choose Video Editor.

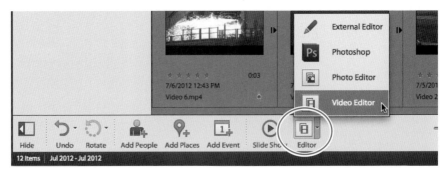

3   If this is the first time you've used this function, you'll see the status message in the next figure. Click OK to close the message.

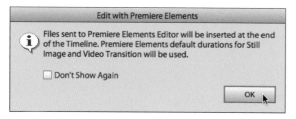

4   If the SmartFix dialog opens, click No.

5   If the Mismatched Project Settings Preset opens, click Yes to use a project preset that matches the clips.

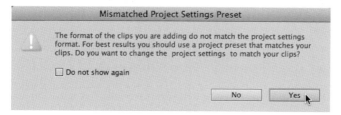

The Save Project dialog opens.

Adobe Premiere Elements opens.

6   On the top bar over the Monitor panel, click the Quick button (if necessary) to enter Quick view. Click anywhere in the timeline, and then press the Backslash (\) key to fit the content over the entire Quick view timeline. Note that the order of videos in your project may be different from that shown in the figure.

The Add Media panel   Monitor panel   Quick view/Expert view toggle   Publish+Share panel

Quick view timeline.   Action bar   Tools panel   Adjust and Applied Effects panels
Toggles to the timeline
in Expert view

Note: Again, the order of content in your application may be different than that shown on-screen. Don't worry, it doesn't impact the exercise in any way.

The Adobe Premiere Elements workspace is arranged in two main panels: the Monitor panel and the Timeline panel. Simply stated, you build your project in the Timeline panel and preview your work in the Monitor panel. In Adobe Premiere Elements 11, the interface has been streamlined to maximize the size of each panel and minimize clutter. Let's walk through the key components of the interface and take a quick look at the differences between the Quick and Expert views. Although every project is different and every editor works differently, the order of the next few sections will roughly follow that of a typical project.

If you haven't spotted this already, take a quick look at the middle of the silver bar at the top of the Monitor panel. You'll see two buttons: Quick (Quick) and Expert (Expert). Click each button to enter its respective view.

Add Media and Project panels

If you don't start your project in the Organizer, you'll probably start by importing content into the project, which you'll do in both views by clicking Add Media on the upper left. In both the Quick and Expert views, you have all the import options shown in Quick view on the left. These include importing videos from the Elements Organizer; from a Flip or AVCHD camera; from a DV camcorder, HDV camcorder, or DVD camcorder; from a PC DVD drive or a webcam; importing photos from a digital still camera or phone; and getting videos, photos, and audio from Files and Folders, which you'll use to retrieve files already existing on your hard drive. (These functions are detailed in Lesson 3.)

In Quick view, all files that you import are immediately moved to the Quick view timeline, where you can trim away unwanted frames, change clip order, and perform other edits. In Expert view, Adobe Premiere Elements stores the files that you select or import in the Project Assets panel shown in Expert view on the right. From there, you can open them in a trim window to remove unwanted frames, and then drag them into the timeline in the desired order.

Quick view

Expert view

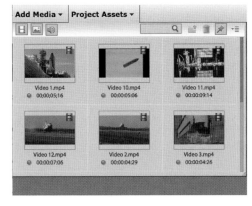

 Note: For Windows users, the Webcam selection will read "Webcam or WDM" for WDM-compatible device, which is not available on the Mac.

If you want to use a video file or other piece of content twice, in Expert view you could just click open the Project Assets panel and drag the content back into the timeline. In Quick view, you'd have to import it again. Or, of course, you could just click into Expert view to make the Project Assets panel available, and then find the content.

This brings up a point that's probably obvious to most readers but worth making anyway: You're not permanently limited in any way by working in Quick view. If you need to perform an edit or access a tool that's available only in Expert view, you can simply click into Expert view. If you prefer working in Quick view, you can then click back into Quick view and continue with the project.

Quick view timeline and Expert view timeline

The timeline lets you assemble your media into the desired order and edit clips. To accomplish this, the timeline presents all movie components in separate horizontal tracks. Clips earlier in time appear to the left, and clips later in time appear to the right, with clip length on the timeline representing a clip's duration.

In the Quick view timeline are four tracks: a title track, a single video track, a narration track, and an audio track for background music or other audio files. These four tracks should be sufficient for most projects, including the project that you'll be working on throughout this book.

Quick view

Expert view

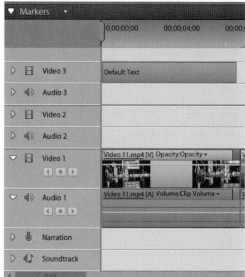

However, if you need additional tracks for audio, video, or both, you'll have to enter Expert view, where you can add dozens of extra tracks if required. Working in Expert view is also useful in other circumstances. For example, although it's not obvious in the previous figure, some edits are driven by information shown by the waveform on the audio track. Quick view doesn't show these audio waveforms; Expert view does.

Again, if you perform edits on tracks in Expert view that aren't available in Quick view, like adding audio/video content to tracks above Video 1/Audio 1, that content isn't eliminated if you enter Quick view. Instead, it's preserved and immediately accessible should you reenter Expert view.

The Monitor panel

The Monitor panel serves multiple purposes. You can navigate to any position in the movie and preview a section or the entire movie using the VCR-like controls beneath the playback window. Other lessons will detail the Monitor panel's controls and operation; here you can experiment with the playback controls to get a feel for how to use them.

In other roles, the Monitor panel also offers tools that let you drag one scene onto another to create picture-in-picture effects and add and customize titles. The Monitor panel adjusts its appearance for some editing tasks. For example, when you're creating menus, the Monitor panel switches to become the Disk Layout panel; in title-editing mode, the Monitor panel displays additional tools to create and edit text.

The Adjust and Applied Effects panels

After selecting a clip on the timeline, click the Adjust button (▦) on the right of the Adobe Premiere Elements interface to open the Adjustments panel, which contains the most common adjustments that you'll use in most projects. Then click the double arrow icon (▶▶) on the top right of the panel to close it, or click the Adjust button again. In essence, these adjustments are effects, but because they're so commonly used, they're not stored with the other effects that you must apply manually. Instead, Adobe Premiere Elements applies them via presets identified by simple visuals, which is more efficient. All you have to do is click the Adjust button and make the necessary adjustments, which are detailed in Lesson 6.

When you're working in Quick view, Adobe Premiere Elements provides access to the one-step SmartFix control, as well as Color, Lighting, and Temperature and Tint adjustments for video, and Volume and Balance for audio. In Expert view, these are supplemented by RGB color and Gamma Correction for video and Treble, Bass, and Audio Gain for audio. The other major difference between the two views is that Expert view lets you animate effects, which you accomplish via controls accessed by clicking the Show/Hide keyframe controls icon (◉) on the upper right of the Adjustments panel. You'll learn how to use keyframes in "Working with keyframes" in Lesson 6.

Quick view

Expert view

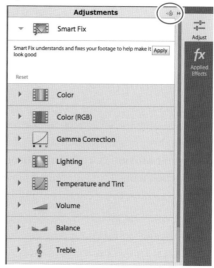

Click the Applied Effects icon (▦) beneath the Adjust icon to open the Applied Effects panel, which contains any effects that you've manually applied to the selected clip, plus the very commonly used Motion and Opacity adjustments. Then click the double arrow icon (▶▶) on the top right of the panel or click the Applied Effects icon again to close it. Note that the Motion effect in particular is one that you'll use in many projects for many different purposes: to create a picture-in-picture, to zoom into or out of a video, or to rotate a video. Remember that it's automatically applied for you and always ready for adjustment in the Applied Effects panel.

Within the Applied Effects panel, the only difference between Expert and Quick views is the ability to keyframe any of the effects in the panel. You can access this capability in Expert view by clicking the Show/Hide keyframe controls icon (◄◉►) on the upper right of the panel.

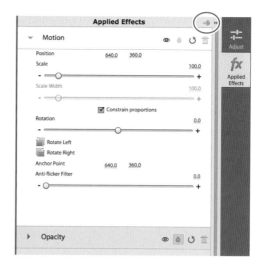

The Action bar

The Action bar sits at the bottom of the interface, providing access to the Instant Movie (Instant Movie) panel, the Tools panel (Tools), and libraries of content and effects, like transitions (Transitions), titles and text (Titles & Text), effects (Effects), music (Music), and graphics (Graphics). Click each button to open the respective panel, and then click it again to close the panel. Here's a brief description of each panel:

- **Instant Movie:** This panel automatically and quickly steps you through the selection and editing portion of movie creation, as well as adding theme-based effects, titles, transitions, and audio. Click Instant Movie (Instant Movie) to open this panel, and click it again to close it.

- **Tools panel:** This panel contains a range of useful tools that you'll use in many projects and is covered in the next section.

- **Transitions:** This panel shows video (both views) and audio transitions (Expert view only) you can use in your movie by dragging them between two clips on the timeline. In Expert view, you can search for transitions by typing all or part of the name into the search box on the upper right of the panel, browse through all available effects, or filter the panel by type and category. Transitions between clips can be as subtle as a cross-dissolve or quite emphatic, such as a page turn or spinning pinwheel. You'll learn more about transitions in Lesson 7.

- **Titles & Text:** This panel shows groups of preformatted title templates you can use in your movie by dragging them onto the title track (Quick view) or any video track (Expert view). In both views, you can browse all available templates or filter the panel by categories. Title templates can include graphic images and placeholder text that you can modify freely, delete from, or add to without affecting the actual templates. You'll learn how to create and customize titles in detail in Lesson 8.

- **Effects:** This panel shows video (both views), audio effects (Expert view only), and FilmLooks (both views) you can use in your movie by dragging them onto any clip in the timeline. In Expert view, you can search for effects by typing all or part of the name into the search box in the upper right of the panel, browse through all available effects, or filter the panel by type and category. Effects in this panel supplement the automatic adjustments available in the Adjust and Applied Effects panels. You can apply video effects to adjust exposure or color problems, apply perspective or pixelate, or add other special effects. Audio effects help you improve the sound quality, add special effects like delay and reverb, and adjust volume or balance. You'll learn about video effects in Lesson 6 and audio effects in Lesson 9.

- **Music:** This panel displays music clips that you can use in your movie by dragging them to the narration or background music track (Quick view) or any audio track (Expert view). This panel also provides access to the SmartSound music-generation application, which lets you create custom-length soundtracks for your movies. You'll learn how to work with SmartSound and other Adobe Premiere Elements audio-related features in Lesson 9.

- **Graphics:** This panel displays graphics elements that you can drag and drop into the movie track (Quick view) or any video track (Expert view) in your projects. In Quick view, you have access to the six most commonly used graphics; in Expert view, you have access to dozens more graphics contained in categories like Animated Objects, Costumes, Baby-oriented clip art, and thought bubbles and similar text-oriented graphics.

Look at the figures below to see the basic differences between Quick view and Expert view discussed in the preceding sections. The figures show the Effects panel where Quick view offers 20 of the most commonly used effects and FilmLooks; Expert view offers dozens more in well-defined categories. For most productions, the effects and transitions in Quick view are more than adequate. However, if you're scratching your head trying to find the perfect effect to apply to your movie or are searching for a particular effect that you've used in the past, click over into Expert view, which has a much greater selection of well-categorized effects.

In addition, when in Expert view, some of the panels in the Action bar, but not all, have search functions accessible by clicking the magnifying lens (🔍) on the upper right of the panel. This search function is not available in Quick view.

Quick view

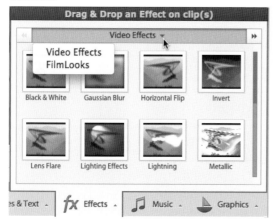

Expert view

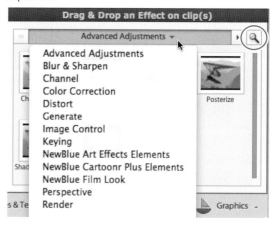

The Tools panel

The Tools panel contains a range of useful tools that you'll use in many projects. To open the panel, click Tools (✕ Tools) in the Action bar at the bottom of the Adobe Premiere Elements interface. To close the panel, click the triangle next to the Tools icon (▲) or just click Tools again. In Quick view, the Tools panel contains the following tools:

- **Adjustments:** For opening the Adjust panel described earlier in the lesson.

- **Freeze Frame:** For capturing a frame from a video and using it in your project. You'll learn how to use this function in "Exporting a frame of video as a still image" in Lesson 11.

- **Movie Menu:** For adding menus to DVDs, Blu-ray Discs, and web DVDs, which is detailed in Lesson 10.

- **Narration:** For adding narration to your project, a function described in "Adding narration" in Lesson 9.

- **Pan & Zoom:** For adding pan-and-zoom effects to pictures and videos, which you'll learn to use in "Creating a Pan & Zoom effect" in Lesson 6.

- **Smart Mix:** For managing the audio levels of foreground and background audio. This function is detailed in "Adjusting project volume with Smart Mix" in Lesson 9.

- **Smart Trim:** For identifying and trimming out low-quality regions within your clips, which you'll learn about in "Working in Smart Trim mode" in Lesson 5.

- **Time Remapping:** For implementing fine control of fast- and slow-motion effects applied to your clips, which is covered in Lesson 6.

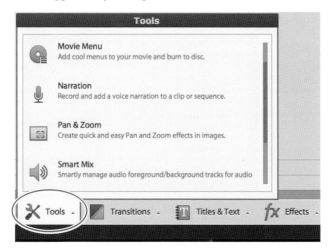

In Expert view, you also have access to the following tools:

- **Audio Mixer:** Another tool for managing audio levels over multiple tracks, which is detailed in "Working with the Audio Mixer" in Lesson 9.

- **Time Stretch:** Another tool for controlling the speed of your clips, also covered in Lesson 6.

Publish+Share panel

After you're finished editing and are ready to share your movie with the world, click the Publish+Share (Publish+Share ▾) button to open the Publish+Share panel. The Publish+Share panel shows buttons for accessing all the different methods for exporting and sharing your movie: web DVD, Disc, Online, Computer, and Mobile Phones and Players. This panel is identical in Quick and Expert views.

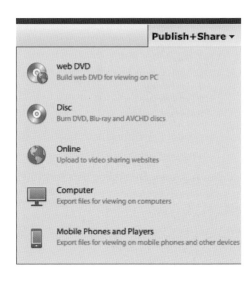

Info and History panels

▶ **Tip:** In addition to the History panel, Adobe Premiere Elements supports multiple undos by choosing Edit > Undo or by pressing Ctrl+Z (Windows) or Command+Z (Mac OS). Each time you press Ctrl+Z (Windows) or Command+Z (Mac OS), you're undoing another step and working back through your edits in order, starting with the most recent. You can also redo a step by choosing Edit > Redo or pressing Ctrl+Shift+Z (Windows) or Command+Shift+Z (Mac OS).

The Info panel displays information about a selected clip in the My Project panel. Among other things, the Info panel can be helpful in identifying the resolution, frame rate, and duration of a clip.

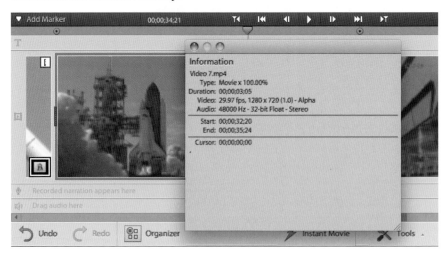

1   To open the Info panel, choose Window > Info. You can then drag the Info panel by its title bar to reposition it on the screen, if necessary.

2   Click to select a clip in the timeline or Project Assets panel. The Info panel displays the clip's name, type, start and end points, duration, video and audio attributes, its location in the timeline, and the position of the cursor.

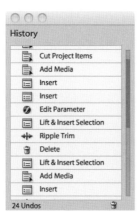

The History panel (Window > History) keeps a running list of every step you take during a project and adds each action to the bottom of its list. To undo an editing step, click it in the History panel. To undo multiple steps, click the earliest step that you'd like to undo, and Adobe Premiere Elements will also undo all editing steps after that point.

These are the most prominent panels and workspaces within Adobe Premiere Elements. By now, you should be familiar with the general project workflow of Adobe Premiere Elements, the key interface elements and functions, and the major differences between Quick and Expert views.

What's new in Adobe Premiere Elements 11

Let's briefly cover some of the new features in Adobe Premiere Elements 11. You've already seen the most significant one: the most sweeping user interface update since the program first appeared. And, there are many more new features for new and experienced Adobe Premiere Elements users. For example, the Mac version of Adobe Premiere Elements now runs in 64-bit mode on 64-bit Mac operating systems, allowing the program to access more memory, which promotes smoother, faster operation. If you're running Adobe Premiere Elements on a 64-bit Windows operating system, you may have noticed these benefits when you installed Adobe Premiere Elements 10, which went 64-bit on Windows.

Time Remapping

All users will appreciate the new Time Remapping feature, which lets you apply forward and reverse speed adjustments to customizable selections in a clip. If you want to slow the launch to half speed right after liftoff and then resume full speed two seconds later, you can do so now with ease-in and ease-out adjustments to make the speed change look even smoother. These are very much like the tools professional editors use for television and movie productions; in Adobe Premiere Elements 11 you can achieve the same polished look. You'll learn how to apply and configure the Time Remapping tool in Lesson 6.

Vignetting

Speaking of polished, you may have noticed the darkness around the edges in the Space Shuttle clip shown in the Time Remapping tool. This is the new Vignetting effect, which you can use to focus a viewer's attention on the central regions in a video or simply to add an elegant look to a video. Configuration options are plentiful and include the amount of the vignette, size, shape, and feathering. You'll learn how to apply and configure the Vignetting effect in Lesson 6.

Temperature and Tint

Many video producers talk about adjusting the warmth or coolness of their videos to achieve a certain feel, but in the past it's been challenging to know which effects to apply to get this done. No more. In Adobe Premiere Elements 11, Adobe introduces Temperature and Tint adjustments with presets and fine-tuning. To add coolness, select a bluish color chip or move the Temperature slider to the left into negative values; to add warmth, click a reddish chip or drag the Temperature slider to the right.

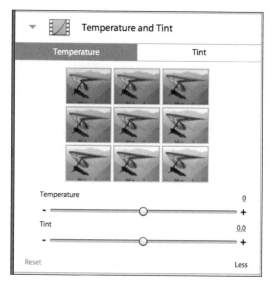

FilmLooks

With some productions, you'll want to create a uniform look across the entire video—perhaps one that suggests a different feel to the production. You can accomplish both by applying the new FilmLooks effect onto your clips. FilmLooks is included in the Effects panel; you'll learn more about FilmLooks in Lesson 6.

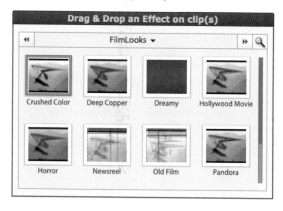

HSL Tuner

If you're used to adjusting colors using Hue, Saturation, and Luminance controls, now you can do that in Adobe Premiere Elements as well using the HSL Tuner, which is only in Expert view. The tool provides exquisite fine-tuning capabilities with separate controls for red, orange, yellow, green, aqua, blue, purple, and magenta in hue, saturation, and luminance ranges.

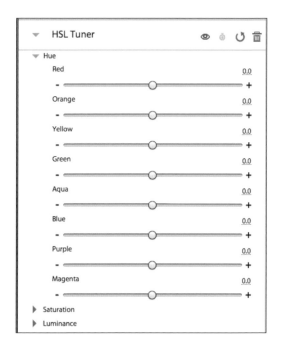

Split Tone effect

The Split Tone effect (only in Expert view) lets you apply a different tint to the highlights and shadows of your clips using different colors with separate hue and saturation adjustments. If you're trying to create a unique and distinctive look and feel for your videos, you'll find this new tool invaluable.

These are the major new features and enhancements; we'll discuss more as we go along.

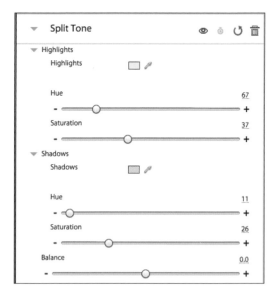

Review questions

1 What are the major differences between Quick and Expert views?

2 What types of projects should you consider starting from the Organizer, and why?

3 What types of effects are in the Adjust panel, and why?

4 Where are Motion adjustments located in the new Adobe Premiere Elements interface?

Review answers

1 Quick view is a streamlined interface that gives you access to the most commonly used editing options, whereas Expert view provides all the functionality in Adobe Premiere Elements. Quick view shows only four tracks, supplies only the most commonly used transitions and effects, and doesn't offer functionality like keyframing or greenscreen overlays. There's also no Project Assets panel in Quick view, so all the content you import into a project is immediately placed on the Quick view timeline.

2 Any project that doesn't involve capture from tape should start from the Organizer. Starting work in the Organizer provides faster access to tagging and sort tools, and direct access to production activities, like creating an InstantMovie or uploading a video to Photoshop.com.

3 The Adjust panel contains the most commonly used color, lighting, and temperature and tint adjustments for video, and volume and balance for audio. These effects are automatically placed in the Adjust panel for efficiency's sake; because they're used so frequently, editors don't need to apply them manually.

4 The motion adjustments are in the Applied Effects panel in both Quick and Expert views.

2 GETTING READY TO EDIT

Lesson overview

Now that you're familiar with the Adobe Premiere Elements interface, you'll learn how to create a project, set relevant user preferences, and configure the interface to your liking. For those tempted to skip this lesson, understand that although Adobe Premiere Elements is a wonderfully flexible and customizable program, once you choose a project settings preset and start editing, you can't change the setting.

Although you can often work around this issue, in some instances you may have to abandon the initial project and start again using a different setting to achieve the results you desire. Invest a little time here to understand how Adobe Premiere Elements works with project settings so you can get your project done right the first time.

In this lesson, you'll learn to do the following:

* Set your Adobe Premiere Elements startup preferences

* Create a new project

* Choose the optimal setting for your project

* Set preferences for Auto Save, ScratchDisks, and the user interface

* Customize window sizes and locations in the workspace

* Restore the workspace to its default configuration

* Enter and work in the Dual Monitor Workspace

 This lesson will take approximately one hour.

Customizing Adobe Premiere Elements' interface
in Quick view.

Setting your startup preferences

Now that you're getting ready to start using Adobe Premiere Elements, let's set your preference for what happens when you actually run the program from the Startup menu, Applications folder, or Dock. By default, the Welcome screen appears, as shown below, which enables you to run either Adobe Premiere Elements or the Adobe Organizer. If you want one program or the other to appear when you start the program, follow this procedure.

1   Launch Adobe Premiere Elements. If it is already open, choose Help > Welcome Screen in the Adobe Premiere Elements main menu to return to the Welcome screen. When the Welcome screen opens, click the Options button on the upper right to open the Options menu.

2   In the On Start Always Launch pull-down menu, choose the desired option. For now, you might want to leave the Welcome Screen open, but later you may choose to run the Video Editor straight away.

3   Click Done to close the Options menu. The next time you run the program, your selected option will launch automatically.

To reverse this decision and open the Welcome screen when you first run the program, choose Help > Welcome Screen in the Adobe Premiere Elements main menu. The Welcome screen appears so you can change your startup preference.

Setting up a new project

Adobe Premiere Elements can work with video from any source, ranging from DV camcorders shooting 4:3 or 16:9 (widescreen) standard-definition (SD) video to the latest AVCHD and Digital Single Lens Reflex (DSLR) cameras. For the best results, you should use a project settings preset that matches your source footage. Fortunately, Adobe Premiere Elements makes that very simple.

There are (at least) three ways to open Adobe Premiere Elements to a new project:

• Run Adobe Premiere Elements, and choose Video Editor > New Project from the Welcome screen.

• If you've elected to bypass the Welcome screen as shown earlier and launch the Video Editor or the Organizer when the application first starts, it opens to a new project.

• With Adobe Premiere Elements open, choose File > New > Project from the main menu.

When you choose either of the first two options, Adobe Premiere Elements deploys the project settings preset from the last project that you worked on, which may or may not be the optimal setting. Only the last option, when you start a new project from within Adobe Premiere Elements, opens the New Project screen shown below, which allows you to choose a project settings preset and, if desired, force the selected project settings on the project. We'll return to this screen after discussing how to choose the optimal project settings for your projects and what happens when you first add content to a project.

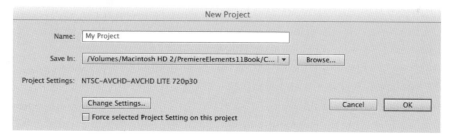

Getting started

Let's load a project to make sure that you're looking at the same content and screens shown in the exercises in this book. Here's the procedure.

1 Make sure that you have correctly copied the Lesson02 folder from the DVD in the back of this book onto your computer's hard drive. For more information, see "Copying the Classroom in a Book files" in the "Getting Started" section at the beginning of this book.

2 Launch Adobe Premiere Elements.

3 In the Welcome screen, click Video Editor, select Existing Project, and click the Open folder.

The Open Project dialog opens.

Note: Depending upon the operating system you are running and the options you've chosen therein, the extension .prel may not be visible. If not, just choose the respective file name for the operating system that you're running and don't worry about the .prel extension.

4 In the Open Project dialog, navigate to the Lesson02 folder you copied to your hard drive. Select the file Lesson02_Start_Win.prel (Windows) or Lesson02_Start_Mac.prel (Mac OS), and then click Open. If a dialog appears asking for the location of rendered files, click the Skip Previews button.

Your project file opens.

5 Choose Window > Restore Workspace to ensure that you start the lesson with the default window layout.

6 If you're not already in Expert view, click the Expert (Expert) button at the top of the Project window.

The project should be open and appear very much like the next figure.

Finding the optimal project setting

You won't need the information contained in this section 99 percent of the time because Adobe Premiere Elements automatically uses the optimal project settings without any action on your part, and you can efficiently start editing. But if you want to be able to diagnose and resolve the issues in the unlikely event that you do have a problem, read on.

Briefly, the project settings are the palette within which Adobe Premiere Elements creates your project. More specifically, a project settings preset defines configuration options for items like video resolution and frame rate. All content added to a project is conformed to that setting. Although you can add files of any configuration to a project using any project settings, Adobe Premiere Elements works most efficiently when the project settings are the same as the content you're editing.

Why? Because Adobe Premiere Elements can work with your source footage natively without conforming it to the configuration of the project settings. As an example, the bulk of the NASA footage in the DVD-based projects has a resolution of 1280x720 and a frame rate of 30 frames per second (fps). This means that it matches the NTSC-AVCHD-AVCHD LITE 720p30 format you see as the project settings in the New Project screen shown in the figure. In essence, when you use this setting, the timeline is configured for a resolution of 1280x720 and a frame rate of 30 fps.

What happens if you add footage to the timeline that doesn't conform to that setting? Adobe Premiere Elements has to render that footage to the configuration of the timeline before playing it in the preview window. Rendering can involve significant CPU resources and can slow down playback. For this reason, you get the most responsive editing when you work with footage that matches the project settings.

Mismatches between your content and your project settings can also cause Adobe Premiere Elements to letterbox your footage, as shown in the next figure. Sometimes you may want or need to use letterboxes, but in many instances, the presence of letterboxes shows that you're using the wrong project settings. As mentioned earlier, because you can't change your project settings after you start editing, it's best to diagnose and resolve these issues before you invest substantial time in the project.

Let's spend a bit of time with the project in the next screen. It's a simple project that uses the NTSC-AVCHD-AVCHD LITE 720p30 project settings preset, which is used in all projects in this book. Note that the project is in Expert view, which is necessary to see the detail in the timeline.

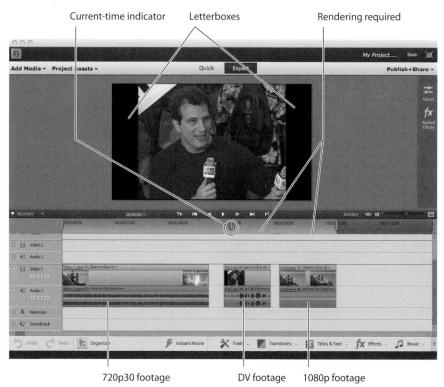

Current-time indicator   Letterboxes   Rendering required

720p30 footage   DV footage   1080p footage

The first video on the timeline is one of the video files you'll be working with throughout the book; the second is a DV file, and the third is a 1920x1080 file from NASA. Note the thin orange lines on the top of the timeline above the second and third clips. This tells you that Adobe Premiere Elements has to render the clip before previewing. There is no similar orange line above the first clip, which means that no rendering is required.

Also note that the current-time indicator, which determines which frame in the project is displayed in the Monitor panel, is over the DV file. As you can see, when the 4:3 DV is displayed in the Monitor of the 16:9 720p project, letterboxes appear on the sides. If you move the current-time indicator (CTI) over either of the other two files, the letterboxes will disappear.

How can you see which project settings preset Adobe Premiere Elements is currently using? From the Adobe Premiere Elements main menu, choose Edit > Project Settings > General to open the Project Settings dialog shown in the next figure. This dialog reveals the key configuration options contained in the project settings preset. The only downside is that there's no direct reference to the actual project settings used, so you can't tell which project settings preset resulted in this configuration. Specifically, although I created this project with the NTSC-AVCHD-AVCHD LITE 720p30 format, it's not obvious from the information in the Project Settings dialog.

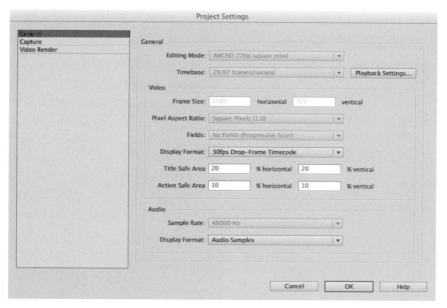

Fortunately, there's a way to identify the current setting that Adobe Premiere Elements is using, and I describe it later in this lesson in the section "Identifying the right project setting." In the meantime, let's agree that the optimal project preset would ensure that no orange lines appear above content in the timeline when it's first imported into the project or any letterboxes (unless desired). Fortunately, that's the project settings preset that Adobe Premiere Elements automatically applies in most instances. Here's how it works.

How Adobe Premiere Elements chooses the project setting

Let's return to where we started. No need to follow along in the application; we're discussing theory here. There are (at least) three ways to open Adobe Premiere Elements to a new project:

- Run Adobe Premiere Elements, and choose Video Editor > New Project from the Welcome screen.

- If you've elected to bypass the Welcome screen and open Adobe Premiere Elements when first running the program, it launches a new project automatically.

- With Adobe Premiere Elements open, choose File > New > Project from the main menu.

When you start a new project using the first two techniques, Adobe Premiere Elements simply uses the project settings preset from the previous project. With the third technique, it uses the project settings preset selected in the New Project dialog.

However, by default, Adobe Premiere Elements will change the project settings when you import content into the project in these instances:

- If you import only a single clip, Adobe Premiere Elements switches the project settings to the settings of that clip.

- If you import multiple clips and all the clips share the same settings, Adobe Premiere Elements switches the project settings to the matching properties.

- If you import multiple clips with various settings, Adobe Premiere Elements switches the project settings based on the first clip's settings.

In my tests, this paradigm worked flawlessly when importing disk-based clips or when importing file-based video from DSLRs and AVCHD camcorders. So, if you're working with file-based content from your hard drive or from a camera, you hopefully should never have to worry about choosing the right preset as long as the first files that you load in the project are the predominant format used in the project. However, you will run into problems if you first load a file that's not the predominant format.

For example, referring to the project you just opened, if the first file I loaded into the project was the DV file, Adobe Premiere Elements would automatically apply the DV Project Settings preset without asking any questions; it just conforms the set-ting. When I subsequently loaded the AVCHD file that I want the setting to match, Adobe Premiere Elements would not do so; it continued to use the DV preset.

There is a way to force Adobe Premiere Elements to use the selected project settings (discussed in the next section), but otherwise, Adobe Premiere Elements will automatically choose the project settings using the rules just described. The only time the program doesn't conform the project settings to the

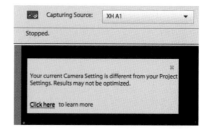

video that you input is when you're capturing from tape-based devices like DV and HDV. In these instances, if the selected preset doesn't match the footage captured from tape, you'll see the error message shown above in the Capture panel.

If you capture the video anyway, you'll have a mismatch between the captured footage and project settings, which means orange lines over the timeline, letterboxes, or both. Accordingly, if you ever see this message and want the project settings to conform to the footage you're about to capture, exit the capture screen, start a new project, and choose the project settings preset that conforms to the tape-based video you're about to import. The next section details how to do this.

In addition, if you ever load your initial files and see letterboxing or the render bar, you'll have to identify the right project setting using the information you'll learn in the section "Identifying the right project setting," and then manually choose your project setting as you'll learn in the next section.

Manually choosing a project setting

Here's the procedure for manually choosing a project settings preset, which might be necessary to address the capture issue addressed in the preceding section. I'll also detail how to force Adobe Premiere Elements to use a selected project settings preset, which might be necessary if the first content you import into a project is different from your main content.

Again, to manually select project settings to use, Adobe Premiere Elements must be running; otherwise, you won't see the New Project screen. Here's the procedure.

1   From the main menu, choose File > New > Project.

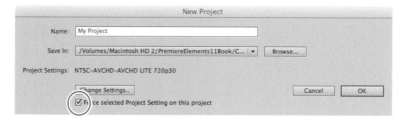

2 Make sure the Project Settings in the lower-left corner of the New Project screen match those of the previous screen. If so, proceed to step 4. If not, click the Change Settings button to open the Setup screen.

3 In the Change Settings dialog, click the preset that matches your content (note that the selected preset isn't the right preset for the source footage provided on the DVD. For that, use the AVCHD LITE 720p30 preset found in the AVCHD folder [NTSC > AVCHD]).

● **Note:** For more information on a preset, click the setting, and Adobe Premiere Elements will display technical details in the Description field.

4 After choosing a preset, click OK to close the Change Settings dialog and return to the New Project screen.

5 Select the "Force selected Project Settings on this project" check box at the bottom of the screen to force Adobe Premiere Elements to use the selected preset.

6 Choose a name and storage location for the new project at the top of the New Project screen. Then click OK to save the new project file.

After you choose a setting, Adobe Premiere Elements automatically uses the same setting for all future projects until you change it manually or it gets changed by Adobe Premiere Elements automatically. When you do change formats, be on the lookout for rendering lines on the timeline and letterboxes that may indicate a content/project settings mismatch, particularly when you're capturing from tape.

Identifying the right project setting

Of course, the aforementioned information assumes that you know which are the "right" project settings for your footage. How can you figure this out? There are two ways: the easy way and the hard way.

The easy way is to let Adobe Premiere Elements tell you. To do this, find a video file in the format that you plan to edit in. Start a new project (File > New > Project), import the file (see "Importing content from your hard drive" in Lesson 3), and then save the project (File > Save). Then start a new project (File > New > Project) and note the project settings in the New Project dialog. That's the preset you should use for future projects with that content.

Note that sometimes this preset may be named differently from the content that you're using. For example, you might import DSLR footage and find that by using this technique Adobe Premiere Elements used an AVCHD preset. No worries; if you use this technique, you should end up with a preset that won't have to render your content before previewing (so no orange lines and no letterboxes).

What's the hard way? Reviewing your camera's documentation and configuration screens to identify the parameters of your source footage and manually determining the right preset from that information. See the next section for more information.

Choosing the correct setting

Adobe Premiere Elements offers dozens of project settings. By far, the easiest way to choose the right preset is to make sure that the first clip you import into your new project is the predominant format and let Adobe Premiere Elements choose the right project settings. If this doesn't work for you and you need to choose your project settings manually, consider these factors:

- **Source:** Choose the source first. For NTSC (North American) camera sources, Adobe Premiere Elements has presets for AVCHD, DSLR, DV, FLIP, Hard Disk and Flash Memory Camcorders, HDV cameras, and Mobile Devices. (Available PAL sources include all of these as well except for FLIP and Mobile Devices.) So first find the presets that relate to your source.

- **Resolution:** Consider the resolution of the video next, which is typically either 1080i or 1080p (1920 horizontal, 1080 vertical, interlaced [i] or progressive [p] —see the following figure); 720i or 720p (1280h, 720v); 720h 480v resolution for DV; and sometimes 480p, which is 640h, 480v resolution. Find a preset that matches your source.

    Complicating this resolution is the pixel aspect ratio issue, which affects AVCHD and HDV camcorders, as well as DV sources. Specifically, all HDV camcorders that shoot in 1080i or 1080p actually capture video at 1440x1080 resolution and then stretch the video to 1920x1080 during display. For that reason, the HDV 1080i 30 HDV preset shows a frame size of 1440h, 1080v and a pixel aspect ratio of 1.333. This tells Adobe Premiere Elements to stretch the 1440 horizontal resolution by 1.333 to display it correctly on the timeline. Although this is confusing, this distinction never causes any problems, because Adobe Premiere Elements knows that all HDV 1080 video is stored in this manner and handles it appropriately.

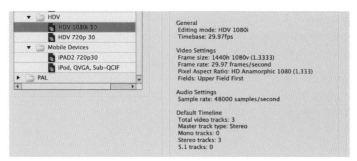

On the other hand, when you're shooting 1080i or 1080p video, all AVCHD camcorders display the video at 1920x1080 resolution. However, like HDV, "HD" AVCHD video is stored by the camcorder at a resolution of 1440x1080, and each horizontal pixel must be stretched by a factor of 1.33 during display to achieve full resolution. In contrast, "Full HD" AVCHD video is captured at 1920x1080 resolution, so no stretching is required to produce the full 1920x1080 display. If you're shooting in AVCHD, check the specs of your camcorder to determine if you're shooting in Full HD or just HD.

Additionally, all DV video is shot at 720x480 resolution, but 4:3 video has a pixel aspect ratio of .9091, which means that the pixels are shrunk about 10 percent during display, achieving the 4:3 aspect ratio. Widescreen DV video has a pixel aspect ratio of 1.2121, so the video is stretched during display, achieving the 16:9 aspect ratio. This is seldom confusing, because you'll probably know whether you shot in 4:3 or widescreen, and you can choose the preset accordingly.

- **Progressive or interlaced:** After you identify the right resolution and aspect ratio, you must determine whether the video is interlaced or progressive. Technically, interlaced video presents each frame in two fields—one consisting of the odd lines and the other of the even lines. Progressive video displays all lines in a frame simultaneously with no fields. Older TV content is almost always interlaced, whereas film-based movies are always progressive. Most modern camcorders shoot in both modes (or at least shoot "natively" in one mode and simulate the other mode); just check the settings on your camcorder to see if you shot in progressive or interlaced, and then choose your preset accordingly. As a rule, I usually shoot in interlaced format when shooting for DVD distribution and shoot in progressive for content bound primarily for web or computer viewing.

- **Frames per second:** Most camcorders can shoot at multiple speeds, including 23.976 fps, 24 fps, 29.97 fps, 30 fps, 59.94 fps, and 60 fps. Again, check the settings on your camcorder to see which frame rate you used, and then choose your preset accordingly.

Once you understand and incorporate all these factors into your preset selection, you should be able to choose the right preset, if it's available. What do you do if you can't find a preset that matches the precise specs that you shot in? Try to find a preset from a different format that matches your specs. In particular, there are lots of AVCHD presets in multiple configurations, so if you're shooting in HDV and can't find a matching preset in that category, look in AVCHD.

Load the preset, drag in your content, and if there are no orange rendering lines or letterboxes, you're home free. If there are, choose another preset, and try again.

Working with project preferences

For the most part, once you have the right project settings selected, you can jump in and begin editing with Adobe Premiere Elements. However, at some point you may want to adjust several program preferences that impact your editing experience. Here are the preferences that will prove relevant to most video editors.

Note: Adjusting these default durations will impact only edits made after the adjustment. For example, if you change the Still Image Default Duration to 120 frames, Adobe Premiere Elements will assign this duration to all still images added to the project thereafter but won't change the duration of still images already inserted into the project.

1 To open the General Preferences panel, choose Edit > Preferences > General (Windows) or Adobe Premiere Elements 11 > Preferences > General (Mac OS). You'll find multiple preferences in this panel; most important are the Video and Audio Transition Default Durations and the Still Image Default Duration. The latter controls the duration of all still images added to your project. As a rule, I typically use a 30-frame transition for DVD-based projects, which is one second long for 30 fps footage, but often shorten it for web-based video where one-second transitions can cause obvious artifacts.

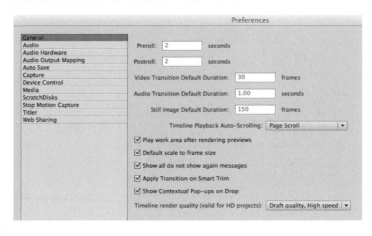

If you plan to use Smart Trim, which is covered in "Working in Smart Trim Mode" in Lesson 5, you should also decide whether to apply transitions to trims made in that mode, which is the default, or to deselect the check box and not use transitions in those instances.

2   Click Auto Save to view Auto Save preferences. Although five maximum project versions are typically sufficient, you might consider shortening the 20-minute Auto Save duration if your computer environment has proven unstable.

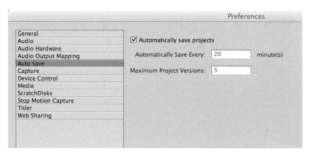

3   Click ScratchDisks to view the ScratchDisks preferences. These preferences identify the folders used to store audio and video clips that Adobe Premiere Elements creates while producing your project. This includes clips captured from your camcorder, video and audio previews, and media encoded for recording onto DVD or Blu-ray Disc. By default, Adobe Premiere Elements stores most of this content in the same folder as the project file. As a result, when you're done with a project, you can delete the project folder, if desired, and reclaim the disk space. The one exception is the Media Cache, which is stored in a centralized location. Let's take a closer look at the Media Cache.

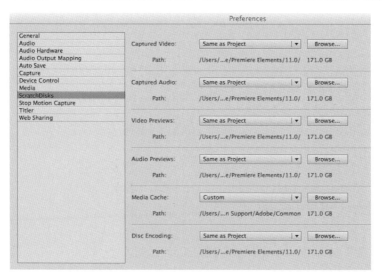

4   Click Media to manage the Media Cache database. According to the Help
    file, the Media Cache contains files that Adobe Premiere Elements creates "to
    improve performance when reading media files." Files in the Media Cache
    accumulate quickly, and because there is no mechanism to automatically delete
    them, they can quickly consume multiple gigabytes of disk space. To manually
    delete these files, click the Clean button in the Media Preferences dialog.
    A good time to do this is just after you finish a large project; if you remove
    these files while working on a project, it could slow performance until Adobe
    Premiere Elements re-creates them. When you're ready, click OK on the bottom
    right to close the Preferences dialog.

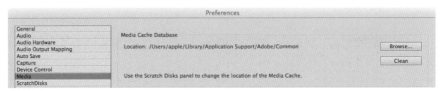

The preceding preferences are the most critical to consider before starting your
first project. With these configured, let's explore other options for customizing your
workspace.

Better saved than sorry

With Auto Save enabled, Adobe Premiere Elements automatically saves a copy
of your project at the specified duration, which you can customize. You can also
change the number of separate projects that Adobe Premiere Elements saves.

Adobe Premiere Elements saves all Auto Save files in a separate subfolder titled
Premiere Elements Auto-Save, which is located in the folder containing your current
project file.

It's good practice to manually save your project periodically during editing to
preserve your work in the event of a power outage or other random crash. Should a
crash occur, you may be able to recover some of the editing that you've done subsequent to your last manual save by loading the most recent project automatically
saved by Adobe Premiere Elements.

You load these projects just like any other project: Choose File > Open Project,
navigate to the Adobe Premiere Elements Auto Save folder, and select the newest
project file.

Customizing the Workspace

If you don't have a project open in Adobe Premiere Elements, go ahead and reopen the Lesson02 project file. As you can see, the default Adobe Premiere Elements application is contained in a single window with movable panels and windows so you can customize the interface to your liking. The following figure shows the project you previously loaded in Quick view, so click the Quick button (Quick) if necessary to change over. In both Quick and Expert views, the interface has two major permanent components: the Monitor panel and the timeline. Click the icon or button to open the panels on the left, right, and bottom, and then click them again to close them.

1 With Adobe Premiere Elements open, notice the small lines on the very bottom right of the application. You can click and drag this handle to increase and decrease the height and/or width of the application window.

2 To adjust the respective size of the Monitor panel and timeline, hover your pointer over the dividing line between the two components until it changes to a two-headed cursor, and then drag it up or down in the desired direction.

3   To adjust the respective size of the Monitor panel and the Adjust or Applied Effects panels, hover your pointer over the dividing line between the two panels until it changes to a two-headed cursor, and then drag it to the left or right in the desired direction.

4   To reset the interface to its default layout, choose Window > Restore Workspace. Notice how everything snaps back to its original position.

Configuring your Dual Monitor Workspace

If you're running Adobe Premiere Elements on a computer with two monitors, you can detach the Monitor panel and timeline, and run them on separate monitors. Here's the procedure.

1   In Expert view, click Window > Dual Monitor Workspace from the Adobe Premiere Elements main menu. Adobe Premiere Elements separates the Monitor panel and the timeline into two separate windows.

2   Drag each window into a monitor and drag the edges to resize as desired.

3   Choose Window > Restore Workspace to return to the default workspace layout.

Review questions

1 What's the most important factor to consider when you're choosing a project settings preset?

2 Why is it so important to choose the right project settings preset at the start of the project?

3 How can you tell if your project settings don't match your content?

4 What is Auto Save, and where do you adjust the Auto Save defaults in Adobe Premiere Elements?

5 What is the Media Cache, and why is it important?

6 What command do you use for restoring your workspace to the default panel configuration?

Review answers

1 Choose a setting that matches the primary video that you will use in the project. For example, if you're shooting in 720p30 AVCHD, you should use the 720p30 LITE AVCHD project settings preset.

2 It's critical to choose the right setting when starting a project because, unlike most Adobe Premiere Elements configuration items, you can't change the project settings after you create the project. In some instances, you may have to start the project over using the correct setting to produce optimal results.

3 Your project settings don't match your content when there are orange rendering lines above the content when it's immediately loaded into the program and/or when there is letterboxing.

4 The Auto Save function in Adobe Premiere Elements automatically saves a copy of the project file at specified intervals, guarding against loss of work due to power outages or other random crashes. You can adjust the Auto Save defaults in the Preferences panel.

5 The Media Cache is where Adobe Premiere Elements creates and stores files that help improve preview and other aspects of program performance. It's important because the Media Cache is in one centralized location and can grow quite large over time. You can delete the Media Cache in the Media tab of the Preferences panel.

6 Choose Window > Restore Workspace.

3 VIDEO CAPTURE AND IMPORT

Lesson overview

This lesson describes how to capture and import video from your camcorder and other devices for editing in Adobe Premiere Elements, and introduces the following key concepts:

- Using the Video Importer to import video from a DSLR or smartphone, an AVCHD or DVD camcorder, or a non-copy-protected DVD

- Connecting a camcorder to your PC

- Capturing video from a DV/HDV camcorder

- Importing audio, video, or still images from your hard drive into an Adobe Premiere Elements project

There are multiple differences between capture and import operation in Quick and Expert views. Most notable is that when you're adding media in Quick view, the new media is inserted directly into the Quick view timeline. When you're adding media in Expert view, the media is inserted into the Project Assets panel unless you opt to add the imported media to the timeline. I'll point out other differences in the relevant sections.

 This lesson will take approximately one hour.

Capturing video from your iPhone camera.

Capturing video with Adobe Premiere Elements

When videographers and video enthusiasts started editing video on computers, the typical source was an analog camcorder. Today, most Adobe Premiere Elements users will start with video shot with an AVCHD, DV, or HDV camcorder; video captured with a digital still camera or DSLR camera; video taken with a smartphone; or even video imported from a previously created DVD.

Whatever the source, Adobe Premiere Elements includes all the tools necessary to capture or import your footage so you can begin producing movies. Although the specific technique will vary depending on the source, Adobe Premiere Elements guides your efforts with device-specific interfaces. All you have to do is connect the device to your computer as described in this lesson, and choose the appropriate icon from the Add Media panel.

Adobe Premiere Elements has two basic interfaces for capturing or importing video. After a quick overview of these interfaces, this lesson will detail how to capture video from a DSLR, AVCHD camcorder, and iPhone, or any other device that stores video on a hard drive, on CompactFlash media (such as an SD card), or on optical media. Then it will detail how to capture video from a tape-based camcorder. All the concepts in this section and the specific Adobe Premiere Elements features that support them are described in more detail in the Adobe Premiere Elements User Guide.

● **Note:** Adobe Premiere Elements lets you add video, audio, graphics, and still images to your project from numerous sources. In addition to capturing footage, you can import image, video, and audio files stored on your computer's hard drive, card readers, mobile phones, DVDs, Blu-ray Discs, CDs, digital cameras, other devices, or the Internet.

Capture interfaces

When you shoot video, it's stored locally on your camcorder, whether on tape, SD media, a hard drive, or even an optical disc, such as a DVD. Before you can edit your movie in Adobe Premiere Elements, you must transfer these clips to a local hard drive. In addition to capturing or importing video from a device, you may have existing content on your hard drive to import into a project.

Tape and live capture vs. clip-based import

Adobe Premiere Elements provides three interfaces for accomplishing captures and imports. If you're importing video clips from a DSLR, smartphone, AVCHD camcorder, or optical media, you'll use the Video Importer shown in the next figure. As you can see, I have three sources connected to my computer: the SD card from a Canon DSLR, my Panasonic AG-HMC150 AVCHD camcorder, and my iPhone. This confirms the point that you use the same interface to capture from all three sources. Again, to open the appropriate interface, just connect your device and click the appropriate icon in the Add Media panel; Adobe Premiere Elements will do the rest.

If you're capturing video footage from a tape-based camcorder, such as a DV or HDV model, or live from a webcam, you'll use the panel shown in the next figure.

If the audio, video, or still image files are already on your computer's hard drive, click the Files and Folders icon in the Add Media panel, navigate to the files, and select them as you normally would. Details concerning this procedure are at the end of this lesson.

Using the Video Importer

As mentioned earlier, you'll use Adobe Premiere Elements' Video Importer to import video clips from AVCHD and DVD-based camcorders, smartphones, and DSLR and other digital cameras that also capture video. You'll also use the Video Importer to import videos from non-copy-protected DVDs. In essence, if the video is stored on a hard drive, SD card, optical disc, or other storage media other than tape, you'll import it with the Video Importer.

In this exercise you'll use the Video Importer to import video from an SD card containing footage from a DSLR camera. Although some DSLR cameras and other devices let you capture footage directly from the camera, my rule of thumb is that

if the video is stored on an SD card, remove the SD card from the device and capture directly from that. It's inevitably faster and simpler. I use an inexpensive card reader from Panasonic, although any card reader should do.

If you don't have a DSLR, you can follow along using video captured on an AVCHD camcorder or other digital still camera, a smartphone, or even a non-encrypted DVD, such as one that you've previously produced with Adobe Premiere Elements. Note that Adobe Premiere Elements will not import video from DVDs that are encrypted, such as most Hollywood DVD titles.

● **Note:** If you're capturing from a device rather than an SD card reader, the connection procedure will vary by device: Some AVCHD camcorders require you to set the camcorder to PC mode before connecting the USB 2.0 cable; others, the reverse. Please check the documentation that came with your camcorder for additional details.

1　Connect your video source (or SD card recorded therein) to your computer via the USB 2.0 or 3.0 port.

2　If you're capturing from a camcorder, turn on the camcorder and set it to PC mode or whichever mode is used to transfer video from the camcorder to your computer.

3　Launch Adobe Premiere Elements. Click New Project in the Welcome screen to start a new project. If Adobe Premiere Elements is running, choose File > New Project, save your current project if desired, choose a project name, and then click OK to save the new project.

● **Note:** Adobe Premiere Elements will conform your project setting to the first video imported into the project, so you don't need to worry about choosing the correct setting in the New Project screen. If you want your project setting to be different from the video that you're importing, choose File > New Project to open the New Project dialog, click the Change Settings button (if necessary) to choose the desired setting, and select the "Force selected Project Setting on this project" check box. Then click OK to open the new project.

4　On the upper left of the Adobe Premiere Elements interface, click Add Media (Add Media ▾) to open the Add Media panel.

5 In the Add Media panel, select Videos from Flip or Cameras (■).

The Video Importer opens.

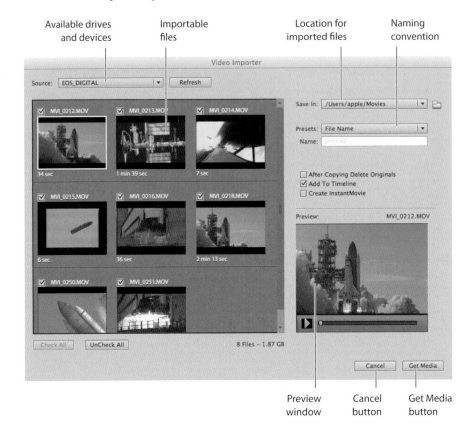

Available drives and devices

Importable files

Location for imported files

Naming convention

Preview window

Cancel button

Get Media button

6 Under Source, choose the drive or device from the drop-down list.

After you choose the drive or device, Adobe Premiere Elements will populate the Video Importer with thumbnails of all available video files.

7 To preview a video file, double-click it, and Adobe Premiere Elements will conform the audio and load it in the preview window on the lower right. Click the Play/Pause button to play the file.

8 To specify a location for the saved files, do one of the following:

- To save files to the default location—which is the location where you previously stored files captured by the Video Importer—leave the location unchanged.

- To specify a new location for saving the files, click the folder icon to open the Browse for Folder window (Windows)/Open dialog (Mac OS) and choose a folder, or click Make New Folder (Windows)/New Folder (Mac OS) to create a new folder.

9 In the Presets list box, choose one of four naming options:

- To use the original filenames created by the camera, choose File Name.

- To name each file with the folder name plus an incremental number, choose Folder Name-Number.

- To name each file with the date plus the original filename, choose Date-File Name.

- To add a custom name and incremental number to each file, choose Custom Name-Number. Then type the desired name into the Name text field beneath the Presets list box. For example, if your project is about a Space Shuttle launch, like the project you'll be starting in Lesson 4, you could name your files "Launch 1," "Launch 2," and so on.

10 In the thumbnail area, select individual files to add to the Media panel. A check mark by the filename indicates that the file is selected. By default, all files are selected. Only selected files are imported. Click a check box to deselect it, thus excluding the related file from being imported. Note the Check All and UnCheck All buttons beneath the thumbnails, which often can speed your selection.

11 Note the three check boxes on the right of the thumbnail area.

- To delete files from your camera or SD card after copying, select that check box.

- To add imported files directly to the timeline, select that check box. Note that this option won't be available when you're importing in Quick view where all imported files are added to the timeline automatically.

- To create an InstantMovie from the imported footage, select that check box. You can learn about InstantMovies in "Creating an InstantMovie" in Lesson 4.

12 Click Get Media to transfer the media to the destination location, which is typically your hard drive. You can click Cancel in the Copying Files dialog at any time to stop the process.

Note: If you've already imported the selected files to your hard drive, Adobe Premiere Elements will present an error message saying so if you try to import the file again. If these files are not currently input into the project, you can add them by choosing Add Media > Files and Folders, a procedure that is documented at the end of this lesson.

Capturing stop-motion and time-lapse video

Using stop-motion and time-lapse video, you can make inanimate objects appear to move (stop motion) or show a flower grow and bloom in seconds (time lapse). In these modes, you capture single video frames at widely spaced time intervals for later playback at normal frame rates. If you're interested in either of these functions, check the Adobe Premiere Elements Help file for more information.

Converting analog video to digital video

Before DV camcorders were widely manufactured, most people used camcorders that recorded analog video onto VHS, 8mm, or other analog tape formats. To use video from analog sources in your Premiere Elements project, you must first convert (digitize) the footage to digital data, because Premiere Elements accepts only direct input from digital sources. To digitize your footage, you can use either your digital camcorder or a stand-alone device that performs analog-to-digital (AV DV) conversion.

You can perform a successful conversion using the following methods:

- **Output a digital signal.** Use your digital camcorder to output a digital signal from an analog input. Connect the analog source to input jacks on your digital camcorder and connect the digital camcorder to the computer. Not all digital camcorders support this method. See your camcorder documentation for more information.

- **Record analog footage.** Use your digital camcorder to record footage from your analog source. Connect your analog source's output to the analog inputs on your digital camcorder. Then record your analog footage to digital tape. When you are finished recording, Premiere Elements can then capture the footage from the digital camcorder. This is a very common procedure. See your camcorder documentation for more details on recording from analog sources.

- **Capture sound.** Use your computer's sound card, if it has a microphone (mic) input, to capture sound from a microphone.

- **Bridge the connection.** Use an AV DV converter to bridge the connection between your analog source and the computer. Connect the analog source to the converter and connect the converter to your computer. Premiere Elements then captures the digitized footage. AV DV converters are available in many large consumer electronics stores.

Note: If you capture using an AV DV converter, you might need to capture without using device control.

—From Adobe Premiere Elements Help

Capturing tape-based or live video

If you're capturing from a DV or HDV camcorder, or a webcam, you'll use the Capture panel, which you access by clicking Add Media (Add Media ▾) to open the Add Media panel and then clicking DV Camcorder (■), HDV Camcorder (■), or Webcam (■) to match your source input. This exercise discusses some preliminary concepts relating to these devices and then details the procedure.

● **Note:** Although it's extremely rare, sometimes when connecting your computer to your camcorder via an IEEE 1394 connector, an electrical charge from the computer can damage the camcorder. To minimize this risk, always turn off both devices before capture, connect the IEEE 1394 cable, turn on your computer, and then turn on the camcorder.

Connecting your device

The best way to capture DV or HDV video is to connect the camcorder to a computer via an IEEE 1394 port. Adobe Premiere Elements supports a wide range of DV devices and capture cards, making it easy to capture DV source files. What can get complicated is the range of connection types, primarily on your computer. In virtually all instances, you'll be confronted with one of the three shown below. First, some background.

4-pin IEEE 1394 400   6-pin IEEE 1394 400   9-pin IEEE 1394 800

The initial IEEE 1394 standard had a maximum speed of 400 megabits per second (Mbps) and was known as IEEE 1394 400. This standard was used for years by Windows and Macintosh computers alike, as well as all DV and HDV camcorders. As shown on the left and in the middle of the previous figure, IEEE 1394 had two connectors: a 4-pin connector and a 6-pin connector.

Virtually all prosumer camcorders used the 4-pin connector, so any cable used for video acquisition had to have at least one 4-pin connector. Most desktop computers and workstations use 6-pin connectors, and most video producers worked on this class of machine, so the typical cable used by video producers was a 4-pin to 6-pin cable shown at right. Although you can pay $20 or more for such a cable, if you shop wisely, you can find them for under $5.

As notebooks became more powerful, many editors started producing on these as well. In the Windows world, your notebook probably has a 4-pin IEEE 1394 connector; if so, you need a 4-pin to 4-pin IEEE 1394 connector. These are less common, but you can still find them for well under $12 or so if you shop around.

In 2002, IEEE 1394 800 was introduced, which ran at 800 Mbps. The target for this standard was primarily computer peripherals, and few, if any, camcorder vendors adopted it. However, in 2009, Apple started using IEEE 1394 800 ports on its Mac computers, which used the 9-pin connector shown earlier. IEEE 1394 is backward compatible to slower speeds, so this caused no serious compatibility issues, but traditional 4-pin and 6-pin cables no longer worked.

If you have a Mac with an IEEE 1394 connector, you have two options. You can buy a custom cable with a 9-pin 800 connector on one end and the required 4-pin or 6-pin 400 connector on the other. Or, you can buy an adapter like the one shown in the next figure, which has a 6-pin 400 connector on one end and a 9-pin 800 connector on the other. These cost less than $5 each, so consider buying more than one; they're about the size of a USB key and are easily misplaced.

Note that in addition to IEEE 1394 ports, some DV and HDV camcorders also have USB 2.0 ports. USB 2.0 is a high-speed transfer protocol similar to IEEE 1394. When present on a DV/HDV camcorder, the USB 2.0 connector is typically used for transferring to the computer only digital still images rather than tape-based video shot by the camcorder. When both connectors are present, use the IEEE 1394 connector for video capture.

System setup

Before you attempt to transfer video from a DV/HDV camcorder, make sure your system is set up properly for working with digital video. The following are some general guidelines for ensuring that you have a DV-capable system:

- **IEEE 1394 port:** Make sure your computer has an IEEE 1394 port. This port may either be built into your computer or available on a PCI or PC card (often referred to as capture cards) that you install yourself. Many currently manufactured computers include onboard IEEE 1394 cards.

- **High data transfer rate:** As long as your computer was manufactured in the last five years or so, your hard drive should be fast enough to capture the 3.6 megabytes per second required by DV and HDV footage. If you're working with an older computer, check your computer's or hard drive's documentation to confirm that it can sustain storage at this rate.

- **Extra storage:** Consider using a secondary hard drive for extra capacity during capture and production, and to enhance capture performance. In general, most internal hard drives should be sufficiently fast for capture and editing. However, external drives that connect via USB 2.0 and IEEE 1394, although excellent for data backup chores, may be too slow for video capture. If you're looking for an external drive for video production, a technology called eSATA offers the best mix of performance and affordability, but you may have to purchase an internal eSATA adapter for your computer or notebook.

- **Sufficient hard drive space:** Make sure you have sufficient drive space for the captured footage. Five minutes of digital video consumes about 1 gigabyte (GB) of hard drive space. The Capture panel in Adobe Premiere Elements indicates the remaining space on your hard drive. Be certain beforehand that you will have sufficient space for the intended length of video capture.

- **Defragment:** Make sure you periodically defragment your hard drive. Writing to a fragmented disk can cause disruptions in your hard drive's transfer speed, causing you to lose or drop frames as you capture. You can use the defragmentation utility included with Windows or purchase a third-party utility.

Capture options

When you're capturing from tape, options in Quick and Expert views differ, primarily in regard to scene detection. Specifically, you can enable scene detection in Expert view but can't in Quick view.

Here's a description of what scene detection is and how it works: During capture, Adobe Premiere Elements can split the captured video into scenes, which makes it much easier to find and edit the desired content. Adobe Premiere Elements can use one of two scene-detection techniques to detect scenes: Timecode-based and Content-based.

Timecode-based scene detection is available only when capturing DV source video. As the name suggests, this technique uses timecodes in the video to break the capture clips into scenes. Specifically, when you record DV, your camcorder automatically records a time/date stamp when you press Stop or Record. During capture, Adobe Premiere Elements can create a new scene each time it detects a new time/date stamp and creates a separate video file on your hard drive for each scene.

Content-based scene detection, which is your only option for HDV or webcam videos, analyzes the content after capture to identify scene changes. For example, if you shot one scene indoors and the next outdoors, Adobe Premiere Elements would analyze the video frames and detect the new scene.

When detecting scenes using Content-based scene detection, Adobe Premiere Elements stores only one video file on your hard drive and designates the scenes in the Project Assets panel and timeline. After capture, while scanning the captured video for scene changes, Adobe Premiere Elements displays a status panel describing the operation and apprising you of its progress.

The screen at right shows the capture interface when opened in Expert view. The Split Scenes option is available, and Content-based scene detection is the only option, which means that Adobe Premiere Elements was capturing HDV. If you were in Quick view, none of the options shown here would appear. Unless you're filming one long event, like a ballet or play, I recommend always capturing with scene detection enabled. When you're working with DV, I recommend using Timecode-based scene detection, because it's faster and more accurate.

About timecode

When capturing video, it's important to understand the basics of timecode. Timecode numbers represent the location of a frame in a video clip. Many camcorders record timecode as part of the video signal. The timecode format is based on the number of frames per second (fps) that the camcorder records and the number of frames per second that the video displays upon playback. Video has a standard frame rate that is either 29.97 fps for NTSC video (the North American and Japanese TV standard) or 25 fps for PAL video (the European TV standard). Timecode describes a frame's location in the format of hours:minutes:seconds:frames. For example, 01;20;15;10 specifies that the displayed frame is located 1 hour, 20 minutes, 15 seconds, and 10 frames into the scene.

—From Adobe Premiere Elements Help

In addition, when you're capturing in Quick view, all clips are automatically added to the timeline, so the Capture To Timeline option does not appear. In Expert view, you can select the Capture To Timeline option to achieve the same result.

Capturing clips with device control

When you're capturing clips, device control refers to the ability to control the operation of a connected video deck or camcorder using controls within the Adobe Premiere Elements interface rather than using the controls on the connected device. This mode of operation is more convenient because Adobe Premiere Elements offers controls like Next Scene or Shuttle that may not be available on your camcorder's controls.

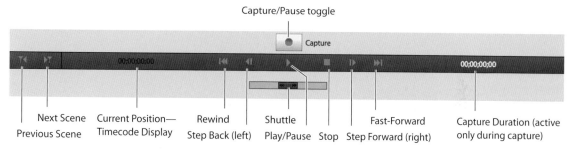

You probably know most of these controls because they're similar to your camcorder or VCR. You may not be familiar with the Shuttle control, which you can drag with your pointer to the left or right to rewind or fast-forward the video. This control is position-sensitive; the farther you drag the shuttle widget from the center, the faster the tape fast-forwards or rewinds. The Previous Scene and Next Scene controls use Timecode-based scene detection to advance backward or forward to the previous or next scenes.

Adobe Premiere Elements should be able to establish device control with all DV and HDV camcorders, but it's not available when capturing from webcams, a WDM Device (Windows)/Webcam (Mac OS), or analog camcorders. You can still capture video from these sources without device control, but the capture procedure is slightly different. Procedures for capturing with and without device control are detailed in the following section.

Capturing with the Capture panel

With the preceding information in this lesson as a prologue, let's look at the process for capturing video via Adobe Premiere Elements' Capture panel.

1   Connect the HDV camcorder to your computer via an IEEE 1394 cable.

2   Turn on the camera and set it to playback mode, which may be labeled VTR, VCR, or Play.

Note: This exercise assumes that you have successfully connected an HDV camera to your computer and that you have footage available to capture. If this is not the case, you can still open the Capture panel to review the interface; however, you will not be able to access all the controls.

Note: If your DV camera is connected but not turned on, your Capture panel will display Capture Device Offline in the status area. Although it is preferable to turn on your camera before launching Adobe Premiere Elements, in most cases turning on your camera at any point will bring it online.

Note: When capturing DV and webcam footage, you will see video in the Preview area of the Capture panel.

3 Launch Adobe Premiere Elements. Click New Project in the Welcome screen to start a new project. If Adobe Premiere Elements is already running, choose File > New Project, save your current project if desired, and then choose a project name and the appropriate preset. Then click OK to save the new project.

4 On the upper left of the Adobe Premiere Elements interface, click Add Media (Add Media) to open the Add Media panel.

5 In the Add Media panel, select HDV Camcorder ( ) to follow along with this procedure. The Capture panel appears. Note that there will be no preview on your computer when capturing HDV video and that you will have to watch the LCD screen on your camcorder to determine when to stop capture.

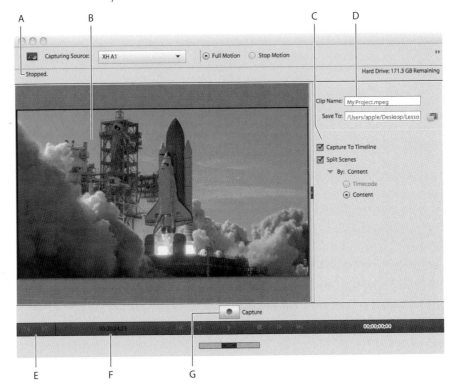

A. **Status area**—Displays status information about your camera.

B. **Preview area**—Displays your current video as played through your camera (DV and webcam only, not HDV).

C. **Capture settings**—Enable you to change the capture settings.

D. **Clip Name**—By default, Adobe Premiere Elements uses the project name to name the AVI or MOV movie clips.

E. **Device controls**—Contains buttons used to directly control your camera.

F. **Current position**—Timecode display. Shows you the current frame of your video, measured in the format of hours; minutes; seconds; frames.

G. **Capture/Pause button**—Starts and stops video/audio capture.

6   In the upper-right area of the Capture panel, type the desired Clip Name and Save To location for the captured files. Note that Adobe Premiere Elements defaults to the project name for Clip Name and uses the folder where you stored your project file for the default Save To location. If desired, change any of the default Capture settings.

● **Note:** When capturing without device control, use the camcorder's playback controls to navigate to a position about 20 seconds before the first scene you want to capture. Click Play, and about 10 seconds before the actual scene appears, click the Capture button (●). Adobe Premiere Elements will start capturing the video, and you should see a red box around the preview screen in the capture window. Capture the desired scenes, and about 10 seconds after the last target frame, click the Pause button (❚❚) to stop capture.

7   At the bottom of the Capture panel, use the navigation controls to navigate to the first scene you'd like to capture.

8   Click the Capture button (●). Adobe Premiere Elements automatically starts playing video on the DV camcorder, captures each scene as an individual movie clip, and adds it to your project.

9   After clicking the Capture button, the button becomes the Pause button (❚❚). To stop capturing video, either click the Pause button or press the Esc key on your keyboard. If enabled, the Auto-Analyze window will appear as Adobe Premiere Elements analyzes the clip and then close. Any clips you have already captured will remain in your project.

10 After you've finished capturing your video, close the Capture panel. If you captured in Quick view, your captured clips appear in the Quick view timeline. If you captured in Expert view, your captured clips appear in the Project Assets panel, and if you enabled Capture To Timeline, Adobe Premiere Elements will also place each clip into your sceneline in sequential order.

● **Note:** If you see the error message shown below, it means that your project setting doesn't conform to the video that you're about to capture. To fix this, choose File > New Project to open the New Project dialog and click the Change Settings button to choose the appropriate setting (HDV for HDV footage, or DV for DV footage). Then click OK to open the new project.

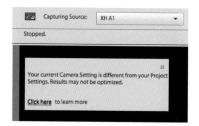

● **Note:** If you receive the error message "Recorder Error — frames dropped during capture," or if you're having problems with the device control, it's likely that your hard drive is not keeping up with the transfer of video. Make sure you're capturing your video to the fastest hard drive available, for example, an external IEEE 1394 drive rather than a hard drive inside a laptop computer.

Debugging device control issues

As mentioned, Adobe Premiere Elements should be able to establish device control with all DV and HDV camcorders. If you see the error message "No DV camera detected" or "No HDV camera detected," Adobe Premiere Elements can't detect your camcorder. In this case, you won't be able to establish device control and may not be able to capture video. Here are some steps you can take to attempt to remedy this situation.

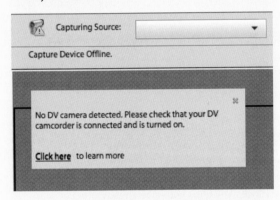

1   Exit Adobe Premiere Elements and make sure your camcorder is turned on and running (and hasn't timed out due to inactivity) in VCR, Play, or other similar mode. Also, check to see that your IEEE 1394 cable is firmly connected to both the camcorder's and computer's IEEE 1394 ports. Then run Adobe Premiere Elements again and see if the program detects the camcorder.

2   If Adobe Premiere Elements still can't see the camcorder, check your project settings and make sure they match your camcorder (DV project if DV camcorder; HDV project if HDV camcorder).

3   If you're still experiencing capture issues, you may have a configuration problem within Adobe Premiere Elements. In the upper-right corner of the Capture panel, click the two triangles to open the Capture panel menu and choose Capture Settings, which opens the Project Settings dialog to Capture Format.

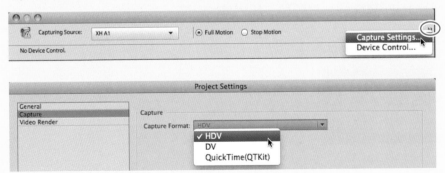

4   In this dialog, choose the correct capture device, either DV or HDV. Note that the Mac OS dialog lists HDV/DV/QuickTime (QTKit) in that order. Close the Project Settings dialog, and then close and reopen the Capture panel. If Adobe Premiere Elements still doesn't detect your camcorder, try step 5.

5   In the Capture panel menu, choose Device Control, which opens the Preferences dialog with the Device Control view visible.

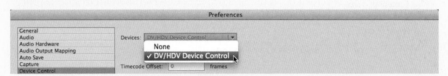

6   In this dialog, make sure that DV/HDV Device Control is selected (note that the Mac OS dialog has only two options: None and DV/HDV Device Control). Close the Preferences panel, and then close and reopen the Capture panel. If Adobe Premiere Elements still doesn't detect your camcorder, try step 7.

7   Most HDV camcorders can also record and play DV video. However, if you're capturing DV video and your camcorder is set to record HDV, Adobe Premiere Elements may detect an HDV camcorder rather than DV (or vice versa). For example, if you shot HDV in your last shoot but were capturing DV video from a previous shoot, Adobe Premiere Elements may detect an HDV camcorder rather than a DV camcorder. In this situation, set the camcorder to record DV video, and when you return to VCR or Play mode, play a few seconds of DV video, which may enable Adobe Premiere Elements to detect the DV camcorder.

Importing content from your hard drive

Follow this procedure to import audio, video, or still-image content that's already on your hard drive.

1　On the upper left of the Adobe Premiere Elements interface, click Add Media (Add Media ▾) to open the Add Media panel.

2　In the Add Media panel, select Files and folders (▢) to follow along with this procedure. The Capture panel appears. Note that there will be no preview on your computer when capturing HDV video and that you will have to watch the LCD screen on your camcorder to determine when to stop capture.

Adobe Premiere Elements opens the Add Media panel.

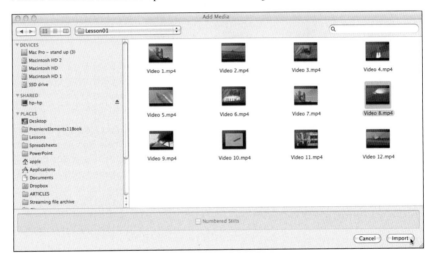

3　To change to a new disk or folder, click the Look In list box (Windows)/Folder list box (Mac OS) and navigate to a new location.

4　To display only certain files types in the dialog, click the Files of Type list box (Windows only), and choose the desired file type. The dialog displays only files of the selected type.

5　To import files, choose them in the dialog as you normally would, and click Open.

Files that you import in Quick view are inserted at the end of the timeline. Files inserted in Expert view are added to the Project Assets panel.

Review questions

1   How do you access the Capture panel in Adobe Premiere Elements?

2   Why is having a separate hard drive dedicated to video a good idea?

3   What is scene detection, and how would you turn it on or off if you wanted to?

4   What is the Video Importer, and when would you use it?

5   What is device control?

Review answers

1   Click Get Media from the Organize Workspace, and then click the appropriate capture icon.

2   Video files take up large amounts of space compared to standard office and image files. A hard drive stores the video clips you capture and must be fast enough to store your video frames. Although office-type files tend to be fairly small, they can clutter a hard drive when scattered throughout the available space; the more free, defragmented space you have on a hard drive, the better the performance of real-time video capture will be.

3   Scene detection is Adobe Premiere Elements' ability to detect scene changes in your video (based on timecode or by content) during video capture and save each scene as an individual clip in your project. You can select or deselect Timecode-based or Content-based in the Capture panel menu.

4   The Video Importer is a feature of Adobe Premiere Elements that enables you to import media from AVCHD camcorders, digital still cameras, mobile phones, other portable media devices, and DVDs, whether from a camcorder or PC DVD drive.

5   Device control is the ability of Adobe Premiere Elements to control the basic functions of your digital video camera (such as play, stop, and rewind) through the interface in the Capture panel. It's available on most DV and HDV camcorders.

4 ORGANIZING YOUR CONTENT

Lesson overview

Fast and efficient movie production requires organization before and during the edit. To help you organize your editing work in Expert view, Adobe Premiere Elements' Project Assets panel lets you search for and deploy content already added to your project.

However, when you're working with content from multiple sources and dates, Adobe Organizer is a very powerful tool for categorizing your content and quickly finding video, audio clips, and pictures to use in your projects. In this lesson, you'll learn how to do the following:

* Create Places in the Organizer and associate your content with those places
* Use Smart Events to quickly find content from specific dates
* Create Events in the Organizer and associate your content with those events
* Rate your clips and find clips based on those ratings
* Create and use keyword tags to find your content
* Use the Auto-Analyzer to split your video into scenes and rate it qualitatively
* Transfer clips from the Organizer to Adobe Premiere Elements

 This lesson will take approximately two hours.

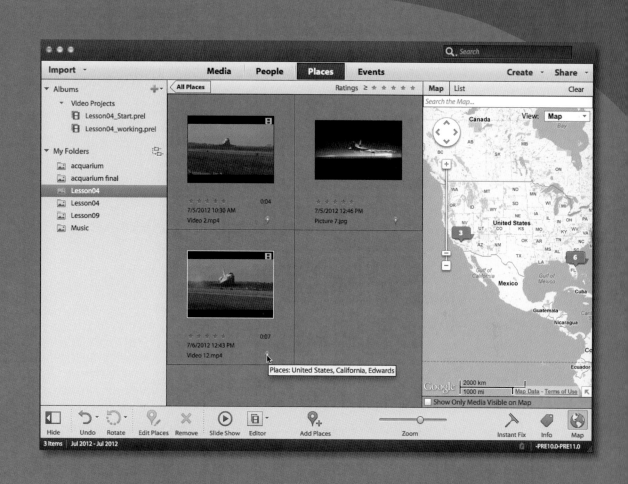

Geotagging content in the Organizer.

Getting started

Before you start working with the footage, let's review a final version of the movie you'll be creating. Make sure that you have correctly copied the Lesson04 folder from the DVD in the back of this book onto your computer's hard drive. See "Copying the Classroom in a Book files" in the "Getting Started" section at the beginning of this book.

1   Launch Adobe Premiere Elements. If it is already open, choose Help > Welcome Screen in the Adobe Premiere Elements main menu to return to the Welcome screen.

2   In the Welcome screen, click Video Editor, select Existing Project, and click the Open folder.

3   In the Open Project dialog, navigate to the Lesson04 folder you copied to your hard drive. Within that folder, select the file Lesson04_Start_Win.prel (Windows) or Lesson04_Start_Mac.prel (Mac OS) and then click Open. If a dialog appears asking for the location of rendered files, click the Skip Previews button.

    Your project file opens.

4   Choose Window > Restore Workspace to ensure that you start the lesson with the default panel layout.

Viewing the completed movie before you start

To see what you'll be creating in this lesson, you can take a look at the completed movie. You must be in Expert view to open the Project Assets panel to view the movie; if you are not, click Expert on the top of the Monitor panel (Expert) to enter that view.

1   On the upper-left side of the Adobe Premiere Elements interface, click the Project Assets button (Project Assets ▾) to open that panel. Locate the file Lesson04_Movie.mov (which should be the only file), and then double-click it to open the video into the preview window.

2   Click the Play button () to watch the video about powering the Space Shuttle
    (all footage was graciously provided by NASA), which you'll build in this lesson.

3   When you're finished, close the preview window.

Working in the Project Assets panel

The Project Assets panel contains all the content that you've input into your project
and is only available in Expert view. As with all panels, you click the Project Assets
button (Project Assets ▾) to open it and then click the button again to close it.

The Project Assets panel's role is to help you organize and find files using different
search methods. Let's load some files into the project so you can work with them
in the Project Assets panel. Again, if you don't see the Project Assets panel, click
Expert on the top of the Monitor panel (Expert) to enter that view.

1   Click Add Media (Add Media ▾) to open the Add Media panel.

2   Click Files and folders (▢) to open the Add Media dialog.

3   Navigate to the Lesson04 folder. While pressing the Ctrl key (Windows) or
    Command key (Mac OS), select the movie clips Video 1.mp4 to Video 12.mp4,
    all digital pictures from Picture 1.jpg to Picture 7.jpg, and the single audio clip,
    narration.wav. Then click Open (Windows) or Import (Mac).

Controls in the Project Assets panel

You can also use controls in the Project Assets panel to create titles, black videos, bars and tones, and color mattes. In this short section, you'll learn how to use the basic tools in the Project Assets panel to find the desired file.

You can perform the following activities in the Project Assets panel to view your files:

- Grab the handle on the extreme lower right of the panel to expand it vertically and horizontally.

- Browse through the entire catalog by using the scroll bar at the right side of Project Assets panel.

A. Show/Hide Video

B. Show/Hide Still Image

C. Show/Hide Audio

D. Search box

E. Go up one folder level

F. Clear

G. Pin view

H. Project Assets menu

Let's work through some of the most common functions of the Project Assets panel.

1 On the upper left of the Project Assets panel, experiment by clicking the Show/Hide Video (▣), Show/Hide Still Image (▣), and Show/Hide Audio (▣) buttons. For example, click the Hide Still Image and Hide Audio buttons so only video files appear in the Project Assets panel. This is a very simple technique for quickly finding the video content that you're looking for.

2   From the Project Assets panel menu, choose View > List view to display the content in this view. Once in List view, click and drag the bottom-right corner to expand the window so all the columns are visible. You can sort your content by clicking the column head of any column. The arrow in the column you choose shows whether the data is sorted in ascending order or descending order. For example, click the Name column head to see how it sorts the content, and then click the Media Duration column head.

3   In the Project Assets panel menu, choose New Folder to create a folder to organize your videos. Adobe Premiere Elements creates a folder named Folder 01 with the text highlighted so it's easy to change the name. Type in the word **Videos** and press Enter or Return, replacing the text Folder 01.

4   Select all files and drag them into the new folder. Click the disclosure triangle next to the Videos folder to close it. Your Project Assets panel is a whole lot tidier. When you're working with large projects with multiple video, still image, and audio files, creating folders is the best strategy for organizing your content and making it easy to find.

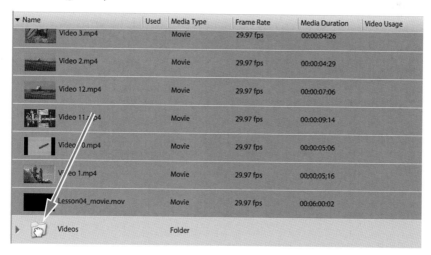

Note: On Windows, you can also create a Universal Counting Leader, a vestigial feature typically used only when writing video back to analog tape.

5 From the Project Assets panel menu, choose New Item to view the new items that you can create from this menu. We'll cover titles in Lesson 8. Bars and Tone is a vestigial concept that is useful for analog projects but has little application for most digital video-based projects. Creating black video and color mattes are useful when you need colored or black backgrounds for titles or other movie elements. Select any of these items and Adobe Premiere Elements will open a format-specific dialog for creating the content and inserting it into the Project Assets panel.

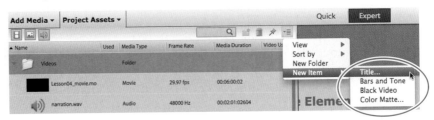

6 Double-click Video 1.mp4 in the Videos folder of the Project Assets panel to open it in the preview window. (If necessary, click and drag the bottom-right corner of the Project Assets panel to make the preview window visible.) The preview window lets you play your content using VCR-like controls before you add it to your project. You can also trim frames from the start and end of the video before adding it to your project. Although you can also trim frames in the timeline, you may prefer to do this in the preview window.

7 Let's trim some frames from the clip. In the Preview window, drag the current-time indicator to the right until the timecode beneath the video reads 00;00;00;09 (see figure on following page), which is nine frames in from the start of the clip and the point at which you can just start to see flames beneath the Space Shuttle's solid rocket boosters. Note that you can also use the left and right arrow keys on your keyboard for precise positioning of the current-time indicator.

8 Click the Set In icon to set the In point, or press the letter I on your keyboard. In essence, you've told Adobe Premiere Elements to ignore the first nine frames when you add the clip to the project and start at frame 10. Of course, the edit is *nondestructive*, so you haven't actually deleted any frames from the video file on your disk. You can always undo this later and show the frames that you just trimmed.

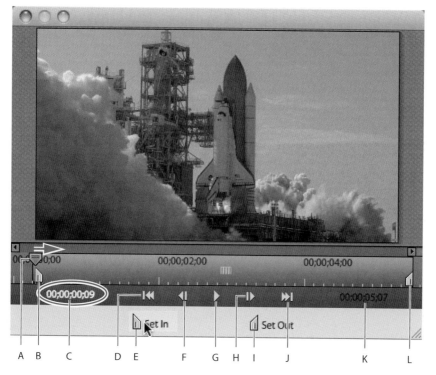

A. Current-time indicator

B. In point handle

C. Current time in movie

D. Rewind

E. Set In point (I)

F. Step Back (left arrow key)

G. Play/Pause toggle (spacebar)

H. Step Forward (right arrow key)

I. Set Out point (O)

J. Fast-Forward

K. Clip duration

L. Out point handle

● **Note:** Rather than moving the current-time indicator to the desired location and choosing Set In point or Set Out point, you can simply drag the In point handle or Out point handle to the desired location.

9 In the preview window, drag the current-time indicator to the right until the timecode beneath the video reads around 00;00;04;05, which is where the Shuttle's nose touches the top of the video frame. Click the Set Out icon to set the Out point, or press the letter O on your keyboard. You've just set the Out point, essentially trimming out all video frames to the right of that point of the video.

10 Click and drag Video 1 in the preview window to the start of the Video 1 and Audio 1 tracks on the timeline as shown in the figure and release. You've just added the trimmed video to the timeline. Click No if Adobe Premiere Elements asks if you want to fix any quality issues in the clip or any other questions.

11 Close the preview window, and then click the Project Assets (Project Assets ▾) button to close the Project Assets panel. Make sure that the current-time indicator in the timeline is at the start of the clip, click anywhere in the timeline, and then press the spacebar to play the clip. Note that it starts and ends on the trimmed frames.

● **Note:** When you set In and Out points in the preview window, they're automatically applied prospectively when you drag the clip into the timeline. But these In and Out points aren't retroactively applied to clips already in the timeline. You'll learn how to trim clips in the timeline in the next lesson.

Tagging in the Organizer

The Project Assets panel is great for quickly finding clips, but the Organizer is Adobe Premiere Elements' best tool for serious organization and search-and-retrieval work. You can open the Organizer by clicking the Organizer icon (📷 Organizer) in Adobe Premiere Elements' Action bar. This exercise details how to perform manual and Smart Tagging in the Organizer, and then how to search for clips using those tags in the Organizer.

People, Places, and Events

Star ratings

Manual tagging with Keyword Tags

Media browser

Smart Tagging

As shown in the figure, there are three ways that the Adobe Organizer helps you organize your clips: by categorizing them into People, Places, and Events; by giving them star ratings on a scale from 1 to 5; and by manually tagging them with keywords and via smart tags. Let's take a quick look at each technique in this introductory overview, and then you'll learn how to use them.

In Adobe Premiere Elements 11, the Organizer's interface has been optimized for three views, as shown on the top toolbar: People, Places, and Events. By associating your video clips with one or more of these categories, you can easily find all clips associated with a person, place, or event. I'll demonstrate how to associate your clips with a place or an event, but not a person, primarily because face recognition—a great feature that the Organizer uses to automate the process of people tagging your still images—is not available for video.

The star ratings system allows you to review and rate all your clips on a scale from 1 to 5; you can later search for only those clips that you rated 4 or higher, for example—an easy way to find high-quality clips and eliminate poor-quality clips. Keyword tags allow you to tag a clip by person, location, event, or other tags and includes customizable categories.

When you run the Auto-Analyzer on a clip, Adobe Premiere Elements analyzes the video to detect scenes based on content and rates the content qualitatively, a process known as Smart Tagging. This allows you to hunt for scenes with faces and identify scenes that are out of focus, shaky, underexposed, or overexposed. Using this qualitative data, Adobe Premiere Elements then categorizes all clips as high, medium, or low quality. This serves a valuable triage function that you can later use to search for the best clips for your movie. This analysis is also used for features like Smart Trimming, which you'll learn in Lesson 5, and Smart Fix, as discussed in Lesson 6.

For example, if you shot an hour of video on your last vacation, Smart Tagging allows you to identify medium-quality-and-higher clips containing faces (presumably family members) and produce a movie containing only these clips. What would literally take you hours to accomplish manually, Smart Tagging can produce in a few moments.

Using all these tags in any combination, you can hunt for clips to manually add to your projects or create an InstantMovie, which is a professional-looking edited movie complete with titles, soundtrack, effects, and transitions. You'll create an InstantMovie in the last exercise in this lesson.

Tagging clips in the Organizer

Let's dive into tagging clips in the Organizer, starting with Places and Events. If you've been following along, your Organizer should just have the content loaded from the Lesson04 folder. To ensure that we're all looking at the same thing, let's reload that content.

1 On the bottom-left corner of the Organizer, click the Show button (⬚) to open the panel. The Show button toggles to the Hide button (⬚).

2 If necessary, click the disclosure triangle next to My Folders to reveal that content. Then click Lesson04. If Lesson04 isn't there, return to the "Working in the Project Assets panel" exercise and load the content as described. Then return to this exercise; the Lesson04 folder should be there.

3 Take these steps to make sure your Organizer looks the same as the figure.

- In the Organizer menu, choose View > Media Types. Make sure photos, video, and audio are all selected.

- Choose View > Details, View > File Names, and View > Grid Lines to show these elements.

- In the Sort By list box on top of the Organizer's Media browser, make sure Oldest is selected.

● **Note:** If you've been working with Adobe Premiere Elements and the Organizer for a while, you'll likely have multiple projects and folders in the panel. Find and click the Lesson04 folder; the content in the Organizer should be close to what you see in the figures.

● **Note:** You can play any video file in the Organizer or view any still image in the Organizer by double-clicking the video or still image in the browser and then clicking the Play button in the preview window that appears. Close the window to return to the Media browser. Still images are displayed in an expanded window in the Media browser; click Grid (Grid) on the left of the toolbar immediately above the image to return to the Media browser.

Now that we're all looking at the same screen, let's start tagging.

● **Note:** The Adobe Organizer can display all clips in a Timeline view (in Media view, click View > Timeline) that displays content by data, which can be a convenient way to find some clips. You just move along the timeline, click any clumps of sequential clips in the timeline, and they appear in the Media browser. Of course, you need clips in the Organizer to create the clumps, so until you populate the Organizer, this view won't provide that much value.

● **Note:** Your screen may not match perfectly what's shown on the page, but the minor differences shouldn't keep you from completing any exercises.

Tagging clips to Places

The NASA clips we're using in this book took place in two basic places: The launch occurred at Kennedy Space Center in Florida, and the other location is somewhere in outer space that, as near as I can tell, Google hasn't yet incorporated into Google Earth. Give it time. Even though the launch and landing took place at Kennedy Space Center, because over 50 Shuttle landings have occurred at Edwards Air Force Base in California and we want to tag two different places in this exercise, we'll tag the landing at Edwards Air Force Base.

At a high level, you'll create two Places in the Organizer—one for launch and one for landing—and then associate some clips with each place. Then, working from the Organizer's Google Maps view, you can click a place and see all clips associated with that place. Let's jump in.

1   On the Organizer's top toolbar, click Places (**Places**).

2   On the Organizer's bottom toolbar, click Add Places (⚑).

3   In the Add Places Search field, type **Kennedy Space Center** and click Search. Note that if you were typing in a street address, you would type in the address as you would on an envelope. For example, if you shot video at the White House in Washington, DC, you could either type in **The White House** or **1600 Pennsylvania Avenue, NW Washington, DC 20500**.

4   If Google Earth finds two locations, click John F. Kennedy Space Center, Florida, USA, not the Visitor Center. The Organizer will create a placeholder into which you will drag all media shot from that location.

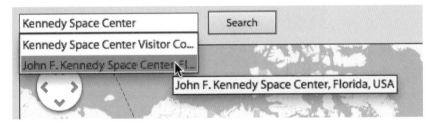

5   Hold down the Ctrl key (Windows) or Command key (Mac OS) and click all the pictures and video in the media bar atop the Add Places dialog associated with that location. Our selections don't have to match precisely, but I selected all take-off related pictures and videos that showed the Shuttle on or near the ground, and didn't select space or landing shots. This totaled six videos.

6   Release the Ctrl key (Windows) or Command key (Mac OS), click any of the
    selected pictures or video, drag them all to the icon beneath the Place 6 Media
    Here text box, release the pointer, and click the green checkmark. Adobe
    Premiere Elements will associate the selected content with that place.

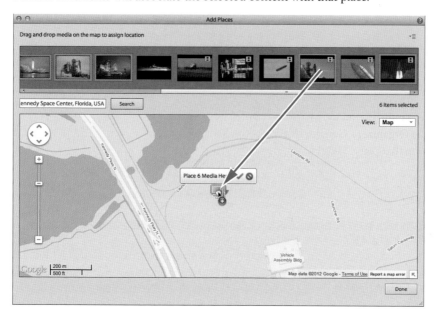

7   On the bottom right of the Add Places dialog, click Done. The Organizer creates
    the place.

8   Repeat the process with the landing shots. Click Add Places again, type
    Edwards Air Force Base in the Search field, and click the location that the
    Organizer finds. Ctrl-click (Windows) or Command-click (Mac OS) the three
    landing shots (two similar landing videos and one still-frame night landing),
    release the Ctrl key (Windows) or Command key (Mac OS), and drag the
    selected content into the icon. Click Done when you're finished.

    You should now have at least two places identified and content associated with
    each. Let's see how this will help you find your content for future projects.

    In the Organizer's top toolbar, click Media (Media) to exit Places view, and then
    click Places (Places) to return to that view. If the Map isn't displayed on the right,
    click the Map icon (🌐) in the lower-right corner of the Organizer interface.

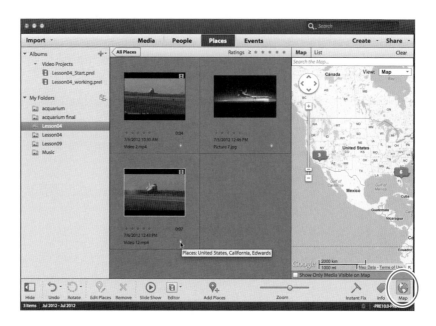

Note: Note that Places has a Map view, shown in the previous figure, and a List view, which might provide better precision for certain search functions.

You may have to adjust the navigational and sizing controls on the upper left of the map, but you should be able to approximate the view shown in the previous figure. Double-click either icon, and the Organizer will display the content from that location in the Media browser, as shown in the figure above. Single-click the icon, and the Organizer will display all content with the content from that location highlighted. If you hover your pointer over the blue icon in each video or still image, you'll notice that it's been tagged to the respective places.

Tagging clips to Events

The Organizer has a Smart Events feature that you can use to find content without any tagging on your part. To see this function in action, click Events (**Events**), and then choose the Smart Events toggle in the Events top toolbar. This shows all content grouped by date in the Media browser, which you can navigate through using the vertical scroll bar on the right of the Media browser. Or, you can narrow your search by choosing a year, month, and/or day using the calendar on the right.

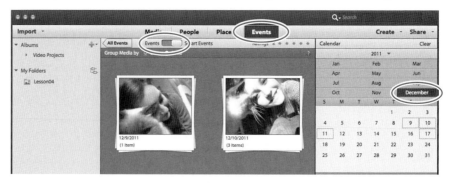

Sometimes, however, you'll want to manually organize clips into Events—perhaps because like the Shuttle flight, the event took place over multiple days. Or, perhaps you shot video and pictures at more than one event on a particular day and need to break them into multiple events, like a wedding ceremony and wedding reception. Here's the procedure for manually creating Events with the Adobe Organizer. For the purposes of this exercise, though our clips were gathered from multiple missions, I'll assume that the Space Shuttle mission was STS-135, the last mission flown.

1   Click Events (Events) to enter Event view. Make sure Events is selected in the top toolbar, not Smart Events.

2   On the Organizer's bottom toolbar, click Add Event ( ). The Add New Event dialog appears on the right.

3   Complete the information in the Add New Event dialog.

   • In the Name field, type **STS-135**.

   • Use the calendar controls to input a Start Date of 7/8/2011 and an End Date of 7/21/2011. It's easiest if you choose the year first and then the date.

   • In the Description field, type **Final Space Shuttle Mission**.

4   Assuming that you still have Lesson04 selected in the panel on the left, all content in the Media browser should relate to this mission. Click anywhere in the media window to select that window, and then press Ctrl+A (Windows) or Command+A (Mac OS) to select all the content in the Media browser, drag it into the window beneath the description, and release your pointer. The Organizer adds this content to the mission event.

● **Note:** While these missions actually occurred and the videos were shot in 2011 and before, the media files that we're using were created from NASA sources in 2012. So don't let the dates in the figure confuse you.

5   On the bottom right of the Add New Event dialog, click Done. The Organizer creates the event.

Let's see how this will help you find your content later on. In the Organizer's top toolbar, click Media (**Media**) to exit Events view, and then click Events (**Events**) to return to that view. You should see the STS-135 event in the Media browser window. If you double-click it, the clips that you associated with the event will appear in the Media browser. If you hover your pointer over the calendar icon for a particular clip in the Media browser, you'll see the event with which it has been associated.

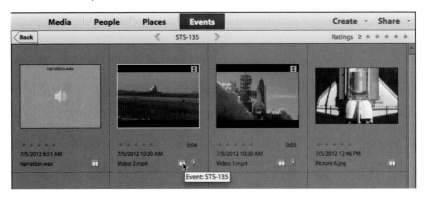

Working with star ratings

As mentioned earlier, star ratings allow you to manually rate your clips on a scale from 1 to 5 and then search for clips based on those ratings. Follow these procedures to apply and delete star ratings, and to search for clips based on the star ratings. Ratings range from 1 (on the extreme left) to 5 (on the extreme right).

1   Click Media to return to Media view. If you don't see the star ratings for your clips, choose View > Details in the Organizer menu.

2   Hover your pointer over the star ratings beneath any clip, and click the star that corresponds to the desired rating for that clip. Go ahead and rate a few clips so you can sort by rating in step 5. These are all five-star clips as far as I'm concerned, but go ahead and rate some across the board.

3   To change a rating, use the same procedure and choose a different rating.

4   To delete the star rating, click the last selected star on the right (the fourth star in a clip rated four stars).

5   To find clips based on their assigned ratings, click the number of target stars in the star Ratings bar on the top right, and in the drop-down list beneath the ratings, choose how to apply the rating. For example, in the next figure, we elected to show all clips with a four-star rating or higher.

6   To stop sorting by star rating and show all clips in the Organizer, delete the star rating on the upper right by clicking the last selected star.

Working with Keyword Tags

Adobe Premiere Elements includes general categories of Keyword Tags that you can apply as is or customize with your own categories or subcategories. In this lesson, you'll create and apply a custom keyword in the Organizer, and then search for clips based on that keyword. To ensure that you're looking at the same content as appears in this book, make sure you've selected the Lesson04 folder in the My Folders section of the Albums and Folders panel on the left of the Organizer. See the first few steps of the earlier section "Tagging clips in the Organizer" to accomplish this.

1   On the bottom right of the Organizer, click Tags/Info (🗨) to open the Tags/Information panel.

2   Below Keyword Tags in the Organizer, click Other.

3   Below Keyword Tags, click the Create New button (🔳) and choose New Sub-Category.

4 In the Create Sub-Category panel, type **Space Shots** in the Sub-Category Name field. Then click OK.

Adobe Premiere Elements creates the new subcategory.

5 Click the orange tag next to Space Shots and drag it onto any of the still images or videos that show the Space Shuttle in space. In the following figure, I've already applied the tag to Picture 6.jpg and Picture 5.jpg and am applying it to Picture 4.jpg.

6 To view the clips that you've just tagged, click the greater than (>) icon to the right of Space Shots, which opens the Tagging Search window that shows Keywords on the upper left and the clips that you just tagged in the Media browser. This window shows all tags created via keywords as well as the People, Places, and Events that you've entered into the system. You can select any check boxes in any of these categories or combination of categories to include content from these sources in the Media browser. You can even apply star ratings to further refine your search.

7 In the upper-left toolbar in the Tagging Search window, click the Back button
(<Back>) to close that search window.

About the Auto-Analyzer

As mentioned earlier, the Auto-Analyzer analyzes your video clips for content and
quality, and is integral to a number of functions, including Smart Tagging, Smart
Trimming, and creating InstantMovies, which you'll learn to do later in this lesson.
You can run the Auto-Analyzer manually, as you'll learn in the next section, or run
it as a background process. In fact, by default, the Auto-Analyzer will run on clips
that you import anytime your system is running and idle.

To access this preference,
in the Organizer, choose
Edit > Preferences > Media-
Analysis (Windows) or Adobe
Elements 11 Organizer >
Preferences > Media Analysis
(Mac OS). In the default
setting, Adobe Premiere
Elements will work in the
background with imported
media, so when you're ready
to edit, you won't have to wait
for the Auto-Analyzer to run.

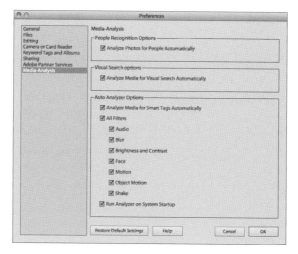

In most instances on most computers, background operation should work just fine. On older, less-powerful computers, and those configured with the minimum RAM, background operation may cause a noticeable drag on foreground operations, particularly when you're working with H.264-based, high-definition formats like AVCHD and video shot by DSLRs. If you notice any sluggishness in your foreground operations after importing footage or experience any system instability, try disabling the Auto-Analyzer as a background operation by deselecting the Analyze Media for Smart Tags Automatically check box.

Running the Auto-Analyzer manually

To manually run the Auto-Analyzer and apply Smart Tags to the project clips, follow these steps. Again, to ensure that you're looking at the same content that appears in the book, make sure you've selected the Lesson04 folder in the My Folders section of the Albums and Folders panel on the left of the Organizer. See the first few steps of the earlier section "Tagging clips in the Organizer" to accomplish this.

1   If the Organizer isn't open, click the Organizer icon ( ) in the Action bar to open the Organizer. If it's already open, press Alt+Tab (Windows) or Command+Tab to switch to the Organizer.

2   Press Ctrl+A (Windows) or Command+A (Mac OS) to select all clips, and then right-click and choose Run Auto-Analyzer. This can take a while, so you might want to try one or two clips first.

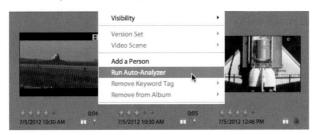

3   The Organizer starts analyzing the clips and displays a progress bar. The duration of the process will vary by clip length, clip format, and the speed of your computer. After completion, Adobe Premiere Elements will display a status message letting you know that the analysis is complete.

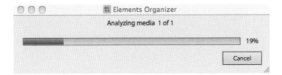

4   In the Organizer, if necessary, press Ctrl+D (Windows) or Command+D (Mac OS) to display file details. A purple tag beneath the clip's thumbnail indicates that Smart Tagging has been applied, and if there are multiple tags (📑), you can hover your pointer over the tags to see which quality-related tags were applied.

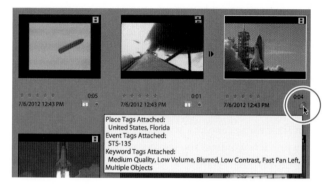

5   To remove a tag, right-click the tag in the Organizer and choose Remove. Repeat as necessary for other tags.

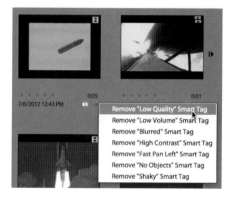

Working with clips after Smart Tagging

Let's take a moment to understand what happens to clips after Smart Tagging. To review, during Smart Tagging, Adobe Premiere Elements breaks the clip into different scenes based on content changes (as opposed to timecode, like DV files); finds different types of content, like faces; and rates the quality of each clip based on factors like exposure, focus, and stability.

In the Organizer, you'll know that the clip has been split into multiple scenes if there is a Step Forward icon (▶) on the right of the clip. Click that icon, and Adobe Premiere Elements displays all scenes separately in the Organizer surrounded by a border that's a different shade of gray from the rest of the Organizer. This lets you know that all the scenes are part of a single clip.

You should see separate scenes in clip Video 6.mp4, although the clip is so short that the difference between the scenes is minimal. With most longer, real-world clips, you'll see more distinct scenes and find that scene detection is quite useful.

 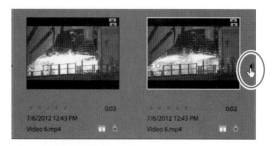

In the Organizer, you can treat each scene as a separate clip—for example, double-clicking it to play it in the preview window. You can consolidate all scenes back into a single frame by clicking the Step Backward icon to the right of the final scene (◀).

From the Organizer to Adobe Premiere Elements

After you've collected the clips you want to use in the Organizer, you have multiple options for transferring them to Adobe Premiere Elements. These options include the following:

- Send them all to Adobe Premiere Elements to start a new project or for insertion at the end of the timeline in an open project. The high-level procedure is to select the desired clips, right-click, and choose Edit with Premiere Elements Editor. Note that you can select complete clips or segments of clips identified by the Auto-Analyzer. The full procedure is documented in "Working in the Organizer" in Lesson 1. This option works well for simple projects because it adds all content to the timeline quickly.

- Drag the clips into the Project Assets panel. You must be in Expert view for the Project Assets panel to be available. Again, the high-level procedure is to select the desired clips, and then drag them into the Project Assets panel. This option gives you the most flexibility because you can add the content to the timeline in any order and at anytime.

- Create an InstantMovie from the content by selecting it in the Organizer and sending it to Adobe Premiere Elements to create the InstantMovie. This is the option explored in the next exercise.

Creating an InstantMovie

In this exercise, you'll create an InstantMovie from the Space Shuttle clips that you tagged in a previous exercise. Again, an InstantMovie is a professional-looking edited movie complete with titles, soundtrack, effects, and transitions that you'll create by following a simple wizard.

You'll start in the Organizer, using the video clips you've been tagging from the Lesson04 folder. Follow the first two steps in "Tagging clips in the Organizer" to make sure these clips are the only ones present in the Media browser. In addition, close Adobe Premiere Elements to start with a clean slate in that program. Do not overwrite the file Lesson04_Start_Win.prel (Windows) or Lesson04_Start_Mac.prel (Mac OS): If you want to save your work, please save it under a different name.

1 Let's start by removing audio and photos from display in the browser. Choose View > Media Types > Photos and then choose View > Media Types > Audio to remove these media types from the Media browser.

2 Press Ctrl+A (Windows) or Command+A (Mac OS) to select all clips in the Media browser, click the Create button (Create) in the upper-right corner of the Organizer, and choose InstantMovie (Instant Movie).

Note: You can create InstantMovies from within Adobe Premiere Elements by adding the desired clips to the timeline in either Quick or Expert view and clicking the Instant Movie button on the Action bar. From there, the procedure is virtually identical to what's described here. Note that when creating an InstantMovie, Adobe Premiere Elements removes all effects, transitions, and titles that you've added to the project, so trim the excess content from your clips, but don't add these elements because they will all be eliminated.

3 Adobe Premiere Elements launches. If the Format Mismatch dialog opens, click Yes to change the project preset to match the clips.

4 If a Save Project dialog opens, name the file **Lesson04_InstantMovie.prel** and save it in the Lesson04 folder.

Note: The "Apply to" radio buttons become active only when you apply a theme to clips already inserted into the timeline, not when you create an InstantMovie from the Organizer.

5   If a dialog opens asking if you want to fix problems in the clips, click No.

6   In the "Choose a movie theme" dialog, choose Pan and Zoom and click Next. If this theme is not available, choose another theme.

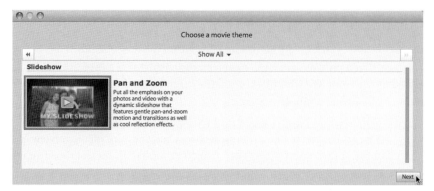

7   Customize the theme as desired. Accept the options as is, *or do any or all of the following:*

•   Customize the Opening and Closing Titles.

•   Select the Auto Edit check box to have Adobe Premiere Elements analyze your clips and edit them to fit the selected theme, which is recommended. If you don't select Auto Edit, Adobe Premiere Elements uses the clips as is and doesn't edit them. Also, choose whether or not to apply the Auto-Analyzer to clips that you haven't previously analyzed.

•   Click the disclosure triangle next to Music to open the Music box. In the Music box, choose the Theme Music radio button to use the background music from the selected theme, or choose the No Music radio button. To use your own background music, click the My Music radio button, and then click the Browse button to choose the song you want. Then drag the Music/Sound FX slider to the desired setting: Drag to the right to prioritize audio captured with the video clips and to the left to prioritize the selected background music. If you have dialogue in your project that you want to retain (which these clips don't), select the SmartMix check box and Adobe Premiere Elements will reduce the volume of the music track when it detects dialogue.

•   Click the disclosure triangle next to Speed and Intensity to open the Speed and Intensity box. In the Speed and Intensity box, adjust the Effects and Cuts sliders as desired.

•   Click the disclosure triangle next to Duration to open the Duration box. In the Duration box, choose the desired option. Match Music produces a movie that matches the duration of the selected music and is recommended. Or, you can specify a duration or choose Use All Clips, which uses all clips at their original duration with no background music.

- Click the disclosure triangle next to Sequence to open the Sequence box. In the Sequence box, choose Theme Order (recommended), which allows Adobe Premiere Elements to use clips as they best match the theme, or choose Time/Date, which uses the clips in the order that they were shot.

- Click the disclosure triangle next to Theme Content to open the Theme Content box. In the Theme Content box, choose the content to incorporate into the InstantMovie and whether to replace any existing content with theme-based content. If a content type is grayed out (like the Intro/Closing Movie for the Pan and Zoom theme), it is not included in that theme.

- Click the disclosure triangle next to Render Preview to open the Render Preview box. In the Render Preview box, click Yes to render a preview of the InstantMovie after completion or No to preview it in real time from the timeline (recommended).

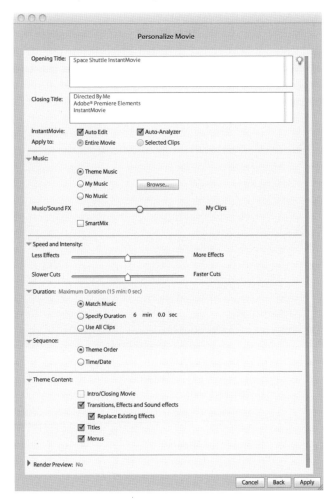

8   After selecting your options, click Apply to create the InstantMovie.

- Click No when the InstantMovie dialog opens and asks if you want to select more clips.

- Click Yes if a dialog opens and asks if you want to replace user-applied effects.

- Click No when Adobe Premiere Elements asks if you want to render the movie.

Adobe Premiere Elements creates the InstantMovie and inserts it into the timeline.

9   Adobe Premiere Elements adds the InstantMovie to the timeline in consolidated form. To separate the InstantMovie into its components to edit them, click to select the new InstantMovie in the timeline, right-click, and choose Break apart InstantMovie.

10 Use the playback controls in the Monitor panel to preview the InstantMovie. If Adobe Premiere Elements asks if you'd like to render effects before playing the movie, click Yes if you'd like to see a perfect rendition, although this may take a good bit of time, depending on your system. Click No if you have a fast system and/or just want to get a quick feel for how the movie looks.

A. Preview area

B. Add Marker

C. Current time

D. Go to Previous Edit Point (Page Up)

E. Rewind

F. Step Back (left)

G. Play/Pause toggle (spacebar)

H. Step Forward (right)

I. Fast-Forward

J. Go to Next Edit Point (Page Down)

K. Render timeline

L. Fit to Visible timeline (\)

M. Zoom Out (−)

N. Zoom control

O. Zoom In (=)

Review questions

1 What view must you be in to see the Project Assets panel?

2 What's the difference between the Organizer that ships with Adobe Premiere Elements and the Organizer that ships with Adobe Photoshop Elements?

3 What are the three main content categories in the Organizer?

4 What is Smart Tagging? Are there any situations in which you wouldn't want to apply Smart Tagging?

5 After creating an InstantMovie, how do you break up the movie to edit it further?

Review answers

1 You must be in Expert view. The Project Assets panel does not appear in Quick view.

2 This is a trick question; there is no difference. If you have Adobe Premiere Elements and Adobe Photoshop Elements installed, both programs can insert content into the same shared database and sort through and retrieve data from that database.

3 The main content categories in the Organizer are People, Places, and Events.

4 When you apply Smart Tagging to a clip, Adobe Premiere Elements analyzes the clip to detect scenes based on content; searches for specific content types, like faces; and ranks the quality of your clips. Other than processing time, there's very little downside to applying Smart Tagging. Your video clips will be divided into useful scenes, and you can find high-quality clips much faster than you could manually.

5 Click the clip with your pointer to select it, and then right-click and choose Break apart InstantMovie.

5 EDITING VIDEO

Lesson overview

In Lesson 4, you learned to organize your video in the Organizer and Project Asset panels. In this lesson, you'll learn how to shape that footage into a cohesive video. You'll apply these basic editing techniques:

- Insert, delete, and rearrange clips in Quick view and Expert view
- Trim and split clips in both views
- Create a slide show with transitions
- Use Smart Trim mode to quickly remove lower-quality segments from your videos

Over the course of this lesson, you'll piece together a short video showing the engines used to power the Space Shuttle with clips graciously supplied by NASA, and some others. You'll be working with video and audio clips provided on the DVD that accompanies this book.

 This lesson will take approximately two hours.

Trimming in Quick view.

Getting started

To begin, you'll launch Adobe Premiere Elements, open the Lesson05 project, and review a final version of the movie you'll be creating. Make sure that you have correctly copied the Lesson05 folder from the DVD in the back of this book onto your computer's hard drive. See "Copying the Classroom in a Book files" in the "Getting Started" section at the beginning of this book.

1   Launch Adobe Premiere Elements. If it is already open, choose Help > Welcome Screen in the Adobe Premiere Elements menu to return to the Welcome screen.

2   In the Welcome screen, click Video Editor, select Existing Project, and click the Open folder.

3   In the Open Project dialog, navigate to the Lesson05 folder you copied to your hard drive. Within that folder, select the file Lesson05_Start_Win.prel (Windows) or Lesson05_Start_Mac.prel (Mac OS), and then click Open. If a dialog appears asking for the location of rendered files, click the Skip Previews button.

Your project file opens.

4   Choose Window > Restore Workspace to ensure that you start the lesson with the default panel layout.

Viewing the completed movie before you start

To see what you'll be creating in this lesson, you can take a look at the completed movie. You'll have to be in Expert view to open the Project Assets panel to view the movie, so if you are not, click Expert (Expert) to enter that view.

1   On the upper-left side of the Adobe Premiere Elements interface, click the Project Assets button (Project Assets ▾) to open that panel. Locate the file Lesson05_Movie.mov and then double-click it to open the video in the preview window.

2   Click the Play button (▶) to watch the video about powering the Space Shuttle (all footage graciously provided by NASA), which you'll build in this lesson.

3   When you're done, close the preview window.

Working in the Monitor panel

When you open the project for this lesson, you'll see multiple clips in the timeline in either Expert view or Quick view. Regardless of which view you choose, you'll preview your work in the Monitor panel, which you'll explore in this exercise. Although the timeline shows your entire project, the Monitor panel shows one frame of the project, and one frame only. The displayed frame is at the location of the current-time indicator (▮), which is sometimes called the CTI or playhead.

After quickly getting familiar with the tracks in Quick view, you'll explore the functions of the Monitor panel. This lesson starts in Quick view, so click Quick (Quick) at the top of the Adobe Premiere Elements interface (if necessary) to shift into that view. Monitor panel functionality is very similar in both Quick and Expert views, so even if you plan on working in Expert view, you should read this section.

1 Select the first clip in Quick view, and note how the current-time indicator shifts to the frame that you clicked and the Monitor panel displays that frame. If you click different frames in the first clip, or any clip in the Quick view timeline, the Monitor panel displays this clip. Briefly, Quick view has four tracks:

- **Title track:** All text titles go here.

- **Audio/Video track:** This single track contains a video file and any audio in that file.

- **Narration track:** Recorded narration is inserted on this track. Alternatively, you can drag any audio file to this track.

- **Background audio track:** Any audio file can be added to this track.

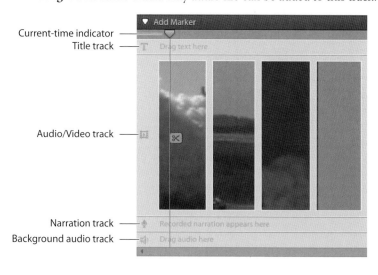

2   If you moved the current-time indicator, return to the first clip and click a spot close to the start of the clip. Then click the Play button (▶) in the Monitor panel to begin playback. As the movie is playing, notice that the timecode in the lower-left corner of the Monitor panel is advancing. To pause playback, press the spacebar, or once again click the Play button, which becomes the Pause button (⏸) during playback.

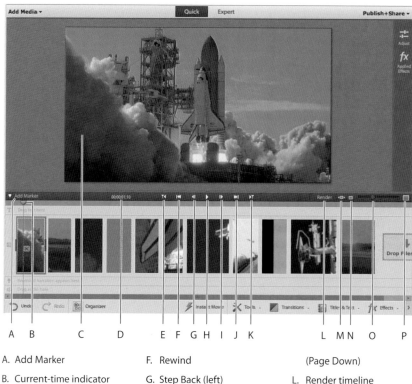

A. Add Marker
B. Current-time indicator
C. Preview area
D. Current time (also called timecode)
E. Go to Previous Edit Point (Page Up)
F. Rewind
G. Step Back (left)
H. Play/Pause toggle (spacebar)
I. Step Forward (right)
J. Fast-Forward
K. Go to Next Edit Point
   (Page Down)
L. Render timeline
M. Fit to Visible Timeline (\)
N. Zoom Out (–)
O. Zoom control
P. Zoom In (=)

3   You can locate a specific frame in your movie by changing your position in time. Place your pointer over the timecode in the lower-left corner of the Monitor panel, and your Selection tool (🖕) will change to a hand with two arrows (✋).

4   Drag the hand with two arrows icon to the right, advancing your video. The pointer will disappear while you're dragging and reappear when you stop and release the mouse button. As long as you keep holding down the mouse button you can move backward and forward through the video. This is known as *scrubbing* through your video.

5   You can move to a specific point in your movie by entering the time directly in the timecode field. Click the timecode in the lower-left corner of the Monitor panel, and it will change to an editable text field. Type **915** and then press Enter (Windows) or Return (Mac OS) to move to a point 9 seconds and 15 frames into the project. Note that you don't have to enter the colons, just the raw numbers.

6   Click the Step Forward (▐▶) button (right arrow key) repeatedly to advance your video one frame at a time. Video is simply a series of frames shown at a rate of approximately 30 frames per second. Using the Step Forward (▐▶) or Step Back (◀▌) button enables you to locate moments in time precisely. You also can use the right and left arrow keys on the keyboard to accomplish the same functions.

7   Click the Go to Next Edit Point button (▶▌) to jump to the first frame of the next clip. Notice in the timeline that the current-time indicator (▼) jumps to the beginning of the next clip representation. Click the Go to Previous Edit Point (▌◀) to jump to the first frame of the previous clip. Or, you can use the Page Up and Page Down keys on your keyboard to accomplish the same functions.

8   Reposition the current-time indicator (▼) by clicking and dragging it to the left or to the right.

9   While editing your project, you will spend lots of time zooming into individual clips for trimming and effect application, and then zooming out to view larger portions of the project. The four controls on the extreme right of the Monitor panel help you accomplish this:

    • Click the Zoom In button (=) (■) to the right of the Zoom slider (▬▬▬▬●▬▬) to zoom into the project. Each video clip becomes larger until it completely fills the timeline. In the next figure, note the scroll bar that appears beneath the Quick view timeline that you can click and drag to navigate around the project.

    • Click the Fit to Visible Timeline button (\) (▣) to make all the content in the project fit within the timeline—no scrolling is necessary. This is a great way to reset your project after some zoomed-in work.

- Click the Zoom Out button (-) () to the left of the Zoom slider ( ) to zoom out of the project, making each component smaller.

- Click and drag the Zoom slider (-) ( ) to customize the content viewable in the Quick view timeline.

10 Press the Home key on your keyboard to position the current-time indicator at the beginning of the movie. Press the End key to position the current-time indicator at the end of the movie. This is useful when you want to add content to the existing sections of your movie.

Previewing in Adobe Premiere Elements

Adobe Premiere Elements attempts to preview all movies at full frame rate and typically can do so when you're simply splitting, trimming, and moving clips around. Once you start to apply the effects discussed in Lesson 6, however, the display rate of the preview may slow down. If this occurs and you need to preview at full frame rate, you can render and play the entire project by pressing the Render (Render) button on the Monitor panel or by pressing Enter (Windows) or Return (Mac OS) on your keyboard, or render a work area using a procedure defined in "Rendering a Work Area" in Lesson 6.

About timecode

Timecode represents the location of the frames in a video. Cameras record timecode onto the video. The timecode is based on the number of frames per second (fps) that the camera records and the number of frames per second that the video displays upon playback. Digital video has a standard frame rate that is either 29.97 fps for NTSC video (the North American broadcast video standard) or 25 fps for PAL (the European broadcast video standard). Timecode describes location in the format of hours;minutes;seconds;frames. For example, 01;20;15;10 specifies that the displayed frame is located 1 hour, 20 minutes, 15 seconds, and 10 frames into the scene.

—From Adobe Premiere Elements Help

Editing in Quick view

As mentioned, Adobe Premiere Elements has two views: a Quick view for basic movie editing and an Expert view for more advanced techniques. You can switch between the two views by clicking Quick (Quick) or Expert (Expert) in the bar above the Monitor panel.

Adding clips in Quick view

In Quick view, each clip is a stand-alone block that makes it easy to arrange clips into coherent sequences, which is called *storyboard-style* editing. In Quick view, you add clips to the project via controls in the Add Media panel, and all content that you add is appended to the end of the project. You learned these techniques in Lesson 3. Or, you can drag and drop clips from Windows Explorer (Windows) or Finder (Mac OS). When you use drag and drop, you can add a clip to any position in the project. In this exercise, you'll use that approach.

This project has 12 clips numbered in order from Video 1.mp4 to Video 12.mp4. Clip Video 7.mp4 is not currently in the project, so you'll add that clip in the desired location.

Everyone uses drag and drop a little differently. One popular technique is to reduce the size of the target window, in this case Adobe Premiere Elements, and the source window, which is either Windows Explorer (Windows) or Finder (Mac OS). Next, place the target window above the source window with the file you want to add visible in the source window. Then simply drag and drop. You can set up your windows whichever way works for you; the drag-and-drop instructions follow in the exercise.

1   If Adobe Premiere Elements is not already in Quick view, click the Quick view button.

2   Click the Fit to Visible Timeline button (⬕) or press the Backslash (\) key so we're looking at the same thing.

3   Press the Home key to move the current-time indicator to the start of the project. Then press the Page Down key or click the Go to Next Edit Point (Page Down) icon in the Monitor panel six times to move to the start of the seventh clip. This is where you want to drag Video 7.mp4. This step isn't absolutely necessary; the current-time indicator doesn't have to be where you add the clip, although it does simplify the operation.

4   In Windows Explorer (Windows) or Finder (Mac OS), navigate to the Lesson05 folder you copied to your hard drive. Within that folder, select Video 7.mp4.

5   Drag Video 7.mp4 to the current-time indicator between the sixth and seventh clips in the timeline. Until you release the pointer, Adobe Premiere Elements displays Trim view in the Monitor panel, which shows the last frame of the clip immediately preceding where you're about to drop the file and the first frame of the clip immediately after where you're about to drop the file. This makes it easy to see if you're dropping the clip in the right location; if your Monitor panel shows the same frames as the screen below, you are, so release the clip.

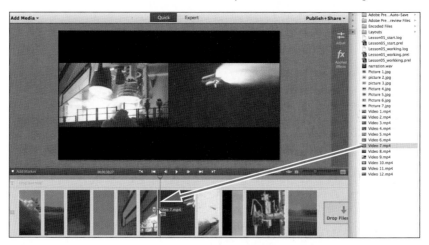

Adobe Premiere Elements adds the clip at the selected location and moves all subsequent clips to the right. If you hover your pointer over a clip, Adobe Premiere Elements will display the filename and other details.

Through the wonders of time-lapse photography, the next figure displays the names of three clips at once, and it looks like the drag-and-drop operation was a success. However, if you hover your pointer over the first few clips in the project, you'll see that some are out of order, which we'll address in the next exercise.

6 Choose File > Save As, and save the project as **Lesson05_working.prel**.

Moving clips in Quick view

Working in Quick view makes it easy to move clips in your movie. If you hover your mouse over the clips at the start of the project, you see that the current order is Video 1.mp4, Video 2.mp4, Video 4.mp4, Video 5.mp4, and Video 3.mp4. You have two options for placing the clips in the proper order: moving Video 3.mp4 two clips to the left or moving Video 4.mp4 and Video 5.mp4 one clip to the right. Let's try both approaches.

1 Video 3.mp4 is the fifth clip in the project, which you can confirm by hovering your pointer over the clip. Click to select Video 3.mp4, and then drag it to the intersection of the second and third clips. Release the pointer when the green vertical line appears at the target location. Note Trim view in the Monitor panel that shows the last frame of the clip immediately preceding where you're about to drop the file and the first frame of the clip immediately after where you're about to drop the file. When you release the pointer, Adobe Premiere Elements inserts the clip at the selected location and moves all subsequent clips to the right.

2   On the bottom left of the Adobe Premiere Elements interface, click Undo (↺ Undo)
    to undo that operation. Alternatively, you can choose Edit > Undo from the
    Adobe Premiere Elements menu, or press the old standbys Ctrl+Z (Windows)
    or Command+Z (Mac OS). Now you'll fix the problem the other way.

3   This time you'll move the third and fourth clips in the project, Video 4.mp4
    and Video 5.mp4, one position to the right. To select multiple adjacent clips,
    press the Shift key and click the clips, release the Shift key, and drag them
    one position to the right, which is the intersection between Video 3.mp4 and
    Video 6.mp4. Release the pointer when a vertical green line appears at the
    desired position.

Note: Although not
shown in this exercise,
a transition following
a scene moves with
the scene.

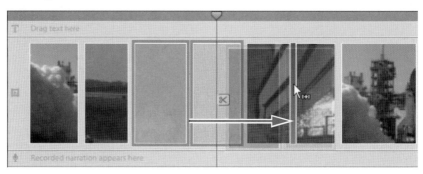

Deleting clips in Quick view

You may find as your project develops that you want to delete clips that you've
added to your project.

Note: When a clip
is deleted from Quick
view, any transitions
associated with the clip,
either before or after,
are also deleted.

To delete a clip, right-click it in Quick view,
and then choose one of the following from
the context menu:

- **Cut:** This option deletes the clip and
  moves all clips following the deleted clip
  to the left to close the gap. This is the
  default behavior when deleting clips in
  Adobe Premiere Elements and is called
  a *ripple deletion*.

- **Delete and close gap:** This option
  does the same thing as Cut; it deletes the clip and moves all clips following
  the deleted clip to the left to close the gap.

- **Delete audio:** This option deletes the audio in the clip but leaves the video
  in place.

Trimming clips in Quick view

In addition to moving clips around, you'll probably also want to shorten your clips by trimming frames from the beginning and end. Here's how you'll accomplish this task.

In editing terminology, the beginning of each clip is called the *In point* and the end of a clip the *Out point*. When you adjust the In and Out points, you don't actually delete frames from the file on your hard drive; you simply point to different frames to start and end playback of that clip on the timeline. When you trim a clip in Adobe Premiere Elements, you are simply changing the In and Out points.

Let's open a new project for the trimming and splitting exercises to follow.

1   With Adobe Premiere Elements open and running, choose File > Open Project.

2   In the Open Project dialog, navigate to the Lesson05 folder you copied to your hard drive.

3   Within that folder, select the file Lesson05_Trim_Win.prel (Windows) or Lesson05_Trim_Mac.prel (Mac OS). Be careful; there are several different lessons in the folder. Do not save changes to the first project, and if a dialog appears asking for the location of rendered files, click the Skip Previews button.

    Your project file opens.

4   Click the Home key to move the current-time indicator to the start of the project, and press the spacebar to start playback. The first six clips are trimmed correctly, so the audio narration matches the videos shown. With the seventh clip, however, that synchronization is lost because Video 7.mp4 is about four seconds too long. More specifically, you need the next clip, Video 8.mp4, to start right around timecode 35:15. You'll fix that now.

5   Move the current-time indicator to timecode 00;00;35;15. To accomplish this, do *either of the following*:

    •   Click and drag the current-time indicator to that location. When you get close to this spot, you can use the arrow keys for frame-by-frame fine-tuning.

    •   Click the Current Time field in the Monitor panel to make it active, type **3515**, and press Enter (Windows) or Return (Mac OS).

6   Hover your pointer over the right edge of Video 7.mp4. The pointer will convert to the drag pointer (⬚).

7   Click and drag the right edge of Video 7.mp4 to the left until it snaps to the current-time indicator at 00;00;35;15, and then release the left mouse button. Adobe Premiere Elements trims about the last four seconds from the end of Video 7.mp4.

Notice that while you drag the edge, the Monitor panel changes to Trim view, showing the clip you're trimming on the left and the next clip on the timeline on the right. As you drag the right edge to the left, Trim view updates the frame on the left, making it easy to see the edge of the clip that you're trimming. You're trimming Video 7.mp4 to where the Shuttle's nose touches the top of the screen.

● **Note:** You may not see the Trim view on all computers, particularly Mac notebooks. If you don't, make sure you've got the latest graphics card driver for your computer.

● **Note:** You don't need to place your current-time indicator at the trim point. You can simply click and drag the edge to the new location. Placing your current-time indicator at that location and then snapping to it as demonstrated is just a bit more precise.

8   Let's trim in the other direction just to learn how. You'll drag the right edge of the clip you just trimmed, Video 7.mp4, back to its original location. To do so, hover your pointer over the right edge of Video 7.mp4 until it becomes the drag pointer (▦), click to grab the edge, drag it to the right as far as you can, and release the pointer. Note that you can drag it only so far and then it stops. As you've probably guessed, the reason it stops is because you can't drag a clip to longer than its original length. When you can't drag any further, you've reached the edge.

9 Either click Undo (↺ Undo) to return the edge of Video 7.mp4 to the 00;00;35;15 spot or repeat steps 5–7.

10 Now let's trim about 3.5 seconds from the start of clip Video 8.mp4. Move the current-time indicator to 00;00;39;01. Then click and drag the left edge of Video 8.mp4 to the right until it snaps to the current-time indicator and release the pointer. Adobe Premiere Elements trims the first 3.5 seconds from the start of Video 8.mp4.

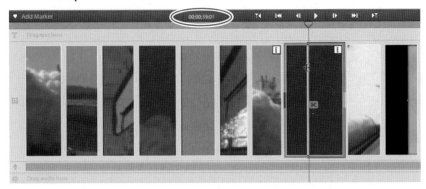

● **Note:** Note the new icons on the top right of Video 7.mp4 and Video 08.mp4 in the Quick view timeline. These let you know that these clips have been trimmed.

11 Let's check the fruits of our labors. Drag the current-time indicator to about 00;00;20;00 and press the spacebar to play the video. The audio should be synchronized with the video until you reach Video 10.mp4, which is about 45 seconds into the project, where there's an issue that you'll resolve in Lesson 6.

Using the Split Clip tool in Quick view

The Split Clip tool allows you to divide single clips into multiple clips. You can use this tool to split a clip into sections so you can delete one of them, which some-times is more convenient than trimming. You can also use the tool to split a long clip into separate clips to edit them individually.

Let's revert back to the most recent project to start with a clean slate.

1 With Adobe Premiere Elements open and running, choose File > Revert, and click Yes to discard any changes. Adobe Premiere Elements discards any changes and returns to the original project file.

2 Move the current-time indicator to timecode 00;00;35;15, and click the file Video 7.mp4 to select it. Clicking the file is important, because if you don't, Adobe Premiere Elements will split all content at that location, including the narration file, which is not what you want.

3 Hover your pointer over the scissors icon (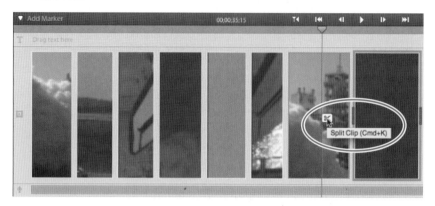) attached to the current-time indicator until it turns white, and then click the icon. Adobe Premiere Elements splits the clip at that location. If you split the audio file beneath the audio/video track, it's because you didn't click Video 7.mp4 before splitting the clip. Undo and start over.

4 You now have two Video 7.mp4 clips in the timeline; you want to delete the second clip. Hover your pointer over the second Video 7.mp4, right-click and choose "Delete and close gap." Adobe Premiere Elements deletes that clip and moves all subsequent files to the left to close the gap.

5 Let's split Video 8.mp4. Move the current-time indicator to 00;00;39;01 and click Video 8.mp4 to select it. Hover your pointer over the scissors icon () attached to the current-time indicator until it turns white, and then click the icon. Adobe Premiere Elements splits the clip at that location.

6 You now have two Video 8.mp4 clips in the timeline; you want to delete the first clip. Click the first Video 8.mp4, right-click and choose "Delete and close gap." Adobe Premiere Elements deletes that clip and moves all subsequent files to the left to close the gap.

7 Drag the current-time indicator to about 00;00;20;00 and press the spacebar to play the video. The clip should be identical to the result produced when you trimmed the clips; the narration and video clips should be in sync until you reach Video 10.mp4, which is about 45 seconds into the project.

8 When you're finished reviewing the movie, choose File > Save As.

9 In the Save Project dialog, name the file **Lesson05_Trim_work.prel** and save it in your Lesson05 folder.

● **Note:** You produced the same result using two different techniques, so which is better? I typically use trim commands when I'm deleting a few frames from the start and end of a clip. And I typically split the clip when I'm doing major surgery—cutting a clip into multiple components or eliminating major segments of the clip.

Working in Expert view

Although you can perform most basic editing tasks in Quick view, you'll use Expert view for many advanced editing tasks, especially those that involve *layering*, which means having multiple clips in the project at the same location. Before you begin working with Expert view, follow the instructions at the start of this lesson to load Lesson05_Start_Win.prel (Windows) or Lesson05_Start_Mac.prel (Mac OS).

1   To enter Expert view, click the Expert button (Expert) at the top of the Monitor panel.

2   If necessary, click the Collapse-Expand track disclosure triangles on Video 1 and Audio 1 to show the content in those tracks.

3   If necessary, click the Zoom in button (■) on the extreme right of the Monitor panel once to approximate the view shown in the next figure.

> ● **Note:** For information on zooming into and out of the timeline and resizing content within the timeline, see "Working in the Monitor panel," earlier in this lesson. The Monitor panel functions very similarly in both modes, and operation in the Monitor panel is addressed in detail in the referenced section.

The Timeline:

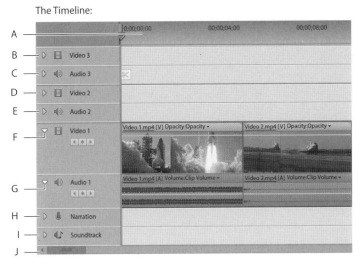

A.	Time ruler	F.	Collapse-Expand video track
B.	Video track 3	G.	Collapse-Expand audio track
C.	Audio track 3	H.	Narration track
D.	Video track 2	I.	Soundtrack
E.	Audio track 2	J.	Timeline slider

> ● **Note:** If you're going back and forth between Quick and Expert views, keep in mind that Video 1/Audio 1 track corresponds with the audio/video track in Quick view, whereas Video 3 corresponds with the Title track in Quick view. If audio or video is placed on any other tracks in Expert view, it won't appear in Quick view. If non-title content is placed on Video 3, it will appear in Quick view, but you won't have a track left for titles.

Adding and deleting tracks

The timeline consists of vertically stacked tracks where you arrange media clips. Tracks let you layer video or audio and add compositing effects, picture-in-picture effects, overlay titles, soundtracks, and more.

You perform most of your editing in the Video 1 and the Audio 1 tracks. Directly above these are the Video 2 and Audio 2 tracks. Note that the stacking order of video tracks is important. The Monitor panel displays (and Adobe Premiere Elements produces) the tracks from the top down. Accordingly, any opaque areas of the clip in the Video 2 track will cover the view on the clip in the Video 1 track.

Conversely, the clip in the Video 1 track will show through any transparent areas of the clip in the Video 2 track. Below the Video 1 and Audio 1 tracks are two more audio tracks, Narration and Soundtrack. Audio tracks are combined in playback, and their stacking order is not relevant.

Adobe Premiere Elements starts with three open video tracks (Video 1, 2, and 3) and five open audio tracks (Soundtrack; Narration; and Audio 1, 2, and 3), which should be sufficient for most projects. Should you need additional video or audio tracks, you can add them by choosing Timeline > Add Tracks. You can delete any empty tracks by choosing Timeline > Delete Empty Tracks.

Changing the height of tracks

You can change the height of each track in the Timeline for better viewing and easier editing of your projects. As a track enlarges, it displays more information. Let's adjust the height of the Video 1 track.

1   If necessary, scroll down in the timeline to see the Video 1 track.

2   Right-click on any open area in the timeline, and choose Track Size > Small, Track Size > Medium, or Track Size > Large to change the track size for all tracks in the timeline.

3   To customize a specific track, at the left side of the timeline, place your pointer between the Audio 2 and the Video 1 tracks. Your pointer should change to two parallel lines with two arrows (⬚). Drag up to expand the height of this track.

Customizing track views

You can display clips in the timeline in different ways, depending on your preference or the task at hand. You can display a thumbnail image at just the beginning of a clip, at the head and tail of a clip, or along the entire duration of a clip, as shown in the previous figure. For an audio track, you can display or hide the audio waveform of the audio contents. Toggle through the various views of the video and audio tracks until you find the one that best suits your eye and working style.

To get a good look at the various styles, it's best to click the Zoom in button (■) on the right of the Monitor panel until only three or four clips are showing on the timeline.

1 By default, Adobe Premiere Elements displays all the frames in a video clip. However, at times you may want to work with fewer visual distractions in your clip. Click the Set Video Track Display Style button (■) to the left of the Video 1 track to set the display style to Show Head and Tail. This will show you the first frame and last frame of all the clips in Video 1.

2 Click the Set Video Track Display Style button again to view only the head of the clip.

3 Click the Set Video Track Display Style button again to view the clip by its name only. No thumbnails will be displayed on the clip.

4 Click the Set Video Track Display Style button one more time to view the default style of all the frames.

5 Click the Set Audio Track Display Style button twice to view the available audio views.

Editing in Expert view

One of the most significant differences between Expert and Quick views is that the Project Assets panel exists in Expert view, but not in Quick view. When you're working in Quick view, all content imported via the Add Media controls is immediately placed at the end of the project in the Quick view timeline. In Expert view, all content imported via the Add Media controls is placed in the Project Assets panel, where you can add the content to your project at any location. So you'll start there, adding content from the Project Assets panel to the project.

Adding clips in Expert view

If you worked through the exercises in Quick view, recall that the initial project was missing the clip Video 7.mp4. For your first exercise in Expert view, you'll add that to the project between Video 6.mp4 and Video 8.mp4. Keep in mind that the Project Assets panel is available only in Expert view, so if you're not in Expert view, click the Expert button at the top of the Monitor panel.

1 On the lower right of the Monitor panel, click the Fit to Visible Timeline button (⬚) or press the Backslash (\) key to fit the project in the timeline.

2 On the upper left of the Adobe Premiere Elements interface, click Project Assets (Project Assets ▾) to open that panel.

3 Click Video 7.mp4 and drag it to the intersection of Video 6.mp4 and Video 8.mp4. Hold the clip for a moment, and notice how Adobe Premiere Elements moves Video 8.mp4 and all subsequent clips to the right to make space for Video 7.mp4.

Also, note how the Monitor panel changes to Trim view to show the last frame of Video 6.mp4 on the left and the first frame of Video 8.mp4 on the right. Before releasing your mouse, drag Video 7.mp4 a bit to the right into Video 8.mp4 to see how this is reflected in the Monitor panel. This view makes it simple to tell when you're not dropping the clip in the right place. When you're ready, release the left mouse button to complete the edit.

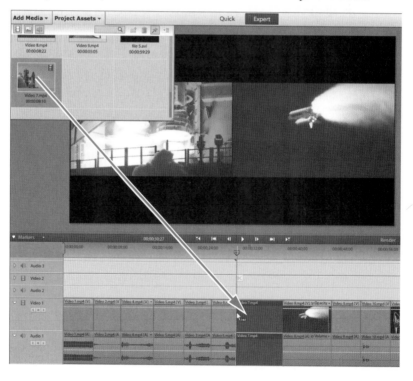

4   Let's have some fun. On the bottom left of the Adobe Premiere Elements interface, click the Undo button, or otherwise undo the edit.

5   Move the current-time indicator between Video 6.mp4 and Video 8.mp4, which should be around 00;00;30;27.

6   In the Project Assets folder, click Video 7.mp4 to select it. Then watch the timeline and press the comma (,) key on your keyboard. Adobe Premiere Elements adds Video 7.mp4 to the timeline at the current-time indicator.

7   Let's have a bit more fun. Undo the edit again.

8   In the Project Assets panel, double-click Video 7.mp4 to open the clip in the preview window. Let's trim those frames you'll be trimming in the next exercise before you add the clip to the project.

9   In the preview window, drag the current-time indicator to the right until the timecode beneath the video reads 00;00;04;13, which is just where the Shuttle's nose starts to leave the frame. Note that you can also use the left and right arrow keys on your keyboard for precise positioning. Click Set Out (Set Out) to set the Out point, or press the letter O on your keyboard. You've just told Adobe Premiere Elements to insert only that portion of the clip up to the Out point.

10 Back in the Adobe Premiere Elements timeline, make sure that the current-time indicator is still between Video 6.mp4 and Video 8.mp4, which should be around 00;00;30;27.

11 Press the comma (,) key again. Adobe Premiere Elements inserts the trimmed version of Video 7.mp4 into the timeline immediately after Video 6.mp4.

12 Click the Project Assets button to close the Project Assets panel and close the preview window as well.

Moving clips in Expert view

Now let's fix the order of clips in Expert view. If you hover your mouse over the clips at the start of the project, you'll see that the current order is Video 1.mp4, Video 2.mp4, Video 4.mp4, Video 5.mp4, and Video 3.mp4. As before, you have two options for placing the clips in the proper order: moving Video 3.mp4 two clips to the left or moving Video 4.mp4 and Video 5.mp4 one clip to the right. Let's try both approaches.

1 Click and hold to select Video 3.mp4, and then press the Alt (Windows) or Option (Mac OS) key. You'll see the rearrange pointer (▣). Drag Video 3.mp4 until the front edge of the clip touches the intersection between Video 2.mp4 and Video 4.mp4. Watch the Trim view in the Monitor panel to make sure that the front of Video 3.mp4 is at the intersection between the two clips. Wait a moment for Adobe Premiere Elements to move all the clips to the right to make a space for Video 3.mp4. Then release your pointer.

2 If Adobe Premiere Elements leaves a gap where Video 3.mp4 used to be, right click the gap, and choose "Delete and close gap" to close the gap.

● **Note:** Using the rearrange pointer is not supposed to leave a gap in the timeline but was doing so during the writing of this book. Adobe says it will address this issue in the short term, so we've documented the way it's supposed to work and caution you that the gap may appear.

3 On the bottom left of the Adobe Premiere Elements interface, click Undo (↺ Undo) twice to undo those operations.

4 This time you'll move the third and fourth clips in the project, Video 4.mp4 and Video 5.mp4, one position to the right. To select multiple adjacent clips, press the Shift key and click the clips, in this case Video 4.mp4 and Video 5.mp4, and without releasing the Shift key, press the Alt (Windows) or Option (Mac OS) key. Then you can release the Shift key and drag the selected clips (pay attention here) until the left edge of the two clips is in the intersection between Video 3.mp4 and Video 6.mp4. Watch the Trim view in the Monitor panel to make sure that you're dropping the two clips at the desired location. Wait a moment for Adobe Premiere Elements to move all the clips to the right to make a space for the two clips. Then release your mouse.

Note: Although not shown in this exercise, in Expert view, any transitions before or after a single clip are deleted during a move. Transitions between multiple adjacent clips that were moved survive the move.

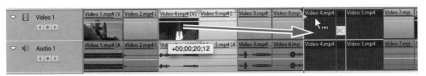

5 If Adobe Premiere Elements leaves a gap where Video 4.mp4 and Video 5.mp4 were previously located, right click the gap, and choose "Delete and close gap" to close the gap.

Deleting clips in Expert view

When you're deleting clips in Expert view, you have a lot more control over the results than you do in Quick view. This section describes the various options.

To delete a scene, you right-click it in the Expert view, and then choose one of the following from the context menu:

Note: When a clip is deleted in Expert view, any transitions associated with the clip, either before or after, are also deleted.

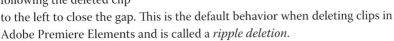

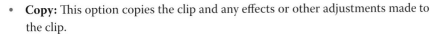

- **Cut:** This option deletes the clip and moves all clips following the deleted clip to the left to close the gap. This is the default behavior when deleting clips in Adobe Premiere Elements and is called a *ripple deletion.*

- **Copy:** This option copies the clip and any effects or other adjustments made to the clip.

- **Paste Effects and Adjustments:** This option pastes any effects or other adjustments from the source clip to the target clip. This can be exceptionally useful when you're applying an effect like an exposure correction to a number of clips from the same scene, and you'll explore it further in Lesson 6.

- **Delete:** This option deletes the clip but leaves a gap at the clip's former location.

- **Delete and Close Gap:** This option does the same thing as Cut; it deletes the clip and moves all clips following the deleted clip to the left to close the gap.

- **Delete Audio:** This option deletes the audio in the clip but leaves the video in place.

- **Delete Video:** This option deletes the video in the clip but leaves the audio in place.

- **Replace Clip From Project Assets:** This option replaces a selected clip on the timeline with a clip selected in the Project Assets panel.

Trimming clips in Expert view

As discussed in the "Editing in Quick view" section, every clip in the timeline has a beginning and an end. In editing terminology these are referred to as the *In points* and *Out points*. Setting In and Out points does not actually delete frames from the hard drive but instead isolates a portion of the clip for use in your movie. When you trim a clip in Adobe Premiere Elements, you are simply changing the In and Out points.

Let's open a new project for the trimming and splitting exercises to follow.

1 With Adobe Premiere Elements open and running, choose File > Open Project.

2 In the Open Project dialog, navigate to the Lesson05 folder you copied to your hard drive.

3 Within that folder, select the file Lesson05_Trim_Win.prel (Windows) or Lesson05_Trim_Mac.prel (Mac OS). Be careful; there are several different lessons in the folder. Do not save changes to the first project, and if a dialog appears asking for the location of rendered files, click the Skip Previews button.

   Your project file opens.

4 Click the Home key on your keyboard to move the current-time indicator to the start of the project, and press the spacebar to start playback. The first six clips are trimmed correctly, so the audio narration matches the videos shown. With the seventh clip, however, that synchronization is lost because Video 7.mp4 is about four seconds too long. More specifically, you need the next clip, Video 8.mp4, to start right around timecode 35:15. You'll fix that now.

5 Move the current-time indicator to timecode 00;00;35;15. To accomplish this, do *either of the following:*

   - Click and drag the current-time indicator to that location. When you get close to this spot, you can use the arrow keys on your keyboard or at the bottom of the Monitor panel for fine-tuning.

   - Click the Current Time field in the Monitor panel to make it active, type **3515**, and press Enter (Windows) or Return (Mac OS).

6 Hover your pointer over the right edge of Video 7.mp4. The pointer will convert to the drag pointer (⊞).

7 Click and drag the right edge of Video 7.mp4 until it snaps to the current-time indicator at 00;00;35;15, and then release the left mouse button. Adobe Premiere Elements trims about the last four seconds from the end of Video 7.mp4.

Note that while you drag the edge, the Monitor panel changes to Trim view, showing the clip you're trimming on the left and the next clip on the timeline on the right. As you drag the right edge to the left, Trim view updates the frame on the left, making it easy to see the edge of the clip that you're trimming. You're shooting to trim Video 7.mp4 about where the Shuttle's nose touches the top of the screen. Note the text box to the right of the pointer that tells you how many seconds you're moving the right edge backward, which is how much time you're trimming from the clip.

● **Note:** You don't need to place your current-time indicator at the trim point. You can simply click and drag the edge to the new location. Placing your current-time indicator at that location and then snapping to it as demonstrated is just a bit more precise.

8 Let's trim in the other direction just to learn how. You'll drag the right edge of the clip you just trimmed, Video 7.mp4, back to its original location. To do so, hover your pointer over the right edge of Video 7.mp4 until it becomes the drag pointer (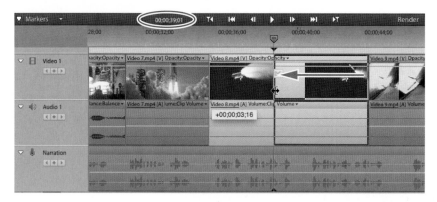), left-click to grab the edge, drag it to the right as far as you can, and release the left mouse button. Note that you can only drag it so far, and then it stops. The reason it stops is because you can't drag a clip to longer than its original length. When you can't drag any further, you've reached the edge.

9 Either click Undo to return the edge of Video 7.mp4 to the 00;00;35;15 spot, or repeat steps 5–7.

10 Now let's trim about 3.5 seconds from the start of clip Video 8.mp4. Move the current-time indicator to 00;00;39;01. Then click and drag the left edge of Video 8.mp4 to the right until it snaps to the current-time indicator and release the left mouse button. As you can see from the text box near the trim pointer, you dragged the left edge of the clip 3:16 to the right, trimming 3 seconds and 16 frames from the start of Video 8.mp4.

11 Let's check the results. Drag the current-time indicator to about 00;00;20;00 and press the spacebar to play the video. The audio should be synchronized with the video until you reach Video 10.mp4, which is about 45 seconds into the project, where there's an issue that you'll resolve in Lesson 6.

● **Note:** Note that the start of Video 8.mp4 and Video 9.mp4 correspond with a new section of narration, as shown by the peaks and valleys in the waveform in the Narration track. One advantage of Expert view as opposed to Quick view is the ability to see waveforms in the audio tracks, which are often the fastest and best guides to show you where to make your cuts.

Using the Split Clip tool in Expert view

The Split Clip tool allows you to divide single clips into multiple clips. You can use this tool to split a clip into sections so you can delete one of them, which sometimes is more convenient than trimming. You can also use the tool to split a long clip into separate clips to edit them individually. Note that this function works identically in Quick view.

● **Note:** You'll remain in Expert view to do this exercise, but it could be completed in either view.

Let's revert back to the original trim project to start with a clean slate.

1   With Adobe Premiere Elements open and running, choose File > Revert, and click Yes to discard any changes. Adobe Premiere Elements discards any changes and returns to the original project file.

2   Move the current-time indicator to timecode 00;00;35;15, and click the file Video 7.mp4 to select it. Clicking the file is important, because if you don't, Adobe Premiere Elements will split all content at that location, including the narration file, which is not what you want.

3   Hover your pointer over the scissors icon (✂) attached to the current-time indicator until it turns white, and then click the icon. Adobe Premiere Elements splits the clip at that location.

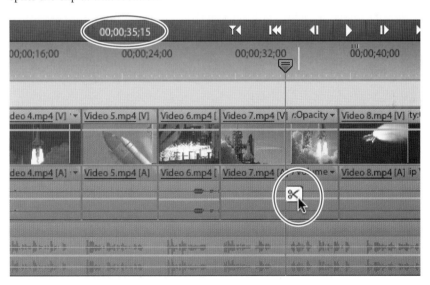

4 You now have two Video 7.mp4 clips in the timeline; you want to delete the second clip. Hover your pointer over the second Video 7.mp4, right-click, and choose Delete and Close Gap. Adobe Premiere Elements deletes that clip and moves all subsequent files to the left to close the gap.

5 Let's split Video 8.mp4 and delete the initial version. Move the current-time indicator to 00;00;39;01. Hover your pointer over the scissors icon () attached to the current-time indicator until it turns white, and then click the icon. Adobe Premiere Elements splits the clip at that location.

6 You now have two Video 8.mp4 clips in the timeline; you want to delete the first clip. Hover your pointer over the first Video 8.mp4, right-click, and choose Delete and Close Gap. Adobe Premiere Elements deletes that clip and moves all subsequent files to the left to close the gap.

7 Drag the current-time indicator to about 00;00;20;00 and press the spacebar to play the video. The clip should be identical to the result produced when you trimmed the clips; the narration and video clips should be in synch until you reach Video 10.mp4, which is about 45 seconds into the project.

8 When you're finished reviewing the movie, choose File > Save As.

9 In the Save Project dialog, name the file **Lesson05_Trim_work.prel** and save it in your Lesson05 folder. Go ahead and replace the previous file if you created one in Quick view.

Creating a slide show in Expert view

In many productions, video enthusiasts often like to integrate video and slide shows, particularly because we tend to shoot so many photos with our smart-phones, tablets, and DSLRs. Adobe Premiere Elements makes this very simple with a Create Slideshow function, which has convenient features like the automatic insertion of transitions between the images. Because you'll be working with pictures in the Project Assets panel, you must be in Expert view to run this exercise.

Note that the slide show function always inserts the slide show at the end of the Video 1 track. To insert a slide show in the middle of project, follow these steps.

1 In the upper-left corner of the Adobe Premiere Elements interface, click Project Assets (Project Assets ▾) to open that panel.

2 To make the photos easier to select in the proper order, let's customize the view:

  • On the upper-left side of the Project Assets panel toolbar, click the Hide Video and Hide Audio icons so that only the still images in the panel are displayed.

  • Click the panel menu in the upper-right corner of the Project Assets panel, and choose View > List view.

- In List view, you can sort by any column by clicking the column head. Click the Name column head until the photos are displayed in ascending order, as shown in the next figure.

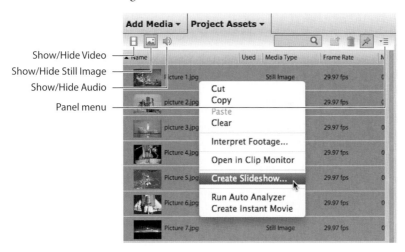

3 Click Picture 1.jpg, press the Shift key, and then click Picture 7.jpg to select all of the pictures. Scroll down to Picture 7.jpg if necessary. Note that if you press Ctrl+A (Windows) or Command+A (Mac OS) to select all of the photos, you'll select all the content in the Project Assets panel, including video and audio content, not just the photos.

4 Right-click any selected image and choose Create Slideshow. If the Smart Fix window appears, click No. The Create SlideShow dialog opens. Note the options in the dialog, which include choosing the Ordering (Sort Order or Selection Order) and Media (Take Video and Audio, Take Video Only, Take Audio Only, although only Take Video will be available here because you're selecting pictures rather than video files with audio), selecting whether or not to Place Images/ Clips at Unnumbered Markers (grayed out because the project has no markers), setting Image Duration, selecting whether or not to Apply Default Transition, and setting Transition Duration. Let's use the default settings.

5   Click OK to create the slide show. Adobe Premiere Elements inserts the slide show with transitions at the end of the Video 1 track.

Working in Smart Trim mode

The Smart Trim editing mode can help you identify suboptimal regions within your videos so you can either fix or delete them. Smart Trim relies on information gathered while Adobe Premiere Elements analyzes your clips, so you must Auto-Analyze your clips before entering Smart Trim mode. You can operate Smart Trim either automatically or manually, although we recommend that you use Smart Trim manually until you understand how it works.

Let's open a new project for this topic.

1   With Adobe Premiere Elements open and running, choose File > Open Project.

2   In the Open Project dialog, navigate to the Lesson05 folder you copied to your hard drive.

3   Within that folder, select the file Lesson05_SmartTrim_Win.prel (Windows) or Lesson05_SmartTrim_Mac.prel (Mac OS). Be careful; there are several different lessons in the folder. Choose No when Adobe Premiere Elements asks if you want to save changes to the current project. If Adobe Premiere Elements asks you where a rendered file is, click Skip Previews.

You can work with Smart Trim in Quick and Expert views; this exercise demonstrates how it works in Expert view, so click Expert (Expert) at the top of the Monitor panel, if necessary, to enter that view. Then click the Fit to Visible Timeline icon (🔲▶) on the extreme right of the Monitor panel to spread the clip over the timeline. When the clip is positioned, in the Action bar beneath the timeline, click Tools, and then click Smart Trim. If you haven't run the Auto-Analyzer, Adobe Premiere Elements will run it now.

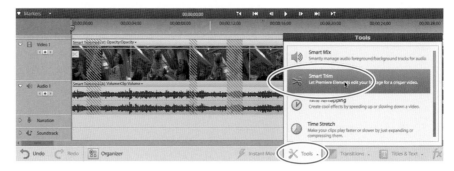

As you can see in the previous figure, Smart Trim identifies problem areas via a zebra pattern. If you hover your mouse over the zebra pattern, a tool tip details the problems with the clip. You have multiple options regarding any clip, or portion of a clip, that Adobe Premiere Elements flags as a problem area.

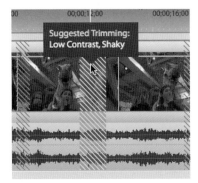

You can right-click the clip, and choose Trim, Keep, or Select All. Trim will delete the selected portion; Keep will retain it and turn off the zebra striping; Select All will select multiple suboptimal regions within the same clip so you can trim or keep them all. In addition to these options, you can trim away any or all of the suboptimal portions of your clip by clicking and dragging an edge to the desired new starting point, just as you would trim any other clip in the timeline.

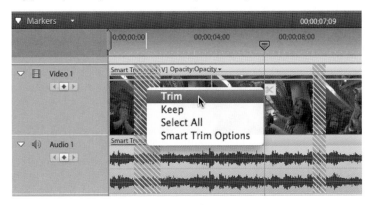

How Smart Trim works

You can also trim a scene by choosing Smart Trim Options and adjusting these options. Let's view the choices available by clicking Smart Trim.mp4 and clicking the Smart Trim Options button in the upper-right corner of the Monitor panel.

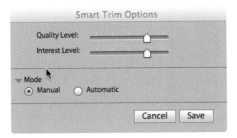

In the Smart Trim Options window, Adobe Premiere Elements uses two variables to identify suboptimal clips: Quality Level and Interest Level. Quality Level is simple to understand: If a clip is shaky, blurry, has poor contrast or lighting, or has other deficits that mar quality, Adobe Premiere Elements identifies the clip in Smart Trim mode as being below the Quality Level threshold, depending on how flawed the clip is and where you positioned the Quality Level slider.

By contrast, Interest Level analyzes qualities, such as the amount of motion in a clip, the presence or absence of dialogue, and other criteria that identify clips that are interesting to watch. If you shot a picture of a blank wall that was sharp, well lit, and completely stable, the Quality Level would be perfect, but Adobe Premiere Elements would flag it as lacking in the Interest Level department. That doesn't do much for those boring conversations with Uncle Harold, because if quality is good, and the audio level sufficient, Smart Trim wouldn't flag the content, so you'll still have to delete those manually.

You can adjust the sliders to set the tolerance levels for either criteria: Moving the slider to the left increases the threshold for suboptimal clips, so that fewer and fewer clips will be flagged. Moving it to the right reduces the threshold so that more clips will be flagged.

For example, if you examine the clips in your project and find that most clips flagged by Adobe Premiere Elements look good to you, move the slider to the left and Adobe Premiere Elements will set the threshold higher and flag fewer clips. If clips left unflagged in Smart Trim mode look suboptimal to you for either Quality Level or Interest Level reasons, move the slider to the right.

Operating modes

Note that there are two operating modes in the Smart Trim Options window: Manual and Automatic. In Manual mode, which is the default, Adobe Premiere Elements displays all suboptimal regions of a clip via the zebra stripes shown and discussed previously. If you opt for Automatic mode, Adobe Premiere Elements immediately deletes all suboptimal regions present on the timeline. Thereafter, when you drag clips with suboptimal regions to the timeline, Adobe Premiere Elements presents a dialog asking if it's OK to remove Smart Trim sections.

There's an awful lot of bad video out there, and Smart Trim mode presents a very efficient way to identify it. In a real project, when you've shot 30–60 minutes of footage and want to quickly isolate the best 3–5 minutes to include in your movie, Smart Trim mode can be a godsend. So check it out on your own projects and see how it works for you.

Two final points: First, when Smart Trim flags quality-related problems, you can either delete the offending sections or try to fix them, which you'll attempt to do in Lesson 6. So even if you decide to leave suboptimal clips in the project, Smart Trim helps by identifying sequences you can improve with corrective effects.

Second, to reiterate a comment made earlier, you should *not* use Smart Trim in Automatic mode. Lots of "must have" sequences in your movies—such as your son blowing out the candles on his birthday cake or your daughter accepting her diploma—may not meet Adobe Premiere Elements' quality thresholds, but you still don't want to delete them. In Automatic mode, you don't get that choice.

That's all for this exercise, so you can close the Smart Trim Options window and exit the project if you'd like, or continue working in the project.

Producing split edits

Sometimes while editing you'll want the audio from a clip to precede the video (a J-cut) or the video to start before the audio (an L-cut). By default, Adobe Premiere Elements links the audio from a clip to the video from a clip; otherwise, your projects would quickly become an audio synchronization nightmare. To produce these edits, you must break this link.

To break the link temporarily, press the Alt (Windows) or Option (Mac OS) key when clicking either the audio or video component of a clip in the timeline. This allows you to drag only the selected media type in either direction, up to the limit of the clip, of course. That's how the audio file in the following figure was dragged to the left—by pressing the Alt (Windows) or Option (Mac OS) key, clicking the waveform on Audio 1, and dragging it to the left, opening a gap where you can add audio from a succeeding file beneath the existing video, a J-cut. When you finish the edit, however, the audio and video components of the clip are relinked.

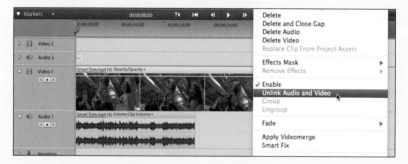

For a more permanent solution, click the target clip, right-click, and choose Unlink Audio and Video, which severs the link between the two clips, allowing you to trim or move either as desired. To link the two components back into a single clip, select them both, right-click, and choose Link Audio and Video. For more information, search for *Extend audio before or after linked video* in the Adobe Premiere Elements Help file.

Wonderful! You've finished another lesson and learned how to cut, trim, split, and arrange your raw video into a cohesive movie. In the next few lessons, you'll polish it into a fine-tuned production.

Review questions

1 What are the key differences between Expert and Quick views from an editing perspective?

2 What are an In point and an Out point, and what can you do with each?

3 What are two methods of shortening your video clips?

4 How does Adobe Premiere Elements combine video tracks at the same position on the timeline?

5 What are the two criteria assessed by Adobe Premiere Elements in Smart Trim mode?

Review answers

1 One of the most significant differences is the ability to see the Project Assets panel. In Quick view, you can only add content to the end of projects via program controls, although you can use drag and drop to add content to the middle of a project. In Expert view, you can drag content from the Project Assets panel to anywhere in the project.

2 An In point is the first frame of your clip as shown in Quick or Expert views, and the Out point is the last frame. In and Out points can be moved to create a shorter or longer clip.

3 You can shorten your clips by trimming their In points and Out points or by splitting the clip and deleting unwanted portions.

4 Adobe Premiere Elements renders the tracks from the top down. Any opaque areas of the clip in the Video 2 track will cover the view on the clip in the Video 1 track. Conversely, the clip in the Video 1 track will show through any transparent areas of the clip in the Video 2 track or if you reduce the Opacity of the clip in the Video 2 track.

5 Quality Level and Interest Level are the two criteria used in Smart Trim mode. The former assesses picture and audio quality on a technical level; the latter assesses multiple qualities, such as the amount of dialogue and motion that tend to indicate whether or not a clip is interesting.

6 WORKING WITH EFFECTS

Lesson overview

Video effects and adjustments allow you to improve the appearance of your clips, add pan and zoom effects, superimpose one clip over another, add special effects like lightning or earthquake motion, and otherwise enhance your video. Learning how to apply and configure these effects is a critical skill and the natural next step of your evolution as a video editor.

In this lesson, you'll learn how to apply effects and adjustments to the NASA Space Shuttle clips that you used in previous lessons, as well as several new clips. Specifically, you'll learn how to do the following:

- Apply video effects to single and multiple clips

- Change effects and settings

- Improve the contrast and saturation of your videos

- Copy effects and settings from one clip to another

- Animate a still image using Adobe Premiere Elements' Pan and Zoom effect

- Render your entire project and a work area within a project

- Control visual effects with keyframes

- Create a picture-in-picture effect

- Composite one video over another with Videomerge

 This lesson will take approximately two hours.

Fixing backlighted video with the
Shadow/Highlight effect.

Getting started

Before you begin the exercises in this lesson, make sure that you have correctly copied the Lesson06 folder from the DVD in the back of this book onto your computer's hard drive. For more information, see "Copying the Classroom in a Book files" in the "Getting Started" section at the start of this book.

Now you're ready to begin working with the Lesson06 project file.

1   Launch Adobe Premiere Elements. If it is already open, choose Help > Welcome Screen in the Adobe Premiere Elements menu to return to the Welcome screen.

2   In the Welcome screen, click Video Editor, select Existing Project, and click the Open folder.

3   In the Open Project dialog, navigate to the Lesson06 folder you copied to your hard drive. Within that folder, select the file Lesson06_Start_Win.prel (Windows) or Lesson06_Start_Mac.prel (Mac OS) and then click Open. If a dialog appears asking for the location of rendered files, click the Skip Previews button.

Your project file opens.

4   Choose Window > Restore Workspace to ensure that you start the lesson with the default panel layout.

Viewing the completed movie before you start

To see what you'll be creating in this lesson, you can take a look at the completed movie. You'll must be in Expert view to open the Project Assets panel to view the movie, so if you're not, click Expert (Expert) to enter that view.

1   On the upper-left side of the Adobe Premiere Elements interface, click the Project Assets button (Project Assets ▾) to open that panel. Locate the file Lesson06_Movie.mov, and then double-click it to open the video into the preview window.

2   Click the Play button (▶) to watch the video about powering the Space Shuttle, which you'll build in this lesson.

3   When you're done, close the preview window.

   ● **Note:** Adobe Premiere Elements offers a large selection of diversified effects. It's a good idea to look up the gallery of video effects in your Adobe Premiere Elements Help file, which gives you a quick overview of all those effects actually applied to an image.

Using effects

The tools that you'll work with in this lesson are located in four different panels. All four panels are different in Quick and Expert views. Quick view contains the most widely used tools or effects in each category, and Expert view contains all these plus a wide selection of other tools and effects.

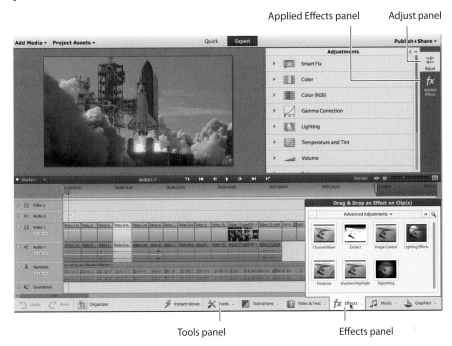

Applied Effects panel — Adjust panel

Tools panel — Effects panel

In terms of workflow, effects in the Adjust (⊞) and Applied Effects (▤) panels are automatically applied to each clip in the timeline. To adjust these, click the clip in the timeline, and then click the respective panel button to open the adjustments.

You'll go through these procedures in various exercises in this chapter, but as an overview, you apply tools by selecting a clip on the timeline, clicking the Tools button (✕ Tools) to open that panel, and clicking the desired tool. Adobe Premiere Elements will apply the tool to that clip and open a customization window unique to the selected tool.

To apply an effect from the Effects panel (ƒx Effects), click the Effects panel button to open the panel, find the desired effect, and then drag it onto the target clip or clips. To adjust the parameters of the effect that you just applied, click the Applied Effects (▤) button to open that panel, which contains all effects that you applied from the Effects panel, plus the Motion and Opacity adjustments.

Now let's take a closer look at the adjustments in each panel.

The Adjust panel

The Adjust panel () contains the most common adjustments that you'll make to your clips in most projects. In essence, these adjustments are effects, but because they're so commonly used, they're not stored with the other effects that you have to apply manually; instead, Adobe Premiere Elements applies them to every clip automatically, which is more efficient.

When you're working in Quick view, Adobe Premiere Elements provides access to the one-step Smart Fix control, as well as Color, Lighting, and Temperature and Tint adjustments for video, and Volume and Balance for audio. In Expert view, these are supplemented by Color (RBG) and Gamma Correction for video and Treble, Bass, and Audio Gain for audio. The other major difference between the two views is that Expert view lets you animate effects by adding keyframes, which you accomplish via controls accessed by clicking the Show/Hide keyframe controls icon (⏱) on the upper right of the Adjustments panel. You'll learn how to use keyframes in "Working with keyframes" later in this lesson.

Quick view

Expert view

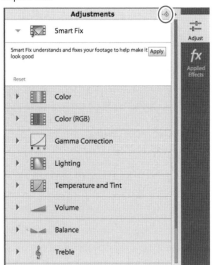

The Applied Effects panel

The Applied Effects panel (🔲) contains any effects that you've manually applied to the selected clip, plus the very commonly used Motion and Opacity adjustments. The Motion effect, in particular, is one that you'll use in many projects for many different purposes: to customize a picture-in-picture, to zoom into or out of a video, or to rotate a video. Remember that it's automatically applied for you and always ready for adjustment in the Applied Effects panel.

Within the Applied Effects panel, the only difference between Expert and Quick views is the ability to keyframe any of the effects in the panel. You access this capability by clicking the Show/Hide keyframe controls icon (⊙) on the upper right of the panel.

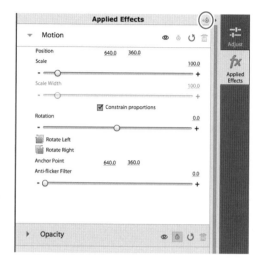

The Tools panel

The Tools panel contains a range of useful tools that you'll use in many projects. To open the panel, click Tools (✕ Tools) in the Action bar at the bottom of the Adobe Premiere Elements interface. To close the panel, click the triangle next to the Tools icon (▲). In Quick view, the Tools panel contains the following tools that we'll discuss in this lesson:

- **Pan & Zoom** is used for adding pan and zoom effects to pictures and videos, which you'll learn to use in "Creating a Pan & Zoom effect" later in this lesson.

- **Time Remapping** is used for fine control of fast and slow motion effects applied to your clips, which is described later in this lesson in "Working with Time Remapping."

In Expert view, you also have access to the Time Stretch tool, which is covered later in this lesson in "Changing playback speed."

The Effects panel

The Effects panel shows video (in Expert and Quick views) and audio effects (in Expert view only), and FilmLooks you can use in your movie by dragging them onto any clip or clips in the timeline. Quick view offers 32 of the most commonly used effects and FilmLooks, whereas Expert view offers dozens more in well-defined categories. In addition, when you're in Expert view, you can search for an effect by clicking the magnifying lens (🔍) on the upper right of the panel. This opens a search box where you can type the name of the effect that you're looking for. This search function is not available in Quick view.

Quick view

Expert view

 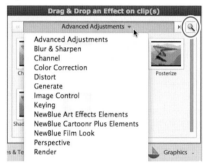

Recommended workflows

From a workflow perspective, it's helpful to think about effects in the following categories. All effects listed are available in Expert view; some are also available in Quick view:

- **Curative effects:** Curative effects correct problems in your video footage, including footage that's too bright or too dark, backlighted video, video that's too shaky because it was shot without a tripod, and even video that's a bit blurry. You should start with the color- and brightness-related curative effects in the Adjustments panel. Beyond these, you can find other curative effects in the Effects panel in the Advanced Adjustments folder; Color Correction folder; Blur Sharpen folder; Image Control folder; and Video Stabilizer folder.

- **Overlay effects:** Overlay effects allow you to composite one image over another. You can find overlay effects in the Keying and Videomerge folders.

- **Pan & Zoom effect:** This effect enables you to pan around and zoom into and out of still images and videos, allowing you to animate still images and add additional motion to videos. You can find this tool by clicking the Pan and Zoom icon (▦) in the Tools panel.

- **Artistic effects:** Artistic effects let you create a different look or feel from the original clip, or add a Lens Flare (Generate folder) or Vignetting (Advanced Adjustments). Most artistic effects are found in the Effects panel, and they can be quite powerful, like the NewBlue Cartoonr Plus effect in the NewBlue Cartoonr Plus Elements folder that converts your videos to cartoons. Other artistic effects let you add lightning to a clip (Lightning effect in the Render folder), add earthquake-like effects (Earthquake effect in the NewBlue Art Effects Elements folder), place a spotlight on a subject (Lighting Effects in the Advanced Adjustments folder), and apply many other looks and characteristics.

- **FilmLooks:** The FilmLooks folder in the Effects panel contains a number of presets that let you quickly and easily add a certain look or feel to your project, like Newsreel, Summer Day, or Vintage.

- **Speed controls:** These controls enable you to speed up, slow down, or reverse your clips by using the Time Stretch and Time Remapping tools in the Tools panel.

- **Motion effects:** Motion effects allow you to zoom into and around your original video clip or still image, and are used to adjust the framing of a video. You adjust these parameters using the Motion controls in the Applied Effects panel.

Although you can apply any and all of these effects at anytime during the course of a project, the recommended workflow is to apply curative filters first, then adjust speed and motion, and then add other artistic effects. You can add an effect to any clip and even apply the same effect numerous times to the same clip but with different settings. By default, when you add an effect to a clip, it applies to the entire clip. If you want to apply an effect to only part of a clip, split it first, and then apply the effect to the desired clip segment.

Working with Smart Fix

Unless you disable the Auto-Analyzer application in the Organizer, at some point Adobe Premiere Elements will analyze your clips, either in the background while you're performing other edits or after capture or import. While analyzing the clips, Adobe Premiere Elements looks for problems in the video.

As you saw with Smart Trim in the previous lesson, Adobe Premiere Elements uses some of this information to recommend which clips to trim away. In addition, if your video or still image is too dark, Adobe Premiere Elements will apply the Shadow/Highlight effect, as you'll see in this exercise. If a standard definition (SD) video is too shaky, Adobe Premiere Elements will apply the Stabilizer effect. If you're working with shaky high definition (HD) video, Adobe Premiere Elements won't apply the Stabilizer effect automatically because it's too processor-intensive, although you can apply the effect manually, as you'll learn in a subsequent exercise.

This is how Smart Fix works.

1 If necessary, click the Expert button (Expert) to enter Expert view.

2 On the bottom right of the Monitor panel, just to the right of the Render button (Render), click the Fit to Visible Timeline button (⬚), or press the Backslash (\) key.

3 On the upper left of the Adobe Premiere Elements interface, click the Project Assets button to open that panel.

4 Right-click Video 4.mp4, and choose Run Auto Analyzer.

5 Click and drag Video 4.mp4 into the Video 1 track on the timeline about an inch after the last picture on that track. Adobe Premiere Elements opens the Smart Fix window. If Smart Fix doesn't run automatically, click Adjust in the Monitor panel, select Smart Fix in the Adjustments panel, and click Apply.

6 In the Smart Fix window, click Yes to fix the quality problem in the clip.

7 Click the Project Assets button to close that panel.

▶ **Tip:** Toggling the effect off (👁) and on (👁) is a great way to see how the effect is modifying your clip. You'll use this toggle frequently with most curative effects.

8 In the timeline, click the copy of Video 4.mp4 you just added to the timeline to select it (if it's not already selected), and then click the Applied Effects button to open that panel. You'll see that Adobe Premiere Elements has applied the Shadow/Highlight effect to the clip.

Drag the current-time indicator over Video 4. Then click the eye icon (👁) next to the Shadow/Highlight effect (officially called the "Toggle the effect on or off" icon) to turn the effect on and off, and you'll see that the Shadow/Highlight effect does a nice job of brightening the shadows without "blowing out" the lighter regions. Although the clip looks a bit pixelated once brightened, this is a function of the compression applied to the clip so that it would fit on the DVD, not a result of applying the effect.

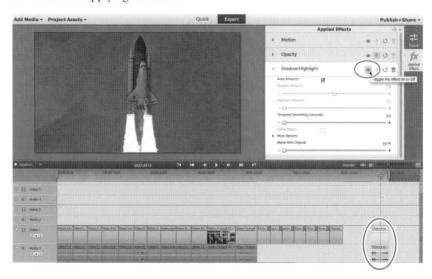

9   Now let's apply Smart Fix to the existing Video 4.mp4 on the timeline. To do so, click the other copy of Video 4.mp4 (between Video 3.mp4 and Video 5.mp4) on the timeline to select it, click the Adjust button to open the Adjust panel, click the disclosure triangle next to Smart Fix to open those options, and click the Apply button (Apply). If Adobe Premiere Elements hasn't auto-analyzed the clip previously, it will do so. In either case, it will then brighten the clip.

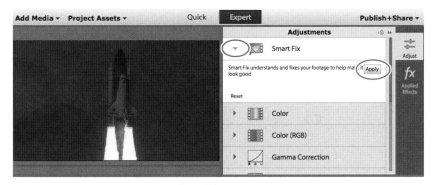

10 Delete the Video 4.mp4 video you added to the end of the timeline by right-clicking the clip and choosing Delete.

▶ **Tip:** You can adjust the setting of any effect applied by Adobe Premiere Elements or disable or delete it. Unless you have a strong reason not to do so, it's generally a good idea to allow Adobe Premiere Elements to apply Smart Fix whenever you add clips to the Project Assets panel. It's not a panacea, but it's a great start toward improving clip quality.

Perfecting your clips

All projects are unique, and all source clips present unique issues. Outdoor projects shot during a nice, bright day are generally fairly simple to perfect. In contrast, indoor shoots typically present a range of problems: Lighting is often inadequate, and camcorders sometimes have problems producing accurate colors when you're shooting under fluorescent or incandescent lighting.

When your personal projects involve indoor shoots, you should experiment with several of the adjustments in the Adjust panel, as well as the Shadow/Highlight effect in the Advanced Adjustments folder in the Effects panel. Often you can produce remarkable improvements in minimal time and with little effort.

Whether you shot the source videos outside, inside, or both, typically you'll apply the curative effects first, fixing brightness, contrast, and color; then remove the shakes; and then reframe the video to get the best presentation possible. Thereafter, you can start to apply artistic effects.

The clips in this project were mostly shot by professionals with high-end equipment. Although they make for an interesting project, they don't leave a lot of major problems to correct. So let's do some fine-tuning, and later you'll perform major surgery on some family vacation videos.

Choosing and applying effects

Move your current-time indicator over Video 5.mp4 in the timeline. To me, the video looks like it could use a boost in color saturation. The sky and fuel tank look faded, and the entire image lacks contrast.

You'll use the Color (RGB) and Lighting effect to repair these problems. You'll be using adjustments available only in Expert view. If necessary, click the Expert button (Expert) at the top of the Monitor panel to enter that view.

1 Click to select Video 5.mp4. Then click the Adjust button to open that panel. As a refresher, all these adjustments are automatically applied to the clip once it is added to the timeline, but with zero values. You don't have to apply these adjustments manually; you just have to configure the values.

2 Click the disclosure triangle to the left of the Color (RGB) adjustment (if you don't see this adjustment, it's because you're in Quick view). This reveals the color chips that you can use to adjust the color values. Experiment by clicking a few of these chips. Change from Red to Green to Blue values by clicking the respective box beneath the Color (RGB) effect text.

   Then click Reset on the bottom left of the Color (RGB) Adjustment panel to reset the values. Note that once you adjust the effect, the "Toggle the effect on or off" eye icon (👁) appears on the upper right of the panel. When you reset, it disappears.

3 Beneath the color chips and to the right, click the More button (More). This reveals separate Red, Green, and Blue adjustments.

4 Change the Red setting to 120 to bring out the orange in the fuel tank, and adjust the Blue setting to 130. To do so, you can do *any of the following:*

- Drag the slider to the desired value.

- Hold the pointer over the numeric value until it becomes the pointer with arrows (🖐). Click and drag to the desired value.

- Click the numeric value to make it active, type the desired value, and press Enter (Windows) or Return (Mac OS).

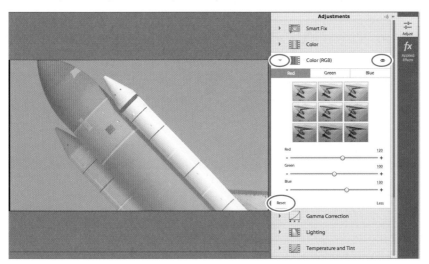

5 Using the eye icon (👁) to the right of Color (RGB), toggle the adjustments on and off. Perhaps you've overcooked it a bit, but the oranges and blues sure look brighter.

6 Click the disclosure triangle to the left of the Color (RGB) adjustment to close the controls. Note the green dot that appears on the right in place of the eye icon, indicating that adjustments have been made.

7 Click the disclosure triangle to the left of the Lighting adjustment to open those controls. Click the More button (More) at the bottom of the Lighting adjustments panel to reveal all controls.

8 Click the Auto Fix button. In this case, there's little benefit, but often Auto Fix works very well for correcting lighting problems, and it's worth a try whenever it's available. Note how when Auto Fix is selected, all controls are grayed out. To customize your controls at this point, deselect Auto Fix.

9 With Auto Fix deselected, experiment by clicking the color chips, switching through the available categories (Brightness, Contrast, Exposure, Black, and White) via the buttons beneath the Lighting adjustment text. Note how clicking the color chips impacts the numerical values beneath the chips.

10 Click Reset on the bottom left to reset the values.

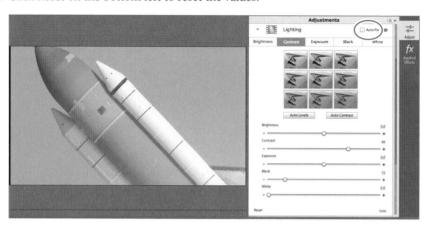

11 Set Contrast to 44 and Black to 15.

12 Toggle the effect on or off to assess the adjustments. Toggle both adjustments off to view the clip as it was before you started, and then toggle them both on to see the final result. Although you probably changed a cloudy day with a faded blue sky to a sunny day with a clear blue sky, the video looks noticeably better. It's a rare clip that can't be improved to some degree using adjustments like these.

13 Choose File > Save As and save your project as **Lesson06_Work.prel**.

Previewing and rendering effects

When you apply an effect or configure an adjustment, Adobe Premiere Elements will show a very close approximation of the result when you preview in the Monitor panel. In most instances, this is good enough to allow you to perfect your configuration options and move on to the next edit.

If the quality isn't sufficient, right-click the frame in the Monitor panel and choose Playback quality > Highest. This tells Adobe Premiere Elements to prioritize frame quality over playback speed. As a result, on slower computers, playback may be jerky, but frame quality should be very good. On the other hand, if playback speed isn't sufficient, right-click in the Monitor panel and make sure that Automatic is selected. This tells Adobe Premiere Elements to prioritize smoothness over frame quality. With Automatic selected, you might see some blurriness or pixelation in the frame, but playback should be smooth.

If neither setting gives you the preview quality that you need to finalize the edit, you'll have to render the clip. If you adjusted the Color (RGB) and Lighting values as detailed in the previous exercise, you should see an orange line above Video 5.mp4 in the timeline.

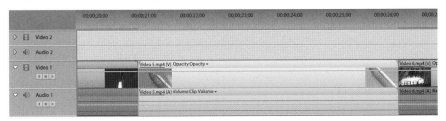

In general, the orange line indicates that some adjustment has been made to the clip that must be rendered before final production. For example, if you apply a title above a clip, you'll see the orange line. If you insert a clip into a project that doesn't match the Project Setting—like the JPEG images inserted into the slide show at the end of the project—you'll see the orange line as well. You don't have to render to preview your work; however, rendering will show you exactly how the final video will look.

To render the entire project, click Enter (Windows) or Return (Mac OS), or press the Render button (Render) on the bottom right of the Monitor panel. Adobe Premiere Elements opens the Rendering dialog, which tells you how many previews need to be rendered and how long it will take. After rendering, Adobe Premiere Elements turns the red bar to green, and you can start previewing your clips from the beginning.

Rendering a Work Area

In most instances, it's not necessary to render every edit, and sooner or later you'll have lots of orange lines over your timeline. At some point, you'll apply an effect that you do want to render. If you press Enter (Windows) or Return (Mac OS) to render, you render the *entire* timeline, which can be time-consuming. As an alternative, you can simply render the Work Area that you're interested in.

The Work Area is a region of the project defined by two vertical Work Area markers (❙) that live in the time scale above the timeline. By default, the Work Area starts at the beginning of the project and ends with the last content on the timeline, and the Work Area expands with your project as you add more content. However, you can drag the Work Area bars to define any region in the timeline, so that you can render only that region. In this exercise, you'll learn how.

1 In the Adobe Premiere Elements menu, choose Timeline > Delete Rendered Files. If that option isn't available, choose Delete Rendered Files for All Projects. This deletes the files that you previously rendered and should turn the green bars above the timeline to orange.

2 Press the Backslash (\) key to show the entire project in the timeline.

● **Note:** Sometimes it may not be convenient to zoom out to see the entire clip and the edges of the Work Area bar. As an alternative to dragging the edges, you can also place the current-time indicator at the start of the Work Area you want to create and press Alt+[(Windows) or Option+[(Mac OS) to set the start of the Work Area. Then drag the current-time indicator to the end of the Work Area and press Alt+] (Windows) or Option+] (Mac OS) to set the end of the Work Area. Then press Enter (Windows) or Return (Mac OS) to render the Work Area.

3 Drag the left Work Area marker (❙) from the very front of the timeline to the start of Video 5.mp4.

4 Drag the right Work Area marker (❙) from the very end of the timeline to the end of Video 5.mp4.

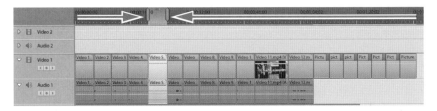

5 Press Enter (Windows) or Return (Mac OS) to render the Work Area. Adobe Premiere Elements will render the Work Area and start previewing at the start of Video 5.mp4. Press the spacebar to stop video playback when ready.

6 Choose File > Save and save your project. This is important because you'll be returning to this project, and you'll want to pick up right where you left off.

Fixing backlighted video

As mentioned earlier, the NASA clips are all professionally shot, so they don't exhibit many of the problems that you'll be facing in your projects. So let's switch to some family vacation videos that have many of these problems. The videos you'll be using were shot in the Toys"R"Us store in Times Square with three girls mugging in front of the lifelike T-Rex in the store, feigning fear.

Because all the lighting is from the ceiling, their faces appear darker than they should be, which is a common problem called *backlighting*. Because these clips were shot without a tripod, they're shaky—the second clip in particular.

You'll apply the Shadow/Highlight effect to brighten just the shadows in the clip without adjusting other regions. You'll adjust the second clip first, and then copy the effect to the first clip in the project. Then you'll apply the Stabilizer effect to reduce the shakes in the second clip.

You'll start by loading the project.

1 Launch Adobe Premiere Elements if it isn't already running.

2 Choose File > Open Project.

3 In the Open Project dialog, navigate to the Lesson06 folder you copied to your hard drive. Within that folder, select the file Lesson06_Backlight_Win.prel (Windows) or Lesson06_Backlight_Mac.prel (Mac OS) and then click Open (Windows) or Choose (Mac OS). If a dialog appears asking for the location of rendered files, click the Skip Previews button.

   The project opens.

4 Choose Window > Restore Workspace to ensure that you start the lesson with the default panel layout.

5 The Shadow/Highlight effect is not available in Quick view, so if necessary, click the Expert button at the top of the Monitor panel to switch to Expert view.

Applying the Shadow/Highlight effect

To begin, apply the Shadow/Highlight effect to the second clip in the project.

1 In the Action bar on the bottom of the interface, click the Effects button (fx Effects) to open the Effects panel.

2 In the list box at the top of the panel, click and select Advanced Adjustments if it's not already selected. Use the slider on the right of the panel (if necessary) to scroll down to view the Shadow/Highlight effect, which is in the bottom row.

3 Drag the Shadow/Highlight effect from the Effects panel onto the second clip in the timeline. If necessary, drag the current-time indicator over the second clip so that you see the three girls in the Monitor panel.

4 Click the Applied Effects (▨) button on the top right to open the Applied Effects panel.

5 In the Applied Effects panel, click the eye icon next to the Shadow/Highlight effect to toggle it off (👁) and on (👁). Note how the effect brightens the darker regions without adjusting the brighter regions like the light in the background behind T-Rex's left shoulder.

6 Click the disclosure triangle to the left of the Shadow/Highlight effect to open the parameter settings.

7 The default parameters may be too conservative for this clip. Let's try to improve the results. To adjust the effect manually, deselect the Auto Amounts check box.

8 To adjust the darker regions, drag the Shadow Amount slider to the right to increase the brightness of pixels in the shadows (including the faces in this clip) and to the left to decrease the brightness. Try to increase brightness as much as you can without fading the video or creating a halo around objects in the video; stop when you've increased it to about 80.

9 If the brightest pixels are too bright, you can drag the Highlight Amount slider to the right to darken them. Experiment with this slider to see the impact, but it's not really a problem with this clip, so drag it back to the left and set it at 0.

10 Click the eye icon (👁) next to the Shadow/Highlight effect to toggle it off and on (👁). It's remarkable how much better the clip looks, particularly given that it probably didn't appear too dark when you first looked at it.

These are the most important manual controls in the Shadow/Highlight effect; to learn about the others, check the Adobe Premiere Elements Help file.

11 Save your project as **Lesson06_Backlight_Work.prel**.

Effect controls

Note the icons to the right of the Shadow/Highlight effect in the Applied Effects panel. We've discussed the "Toggle the effect on or off" eye icon; let's quickly cover the others. The stopwatch icon is called *Toggle animation* and lets you animate the effect with keyframes, which is covered later in this lesson in "Working with keyframes." The Reset icon resets the effect to its default parameters, and the trash can icon deletes the effect. Note that you can't delete any adjustments in the Adjustment panel or delete the Motion or Opacity effects in the Applied Effects panel.

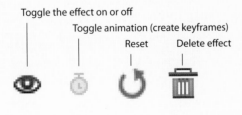

Copying effects from one clip to another

When you adjust one clip shot at a particular location, like the Toys"R"Us Times Square store, you'll probably need to apply the same adjustments to other clips shot at that location. Fortunately, Adobe Premiere Elements provides several simple ways to copy effects and their settings from one clip to another.

Note that neither of the techniques discussed in this section—copying effects from one effect to another and creating effect presets—works with adjustments in the Adjustment panel. Rather, you must copy and paste the adjustment on the timeline using a technique demonstrated later in this lesson in "Reframing an image with Motion controls."

Let's copy the Shadow/Highlight effect from the second clip in the timeline to the first.

1 Click the second backlight.mp4 in the timeline to select it.

2 If necessary, click the Applied Effects button to open that panel.

● **Note:** You can also click to select the effect and choose Edit > Copy, or press Ctrl+C (Windows) or Command+C (Mac OS) to copy the selected effects.

3 Right-click the Shadow/Highlight effect and choose Copy.

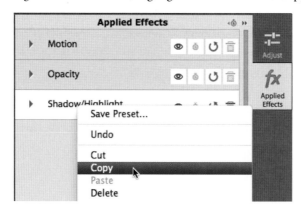

4 Click the first backlight.mp4 clip to select it. If necessary, click the Applied Effects button to open that panel.

5 Right-click in the blank area beneath the Opacity effect in the Applied Effects panel, and then choose Paste. Adobe Premiere Elements applies the Shadow/Highlight effect to this clip with the same properties.

6 Click the eye icon (👁) next to the Shadow/Highlight effect to toggle it off and on (👁). Again, you see quite an improvement for a clip that didn't look that bad at first glance.

Saving a preset

After you've created the ideal Shadow/Highlight configuration for a particular scene, you'll probably want to apply it to all clips in that scene. The easiest way to do this is to save it as a preset.

1   If necessary, click the first backlight.mp4 clip to select it. If necessary, click the Applied Effects button to open that panel.

2   In the Applied Effects panel, right-click the Shadow/Highlight effect and choose Save Preset. The Save Preset dialog opens.

Note: Anchor to In Point and Anchor to Out Point control how clips with keyframes are applied to new clips. Because there are no keyframes in the Shadow/Highlight preset, choose Scale to apply the effect to the entire clip.

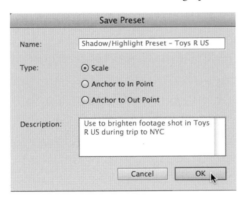

3   For Type, choose Scale, and complete the name and any description. Then click OK to save the preset.

4   To view a custom preset, choose the My Presets folder from the drop-down list in the Effects panel, which is only visible in Expert view. From there, you apply it by dragging the effect onto a clip or clips, just like any other effect.

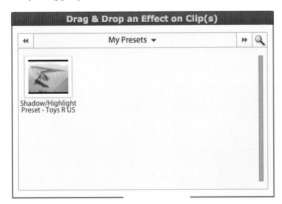

Stabilizing shaky footage

One common problem with vacation video footage is excessive shakiness, which can occur anytime you don't use a tripod. Via the Smart Fix function, Adobe

Premiere Elements stabilizes the worst of the SD clips, but for HD clips like those we're using in this project, you'll have to do it manually. I didn't bring a tripod into Toys"R"Us, and the second backlight.mp4 clip is particularly shaky. In this exercise, you'll apply the Stabilizer effect to correct this problem.

Note that the Stabilizer effect is available in the Effect panel in both Quick and Expert views. In Quick view it's in the Video Effects folder; in Expert view it's in the Video Stabilizer folder.

1 In the Action bar on the bottom of the interface, click the Effects button (fx Effects) to open the Effects panel.

2 In the list box at the top of the panel, click to select the Video Effects folder (Quick view) or Video Stabilizer folder (Expert view). In Quick view, use the slider on the right of the panel to scroll down to the Stabilizer effect, which is on the fourth row.

3 Drag the Stabilizer effect from the Effects panel onto the second clip in the timeline. If necessary, drag the current-time indicator over the second clip so that you see my three daughters in the Monitor panel.

4 Click the Applied Effects (▤) button on the top right of the Monitor panel to open the Applied Effects panel.

5 In the Applied Effects panel, click the disclosure triangle to the left of the Stabilizer effect to open the parameter settings.

6 Render and preview the clip. Then click the eye icon (👁) next to the Stabilizer effect to toggle it off and on (👁). Note how Adobe Premiere Elements zoomed into the frame when it stabilized the video.

7 There's no problem with this application of the Stabilizer effect, but sometimes you'll notice a black bar on the top, bottom, or sides of the clip where the adjustment was too strong and extended beyond the frame's edge. To correct this, in the Applied Effects panel, select the Limit To Zoom check box, which limits the stabilization to the edges of the frame.

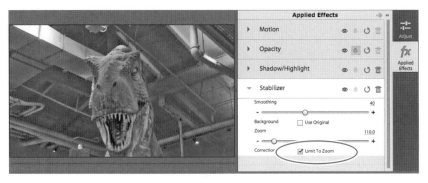

8 Scrub through the other portions of the clip to see if any bars appear. If not, you're ready to move on to your next edit.

Play the clip while using the eye icon to the left of the Stabilizer effect to toggle it on and off. The clip is definitely easier to watch with the Stabilizer effect applied.

Working with Time Remapping

Time Remapping lets you adjust the speed of a clip—forward or backward—and then return to the original speed of the clip. This can produce very elegant, TV- and movie-like results. We'll return to the Space Shuttle project to apply a global speed change to a clip; in this exercise, you'll use Time Remapping to analyze the author's golf swing. After you've done this, you'll reframe the clip using Motion controls to center the video.

Let's start by loading the project.

1 Launch Adobe Premiere Elements if it isn't already running.

2 Choose File > Open Project. Click No and don't save any changes to the existing project if this screen appears.

3 In the Open Project dialog, navigate to the Lesson06 folder you copied to your hard drive. Within that folder, select the file Lesson06_Driver_Win. prel (Windows) or Lesson06_Driver_Mac.prel (Mac OS) and then click Open (Windows) or Choose (Mac OS). If a dialog appears asking for the location of rendered files, click the Skip Previews button.

   The project opens.

4 Choose Window > Restore Workspace to ensure that you start the lesson with the default panel layout.

5 Time Remapping is available in Quick and Expert views, so you can work in either view.

Time Remapping your clips

The original clip is a little less than eight seconds long; the first four seconds are the setup and then the swing and transition. In this exercise, you'll use reverse motion to create an instant replay, and then slow down the swing to painful slow motion to analyze the flaws.

As with many Adobe Premiere Elements tools, Time Remapping has a dedicated workspace for configuring and resetting the effect. In fact, it resembles Quick view to a great degree because it has a very similar Monitor panel and timeline. However, instead of the Action bar you'll find configuration options for the Time Remapping function.

Operationally, you'll create one or more TimeZones, which produce the desired speed changes. You don't have the option to slow or accelerate audio, so you can either keep the original audio, which obviously won't match the video, or remove the audio, which seems like the right decision in most applications.

1 Click to select driver.mp4 in the timeline.

2 In the Action bar on the bottom of the interface, click the Tools button (✖ Tools ▾) to open the Tools panel.

3 Use the slider on the right of the panel to scroll down to the Time Remapping tool, which is at or near the bottom in both Quick and Expert views. Then click Time Remapping in the Tools panel to apply the tool to the selected clip and open the Time Remapping panel.

4 Drag the current-time indicator to about 00;00;04;05 in the Monitor panel, and then click the plus sign (⊞) next to the current-time indicator to create a TimeZone. By default, Adobe Premiere Elements creates a 17-frame TimeZone.

5   Click and drag the right edge of the TimeZone to about 00;00;07;00. This
    applies the effect to the selected 2.8 seconds in the clip. If you know the
    duration to which you want to apply the effect, you can enter the desired time
    in the Duration field on the lower right rather than dragging the edge of the
    TimeZone.

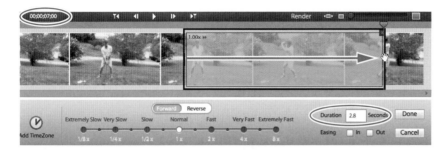

6   Note the Forward/Reverse toggle in the Action bar area. Select Reverse and
    then click the 8x button on the Time Control slider to move the speed selector
    to 8 times faster than real time. You could also click and drag the speed selector
    to that location.

7   Click the Home key to return the current-time indicator to the start of the clip,
    and then press the spacebar to play the clip. The video will play at normal speed
    until it reaches the end of the TimeZone, return at 8x speed to the 4:05 mark,
    and then play the swing again at full speed.

Creating variable-speed, slow-motion effects

OK, let's focus on forward action and really analyze that swing. You'll slow down
the takeaway to 50 percent speed, and then, at the top of the backswing, slow the
speed to 25 percent during the critical downswing. At the end, you'll return the clip
to 100 percent speed.

1   To start, click the Reset button (⬚) on the lower left, and click Yes to remove all
    TimeZones.

2   Drag the current-time indicator to about 00;00;04;05 in the Monitor panel,
    or click the monitor timecode, enter **405**, and then press Enter (Windows)
    or Return (Mac OS). Then click the plus sign (⬚) next to the current-time
    indicator to create a TimeZone.

3   Click and drag the right edge of the TimeZone to about 00;00;05;00, just
    before the downswing begins. In the pre-release programs that I was using, I

had to drag the edge to 00;00;05;01 to make the current-time indicator stay at 00;00;05;00 once I released the edge.

4 Make sure that Forward is selected in the Forward/Reverse toggle. Then click the 1/2x button on the Time Control slider to move the speed selector to that value. You could also click and drag the speed selector to that location. This slows the clip to half speed.

5 On the bottom right of the Time Remapping panel, select the Easing In check box, which smooths the shift from 1x to 1/2x speed at the start of the effect. Because you want to transition directly from 1/2x speed to 1/4x speed in the next TimeZone, you don't want to select the Easing Out check box, which will ease out to the original 1x speed.

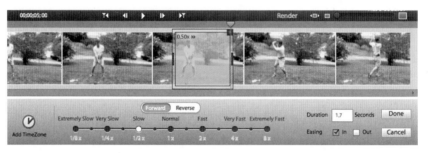

6 Click and drag the current-time indicator as close to the right edge of the previous TimeZone as possible while still seeing the plus sign (⊞), which should be around 00;00;05;11. If you drag it so that it touches the right edge of the first TimeZone, the plus sign will disappear.

7 Click the plus sign to create another TimeZone, and drag the right edge to about 00;00;06;18. Again, you may have to drag a bit past this timecode to make the timecode stop at 00;00;06;18 when you release the TimeZone edge.

Make sure that Forward is selected in the Forward/Reverse toggle. Then click the 1/4x button on the Time Control slider to move the speed selector to that value and select the Easing In and Easing Out check boxes. This will smooth the transition from 1/2x to 1/4x speed at the start of the effect and then transition from 1/4x to 1x at the very end.

● **Note:** When not selected, TimeZones with forward motion are light green; TimeZones with reverse motion are light orange. All TimeZone speed and direction indicators are on the upper right.

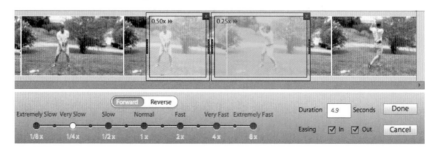

8   Press the Home key to return the current-time indicator to the start of the clip, and then press the spacebar to play the clip. The video will play at normal speed to the 4:05 mark, ease to 1/2 speed, then ease into 1/4 speed, and then ease back to full speed at the very end.

9   On the bottom left of the Time Remapping panel, click the Remove Audio button (⊡) to remove audio from the clip. Click Yes to confirm that you do want to remove the audio.

10 On the bottom left of the Time Remapping panel, click the Frame Blending button (⊡) to apply frame blending to the slow motion effect. Frame blending can smooth the appearance of slow motion but sometimes can introduce blurriness in the clip. Click the Render button (Render) on the bottom right of the Monitor panel in the Time Remapping tool to render the effect; then play back the clip with and without Frame Blending, and choose the option that you prefer.

11 On the bottom right of the Time Remapping panel, click Done to apply Time Remapping, close the panel, and return to the main interface.

▶ **Tip:** To change any Time Remapping options or to remove Time Remapping from a clip, follow steps 1–3 of this exercise to open the Time Remapping panel, and click Reset (⊡) on the bottom left. When you close the panel, Adobe Premiere Elements removes the effect.

● **Note:** When you apply Time Remapping to a clip in the timeline, Adobe Premiere Elements adjusts all subsequent clips on the timeline accordingly. If you slow down the clip, all subsequent clips will be pushed to the right. If you accelerate the clip, Adobe Premiere Elements will shift subsequent clips to the left to close any gap.

Reframing a clip using Motion controls

Time Remapping is working, but the framing of the shot is off: There's too much space over the subject's head, and he needs to be more centered in the frame. You can improve both problems using the Motion controls. In this exercise, you'll learn how to use Motion controls to reframe a video; later in the lesson, you'll learn how to use these controls to reframe pictures.

Motion controls are available in Quick and Expert views. There are no screen shots that show either view in this exercise, so you can work in the view in which you feel most comfortable.

1   Click driver.mp4 to select the clip in the timeline.

2   Click the Applied Effects (⊡) button on the top right of the Monitor panel to open the Applied Effects panel.

3   In the Applied Effects panel, click the disclosure triangle to the left of the Motion effect to open the parameter settings.

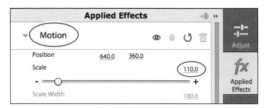

4   Zoom into the video and make it larger. *Do any of the following:*

- Drag the Scale slider to the right to a value of 110.

- Click the numeric entry to make it active, type **110**, and then press Enter (Windows) or Return (Mac OS).

- Hold the pointer over the numeric value until it becomes the pointer with arrows (). Click and drag to the right to 110.

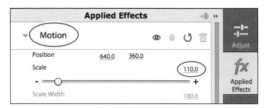

5   Now you'll reframe the image. In the Monitor panel, right-click the frame and choose Magnification > 50%. If you're working on a notebook computer or very small monitor, choose Magnification > 25%.

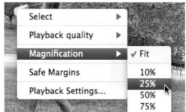

6   Click the frame in the Monitor panel to make the center crosshair active. You should see a white box outside the visible frame in the Monitor panel. (If you can't see the top and bottom outlines of the box, expand the entire Adobe Premiere Elements window, or if you don't have room on your screen, decrease Magnification following the instructions in step 5.) As you've probably guessed, this is an outline of the entire video, which you can drag around to optimize positioning within the preview area in the Monitor panel. As you drag the frame around, note that the numeric Position parameters on the right are updated as you move it. You can position the frame either by dragging it directly as you just did or by typing in new numeric parameters. I typed in 700 and 328, which shifted the video to the right and up a bit.

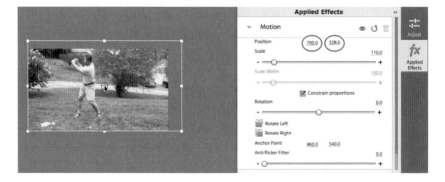

7 In the Monitor panel, right-click the frame and choose Magnification > Fit. This sets your preview to the largest possible size while showing all the pixels in the video, which is helpful when you're previewing Motion control adjustments.

8 Click the eye icon next to the Motion effect to toggle it off (👁) and on (👁). You'll see that you've increased the size of the subject of the video and moved it toward the center. It's not a huge difference, but even a small improvement is welcome.

9 Press the Home key to return the current-time indicator to the start of the clip, and then press the spacebar and watch the entire clip. Whenever you adjust the size or positioning of a video, as you've done here, it's possible that you may have pushed other critical content located elsewhere in the clip out of the viewing window. Either preview the entire clip that you've adjusted, or for longer clips, drag the current-time indicator through the clip slowly to identify any problem areas.

10 Let's review some of the other options and controls in the Motion effect:

- **Constrain proportions:** By default, Adobe Premiere Elements constrains the proportions of your size adjustments, adjusting horizontally and vertically to preserve the aspect ratio of your video. That's why the Scale Width slider and numeric entry are grayed out. If you deselect the Constrain proportions check box, the Scale Width slider will become active, and the Scale slider will convert to a Scale Height slider. You can then adjust the two controls separately. This can distort your video or still images, so be careful if this isn't the look you're seeking.

- **Rotation:** Rotation controls allow you to level out videos shot a bit off kilter and easily shift still images shot in portrait mode to landscape, and vice versa.

- **Anchor Point:** This is the point around which all Motion controls, including positioning and rotation controls, operate. By default, it's set to the center of the image or video.

- **Anti-flicker Filter:** Reduces flicker in pan-and-zoom effects created using the Motion controls. If you are using the Motion controls to create a pan-and-zoom effect and see flicker in the result, try dragging the Anti-flicker Filter slider to the right. Always render and gauge the results before applying the filter because it can cause blurriness.

11 If you want to save your work, now would be a good time, although you won't be returning to this project.

Reframing an image with Motion controls

Although we're sure that you'd love to work on that golf swing for a few more exercises, it's time to start adding the finishing touches to the Space Shuttle clip.

1 Launch Adobe Premiere Elements if it isn't already running.

2 Choose File > Open Project. Click No and don't save any changes to the existing project if this screen appears.

3 In the Open Project dialog, navigate to the Lesson06 folder you copied to your hard drive. Within that folder, select the file Lesson06_Work.prel and then click Open (Windows) or Choose (Mac OS). If a dialog appears asking for the location of rendered files, click the Skip Previews button.

The project opens.

Note: Although Motion controls operate identically in Quick and Expert views, we'll be working in the latter, so you should work in Expert view if you want your screens to match those in the book.

4 Move the current-time indicator over the first picture in the slide show at the end of the videos. Notice in the Monitor panel that the picture has black vertical bars, or *letterboxes*, on the sides. If you drag your current-time indicator over the rest of the clips, you'll see that the other pictures have letterboxes as well. The reason is that like many pictures, they were shot with an aspect ratio of 4:3 and this project uses an aspect ratio of 16:9. Next, you'll eliminate those letterboxes in the first picture and then fix the others.

5 Click Picture 1.jpg to select it.

6 Click the Applied Effects (▤) button on the top right of the Monitor panel to open the Applied Effects panel.

7 In the Applied Effects panel, click the disclosure triangle to the left of the Motion effect to open the parameter settings.

8 Zoom into the picture and make it larger. *Do any of the following:*

- Drag the Scale slider to the right to a value of 120.

- Click the numeric entry to make it active, type **120**, and then press Enter (Windows) or Return (Mac OS).

- Hold the pointer over the numeric value until it becomes the pointer with arrows (🖑). Press your left mouse button and drag to the right to 120.

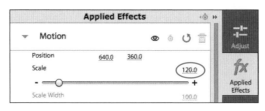

9 Because all the pictures have the same letterboxes, let's copy and paste that adjustment to all other pictures. Right-click Picture 1.jpg on the timeline and choose Copy.

10 Press the Shift key and click to select all other pictures on the timeline. Then right-click and choose Paste Effects and Adjustments. Adobe Premiere Elements adds the same motion adjustments to all pictures. If you drag your current-time indicator over the other clips, you'll see that the letterboxes no longer appear in those as well.

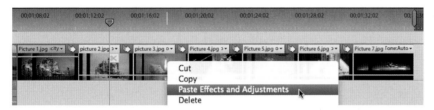

● **Note:** Paste Effects and Adjustments pastes all effects and adjustments from the source clip to the target clips. For this reason, you must be careful when you use it. For example, had we configured the color or lighting adjustments for Picture 1.jpg, Adobe Premiere Elements would have pasted these adjustments as well, which may not be appropriate given the disparity in appearance between all the clips.

11 Click any empty area of the timeline to deselect the group of clips. Then drag the current-time indicator over Picture 5.jpg, at about 00;01;26;00 and click Picture 5.jpg to select it. The adjustment has dropped the shuttle to the bottom of the image. Let's fix that. Hold the pointer over the second position number, which is the vertical adjustment, until it becomes the pointer with arrows (🖑). Click and drag to the left to 310. That looks better. If you click over to the other images, you'll see that all of them could use some fine-tuning. For example, Picture 6.jpg might look better if you dragged the vertical adjustment to about 425.

You'll use these Motion controls a lot when you're working with still images on the timeline, so take some time to experiment with the other images.

Changing playback speed

Although Time Remapping is an awesome feature, sometimes you just want to quickly change the speed of a clip, and there's a simpler way to get that done. If you move the current-time indicator to around 00;00;45;00 and press the spacebar to play the video, you'll note that the narration about the fuel tank continues into Video 11.mp4. You need to slow down Video 10.mp4 to make room for the narration. In this exercise, you'll learn how.

There is no difference between Quick and Expert views for this exercise, so you can do the exercise in either view.

1 Right-click Video 10.mp4 and choose Time Stretch. Adobe Premiere Elements opens the Time Stretch panel. Time Stretch is also available in the Tools panel.

2 Type **60** in the Speed box (where it will appear as 60%), and select the Maintain Audio Pitch check box.

● **Note:** As you can probably guess, the Reverse Speed check box, when selected, will reverse the clip, making the video play backward.

3 Click OK to close the panel. Adobe Premiere Elements extends the clip to its new duration and pushes back all subsequent files. Drag the current-time indicator back to 00;00;45;00, press the spacebar to play the clip, and observe the timing, which is now perfect. Don't worry about the man talking at the start of the clip; you'll cover it up with narration and some music in Lesson 9.

4 Choose File > Save As and save your project.

Creating a Pan & Zoom effect

If you use still images a lot in your productions, you've probably wanted to add motion to those images. Adobe Premiere Elements' Pan & Zoom tool is a great tool for doing just that.

Let's apply the Pan & Zoom tool to Picture 5.jpg and have a look at the interface; in the next exercise you'll customize the Pan & Zoom effect. You can be in either Quick or Expert view for this and the following exercise.

1 Click Picture 5.jpg to select it.

2 In the Action bar on the bottom of the interface, click the Tools button (✕ Tools) to open the Tools panel.

3 Use the slider on the right of the panel to scroll down to the Pan & Zoom tool (▦), which is near the middle in both Quick and Expert views. Then click Pan & Zoom in the Tools panel to apply the tool to Picture 5.jpg and open the Pan & Zoom tool.

4 On the bottom of the Pan & Zoom tool, click Play Output (Play Output ⦿) to watch the effect.

5 In the upper-right corner of the tool, click Exit Preview (✕ Exit Preview). Then, in the thumbnail view on the bottom of the Pan & Zoom tool, click the second thumbnail. Your screen should look very similar to the following screen.

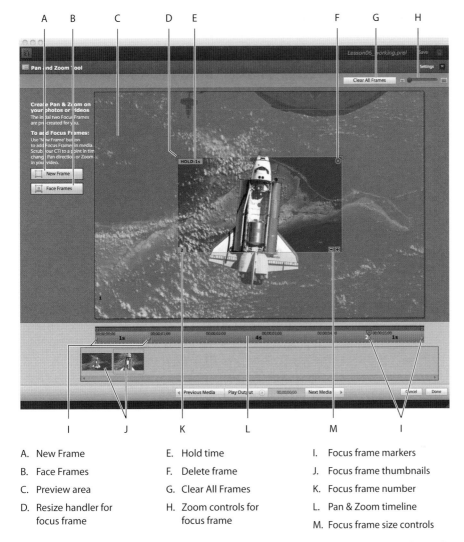

A.   New Frame

B.   Face Frames

C.   Preview area

D.   Resize handler for focus frame

E.   Hold time

F.   Delete frame

G.   Clear All Frames

H.   Zoom controls for focus frame

I.   Focus frame markers

J.   Focus frame thumbnails

K.   Focus frame number

L.   Pan & Zoom timeline

M.   Focus frame size controls

The basic unit of operation of the Pan & Zoom tool is the focus frame, and the tool creates motion by moving from focus frame to focus frame. You control three basic variables: the size and location of each focus frame, its duration (or how long the frame stays at that location), and how long it takes to move from focus frame to focus frame.

Any timing changes made in the Pan & Zoom tool are reflected in the timeline with all subsequent content on that track adjusted accordingly. For example, in the following exercise, you'll increase the duration of the image from 4 seconds to 11 seconds and the pictures on the timeline after Picture 5.jpg will be pushed back.

If your picture has faces, click Face Frames (Face Frames) on the left, which tells Adobe Premiere Elements to create a project that inserts a focus frame on each face and pans to all faces in the project. If there are no faces, as with the picture in this example, Adobe Premiere Elements starts with a wide shot and then zooms into the center of the image for a close-up.

The focus frames in the image are presented in the thumbnail view at the bottom of the dialog. To choose a focus frame and edit any parameters, just click the focus frame in the thumbnail view. When you hover your pointer over the focus frame, as the pointer is hovering over the second focus frame in the figure, its parameters will appear.

You can change the order of focus frames by dragging the thumbnails into the desired order. Click Play Output to preview the Pan & Zoom effect at anytime, after which you must click Exit Preview (✱ Exit Preview) to exit the effect.

In the timeline above the thumbnail view, the green area is hold time and the blue area is pan time. The duration of each is shown in seconds.

Customizing the Pan & Zoom effect

Now that you have a bit of background, let's customize the Pan & Zoom effect. In general, you want to start out with a wide shot, then zoom into the nose, and then tilt down to the tail.

1   If you're still in Preview mode, click the Exit Preview button on top of the preview window (or press Esc on your keyboard) to exit Preview mode. In the Pan & Zoom thumbnail view, click the first thumbnail to select it. Then use the resize handlers at the corners of the image to make it a little smaller and more focused on the shuttle. After you resize the focus frame, you can click anywhere within the frame to move it to the desired location.

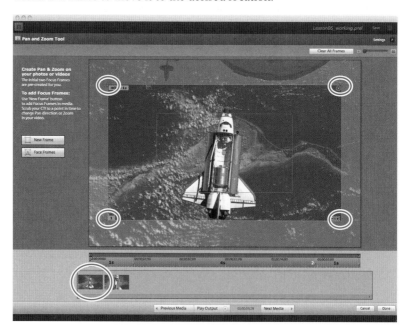

2   Watching the timecode located immediately to the right of the Play Output button (Play Output), drag the current-time indicator to 00;00;03;00.

3   On the left toolbar, click New Frame (New Frame). The Pan & Zoom tool creates a new focus frame between the original two and selects that focus frame.

4   Within the new frame, click the plus sign (⊕) on the bottom right three times to increase its size. Then click inside the focus frame and drag to the nose of the shuttle.

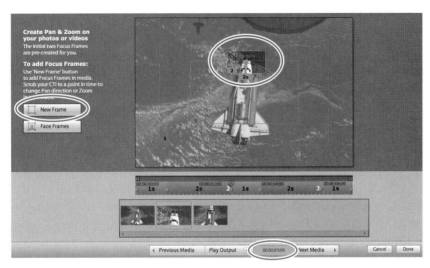

5   The blue line leading from the center of the first focus frame to the center of the second is the pan line, and 2s is the pan duration. Let's increase the pan time from two seconds to three seconds. Click 2s to open the Pan Time dialog. Click and drag the time to the right so that it equals 00;00;03;00, and click OK to close the dialog. On the timeline, notice how the blue pan time from the first focus frame to the second is now 3 seconds.

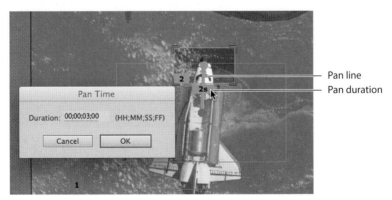

6 Hover your pointer over the second focus frame until the HOLD: 1s hold time appears. Click that to open the Hold Time dialog. Click and drag the time to the right so that it equals 00;00;02;00, and click OK to close the dialog.

7 In the Pan & Zoom thumbnail view, click the third thumbnail to select it. Use the resize handlers at the corners of the image to make it a little smaller and drag it down to focus on the shuttle's tail.

8 Click the pan time to open the Pan Time dialog and change the value to 00;00;03;00; click OK to close the dialog.

9 In focus frame 3, click the hold time to open the Hold Time dialog, change the value to 00;00;02;00, and click OK to close the dialog.

● Note: You can use the Pan & Zoom tool with video, but you can't use the Face Frames option.

10 Drag the current-time indicator to the start of the timeline, and then on the bottom of the Pan & Zoom tool, click Play Output (Play Output ⚬) to watch the effect. Then click Done on the bottom right to close the Pan & Zoom tool dialog. If necessary for smooth preview back in the main interface, click the Render button (Render) on the lower right of the Monitor panel.

Working with keyframes

Every clip in the timeline, and most effects and adjustments that you apply to them, can be modified over time. This involves a concept called *keyframing*. Essentially, a keyframe is a location in the timeline where you specify a value for a specific property. When you set two keyframes, Adobe Premiere Elements interpolates the value of that property over all frames between the two keyframes, effecting a change gradually over time and basically creating an animated effect. For example, in the next exercise, you'll use keyframes to animate the appearance of an effect.

Keyframes give you significant flexibility and creativity in your projects. Although they sound challenging at first, if you work through the next few exercises, you'll quickly grasp their operation and utility.

Using keyframes to animate effects

Animating an effect using keyframes is a very powerful capability: Essentially, it lets you create custom transitions using any Adobe Premiere Elements effect. Keyframing is available only in Expert view, so click over to that view if necessary.

One word of caution: This section is more advanced than some users of Adobe Premiere Elements may need, so feel free to skip this lesson. But before you do, you should know that keyframing unlocks an immense well of creativity in Adobe Premiere Elements, and a few minutes of focused time here could quickly pay dividends in more creative projects. Of course, if you do choose to skip it now, you can always revisit it later.

In this exercise, you'll animate the Vignetting effect to add a unique transition to the start of the project. The Vignetting effect is a great tool for focusing the viewer's attention on a specific portion of the video; think of a soft hazy circle surrounding the happy bride or graduate. Our use here isn't a classic use case, but it should serve to illustrate the effect.

Let's get started. If the Lesson06_Work.prel project is not open, open it by choosing File > Open Recent Project and selecting it from the menu that appears.

1   In the Action bar on the bottom of the interface, click the Effects button (*fx* Effects) to open the Effects panel.

2   In the list box at the top of the panel, click and select the Advanced Adjustments folder. If necessary, use the slider on the right of the panel to scroll down to the Vignetting effect, which is the last one in the folder.

3   Drag the Vignetting effect from the Effects panel onto the first clip in the timeline (Video 1.mp4).

4   Click the Applied Effects (▣) button on the top right to open the Applied Effects panel.

Tip: On the Mac, in the Applied Effects panel, the Show/Hide keyframe toggle works only when the disclosure triangle for a particular effect has been clicked and those parameters are displayed. If it seems like nothing is happening when you click this button, check to make sure you've completed step 5.

5 In the Applied Effects panel, click the disclosure triangle to the left of the Vignetting effect to open the parameter settings.

6 In the upper-right corner of the Applied Effects panel, click the Show/hide keyframe controls ( ) icon.

● **Note:** Be sure to click the stopwatch icon only once when you're animating a property. If you accidentally click it twice, a dialog will appear asking you if you want to delete existing keyframes for the clip. Click Cancel, and continue with the exercise.

7 Note the mini-timeline at the top of the Vignetting effect, which has the same values as the main timeline for the selected clip and has a matching current-time indicator. Move the current-time indicator to the start of the clip, and click the small stopwatch ( ) to the left of the Amount control to animate this property. After you click the stopwatch, a small diamond appears in the mini-timeline within the Applied Effects panel to the right of the configurable properties in the Amount control. This is the initial keyframe for the Amount value for this effect.

8 Drag the Amount slider all the way to the left to a value of –100.

9 Let's configure two other properties in the effect. Click the stopwatch to the left of the Size option and drag the slider to the left to the 0 value.

10 Click the stopwatch to the left of the Roundness option and drag the slider to the right to 100. You should now have a focused, round vignette around the shuttle.

Tip: Because we didn't create a keyframe for the Feather option, the 45 configuration is applied universally over the entire clip. If you changed that from 45 to 100, the new value would be applied universally. Keyframes allow you to apply specific values to specific regions of the clip; when you have no keyframes, the selected values apply to the entire clip.

11 Now you'll set the second keyframe. In the mini-timeline in the Applied Effects panel, drag the current-time indicator to the right about four seconds into the clip.

12 Drag the Amount slider to the middle to a value of 0, which essentially turns off the effect.

Changing the value automatically adds a second keyframe, which is represented as a second diamond in the mini-timeline in the Applied Effects panel. After you turn on the animation, Adobe Premiere Elements automatically animates the effect between the two values. Note that Adobe Premiere Elements didn't create a new keyframe for the Size or Roundness parameters because you did not adjust either option.

▶ **Tip:** With many (if not most) effects, you'll have to adjust all the options that you initially keyframed to completely remove the effect. Just repeat step 12 for each option, finding the value that zeroes out the effect.

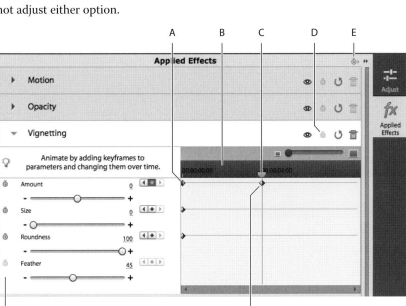

A. Initial keyframes

B. Mini-timeline

C. Current-time indicator

D. Universal toggle animation button (enables keyframes for all options in effect)

E. Show/Hide keyframes

F. Keyframable configuration options in the Vignetting effect

G. Second keyframe

▶ **Tip:** If you click the universal toggle animation button for an effect, you create a keyframe at the location of the current-time indicator for every keyframeable value in the effect. This becomes a hassle if you want to adjust any particular value *universally* for the entire clip. It's usually simpler to click the stopwatches next to the configuration options that you want to keyframe, as you did in the exercise.

13 Press the Home key to move the current-time indicator to the start of the timeline, and then press the spacebar to play the clip. The clip starts out with the vignette in full effect and returns to a normal appearance at the 00;00;04;00 mark. Press the spacebar again to stop playback.

14 Choose File > Save As and save your project as **Lesson06_Work.prel**.

● **Note:** If you hadn't set the second set of keyframes, the Vignetting effect would have continued without change through the end of the clip but wouldn't continue on to subsequent clips.

Creating a fade out using keyframes

Fading to black is one of the most common effects producers use at the end of their projects. Adobe Premiere Elements makes this simple to do with a control in the Applied Effects panel, although often you'll want to customize the effect. In this exercise, you'll learn how to fade to black and how to control keyframes in two locations in Adobe Premiere Elements: the Applied Effects panel and the timeline.

1 Click to select the Picture 7.jpg image, which is the last image in the timeline. You may need to scroll to the right in the timeline to fully see the image.

2 Let's make the video tracks as large as possible to provide some working space. To the right of the Picture 7.jpg clip, right-click a blank area on the timeline and choose Track Size > Large. You may have to adjust the scroll bars on the right of the timeline to see the clip after adjusting the track size.

3 Drag the current-time indicator to about two seconds from the end of the project.

4 If necessary, click the Zoom In tool (■) in the Monitor panel to increase your view of the clip.

The orange line spanning horizontally across the clip is the connector line (or graph) between keyframes. As you'll see, you can access any keyframeable value for any applied effect via this graph, although by default, the graph initially controls the Opacity property. You can tell because the text right after the name Picture 7 in the Video 1 track says Opacity: Opacity. This means that the orange line represents the Opacity value in the Opacity effect, which has only that one value.

5 To the right of the Monitor panel, click the Applied Effects button to open that panel, and then click the disclosure triangle next to the Motion effect.

6 Back in the timeline, click the Opacity: Opacity disclosure triangle above Picture 7.jpg to open the list box. Choose Motion > Position and hold your pointer there. Notice that the parameters that you can choose on the timeline are identical to those in the Applied Effects panel. In essence, although you can apply and adjust keyframes to only one parameter at a time on the timeline, you can access any parameter available in the Applied Effects panel. Most of the

time, it's most convenient to adjust these options in the Applied Effects panel. One notable exception is the Opacity value, which is used to fade to black.

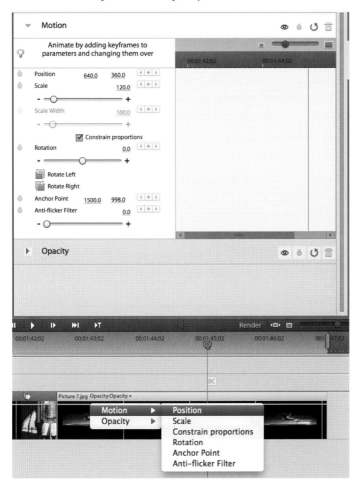

7   In the timeline, in the list box next to the Picture 7.jpg title, choose Opacity > Opacity. Now the orange keyframe graph controls Opacity, or the transparency values of the picture. To fade to black, you'll adjust from 100% opacity to 0%.

8   Working with the Picture 7.jpg file, place your pointer over the orange connector line. The pointer changes to a double-arrow icon (■).

9 Click and drag the connector
line down toward the
bottom of the clip. As you
drag, you'll see a small
window with changing
numbers that represent the

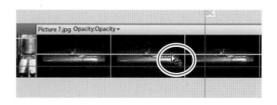

Opacity values. Drag the Opacity value to 0% and you'll see the Monitor panel
fade to black. When you finish experimenting, drag the connector line back up
toward the top of the clip to restore the clip's opacity to 100%.

Now you'll add keyframes to help Adobe Premiere Elements create a fade to
black at the end of the movie.

10 The current-time indicator should be positioned about two seconds from the
end of the clip. Press the Ctrl key (Windows) or Command key (Mac OS), and
position your pointer on the orange connector line where it intersects with the
current-time indicator line. Your pointer will change to a small cross icon (),
which is the create keyframe pointer.

11 Click the connector line once right at the current-time indicator. You should see
a small yellow diamond added to the orange connector line, representing your
first keyframe.

12 Press the Page Down key to move the current-time indicator to the end of the
movie. Repeat step 11 to create a keyframe at that location.

13 Click the keyframe at the end of the movie clip and drag it down to the bottom
of the track. The number on the right of the yellow box next to the pointer is the
Opacity value; drag it until that value equals 0.00.

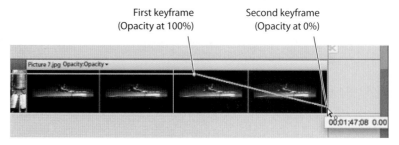

First keyframe
(Opacity at 100%)

Second keyframe
(Opacity at 0%)

14 To view the Opacity fade out, move your current-time indicator to the beginning of the Picture 7.jpg clip, and then press the spacebar.

15 Save your project as **Lesson06_End.prel**.

In Lesson 7, you'll learn how to create a similar effect using the Dip to Black transition. Although the visual effect is similar, working with keyframes lets you customize the effect to a much greater degree.

Adjusting keyframes

After you've set a keyframe, you can modify it by dragging it to a new location or value. To delete a keyframe, right-click it and choose Delete.

As mentioned earlier, you can access all keyframes inserted on the timeline in the Applied Effects panel. Select Picture 7.jpg, and then click the Applied Effects button to open the Applied Effects panel (if it's not already open). If keyframes are not displayed, click the disclosure triangle to the left of the Opacity effect to open the parameter settings, and then click the Show Keyframes (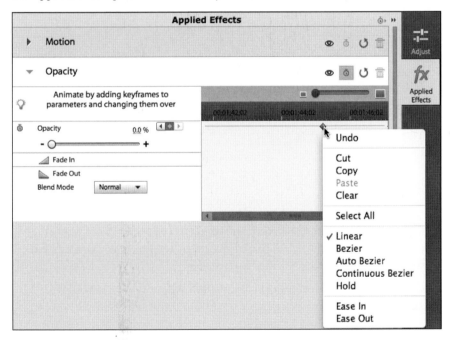) icon at the top right in the Applied Effects panel to view the keyframes.

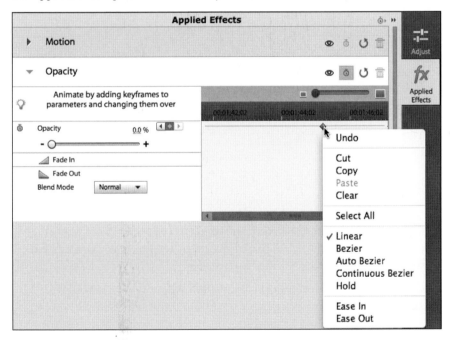

You can set and modify opacity-related keyframes in either or both locations. In general, the timeline is best for fast and simple adjustments, like the fade out that you just applied, whereas the Applied Effects panel is a better choice for complicated, more precise adjustments.

The other keyframe-related controls shown in the context menu in the previous figure are advanced options that control the rate and smoothness of change applied by Adobe Premiere Elements. For more on those options, search the Adobe Premiere Elements Help file for "Controlling change between keyframes."

Applying FilmLooks

FilmLooks are configured effects or collections of configured effects that give your video a certain look or feel. They are available in both Quick and Expert views, and are very easy to apply. Because FilmLooks remove all applied effects and reset all adjustments, they're best used early in the project design process. Although you can apply them to one clip, a selected group of clips, or all clips in the project, let's explore the final option to learn how to apply a single effect to all clips in the timeline.

1   Click the timeline to select it, and press Ctrl+A (Windows) or Command+A (Mac OS) to select all content in the timeline.

2   In the Action bar on the bottom of the interface, click the Effects button (*fx* Effects) to open the Effects panel.

3   In the list box at the top of the panel, click and select the FilmLooks folder.

4   Drag the Newsreel effect from the Effects panel onto any clip in the timeline.

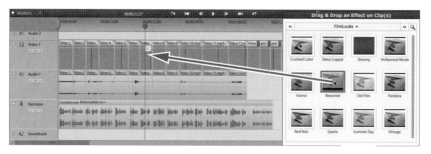

5   Click Yes when Adobe Premiere Elements asks if you want to remove existing effects. If you click Yes, all applied effects will be removed and all adjustments will be reset. If you click No, the Newsreel effect won't be applied.

6   Click the Home key to move the current-time indicator to the start of the project, and then press the spacebar to preview the project. If playback isn't smooth enough to gauge the quality of the FilmLook, render the project by pressing Enter (Windows) or Return (Mac OS), or by clicking the Render button (Render) on the bottom right of the Monitor panel.

7   Click the Applied Effects (▣) button on the top right to open the Applied Effects panel. Click any clip in the timeline to select it.

8   In the Applied Effects panel, click the disclosure triangle to the left of the Old Film effect to open the parameter settings. The Newsreel effect is a preconfigured version of the Old Film effect. Many FilmLooks are comprised of a single effect or a single effect plus preconfigured adjustments applied in the Adjustment panel. The main difference between a FilmLook and a preset that you create is that the FilmLook removes all previously applied effects and resets all adjustments, whereas your preset doesn't.

This concludes the main lesson. Next, you'll learn how to implement several additional effects using other source clips in a separate project file. If you want to save the project you just created, you can do so when you load the next project.

Creating a Picture-in-Picture overlay

Adobe Premiere Elements can superimpose multiple tracks of video over other tracks. In this exercise, you'll superimpose one video clip in a small frame over a preexisting background clip that covers the entire screen. This effect is called a Picture-in-Picture (PiP) overlay. Click over to Expert view, if necessary, for this exercise.

1   To load the project file containing the new content, choose File > Open Project, and then navigate to the Lesson06 folder you copied to your hard drive.

2   Within that folder, select the file Lesson06_Videomerge_Win.prel (Windows) or Lesson06_Videomerge_Mac.prel (Mac OS), and then click Open (Windows) or Choose (Mac OS). If you want to save the project you were working on, you know the drill. If a dialog appears asking for the location of rendered files, click the Skip Previews button.

3   Choose Window > Restore Workspace to ensure that you start the lesson with the default panel layout.

4   If necessary, press the Home key to move the current-time indicator to the start of the project.

5   Click the Project Assets button to open that panel, and locate Greenscreen.mov. Click once to select the clip, hold down the Shift key, and drag the clip toward the lower-left corner of the clip in the Monitor panel.

● **Note:** If you need room in the Monitor panel, grab the bottom-right edge of the Project Assets panel and drag it upward and to the left to minimize the panel as much as possible, as I've done in the figure.

6   Release the pointer and choose Picture-in-Picture from the menu that appears.

7   Click No in the Videomerge panel (if it appears).

8 The superimposed clip will have handles on the edges, indicating that the clip is active. Click anywhere in the clip and drag it to a position that approximates that shown in the next figure.

● **Note:** If the superimposed clip is longer than the background clip, it appears over successive clips in the timeline for its entire duration and appears superimposed over those clips during playback.

9 Click the Applied Effects button to open the Applied Effects panel.

10 In the Applied Effects panel, click the disclosure triangle to the left of Motion to reveal its properties. Make sure the Constrain proportions check box is selected.

11 Place your pointer over the value for Scale, and then drag the value to 45. As you change the scale, the Greenscreen.mov clip expands to 45 percent of its original size.

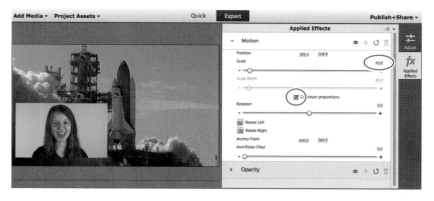

12 If necessary, you can reposition the clip using the Position controls, or simply drag the clip to the desired position in the Monitor panel.

13 With Greenscreen.mov still selected, click the disclosure triangle to the left of the Opacity effect to reveal those properties. Click the Fade Out icon to fade the Greenscreen.mov clip at the end.

14 Now, let's fade out the background clip as well. In the Video 1 track in the timeline, click the Background.mp4 clip to select it. In the Applied Effects panel, click the disclosure triangle to the left of the Opacity effect to reveal those properties. Click the Fade Out icon to fade the Background.mov clip at the end.

15 Press the Home key to go to the start of your project, and then click the Play button or press the spacebar to review your work.

16 Save your project as **Lesson06_pip.prel**.

● **Note:** You could, of course, drag the right edge of Background.mp4 to the left so that the duration of the two clips is the same, but to me, ending that way was too abrupt. Try it both ways and see what you think.

Compositing two clips using Videomerge

Compositing is the process of merging two clips together, one on top of the other, while removing the background color of the top clip to reveal the second. This allows you to place your subject in a variety of environments, both real and simulated.

Adobe Premiere Elements' Videomerge effect makes compositing as easy as drag and drop. Videomerge automatically determines the background of the top clip and makes it transparent. Video or image clips on the tracks below it become visible through the transparent areas. You'll get the best results with Videomerge if you shoot the clip to be composited using the following rules:

• Create a strong (preferably dark or saturated), solid, uniform-color background to shoot against.

• Make sure the background is brightly and uniformly lit to avoid shadows.

• When you're choosing a background color, avoid skin tones and colors that are similar to the subject's clothing or hair color. (Otherwise, the skin, clothes, or hair will become transparent, too.) Bright green and blue are the best choices.

With this information as background, reload the Lesson06_Videomerge_Win.prel (Windows) or Lesson06_Videomerge_Mac.prel (Mac OS) project file (you should have already saved the first project as Lesson06_pip.prel) and follow this procedure.

1 In the timeline, press the Home key to make sure that the current-time indicator is at the beginning of the video.

Note: If you need room in the Monitor panel, grab the bottom right edge of the Project Assets panel and drag it upward and to the left to minimize the panel as much as possible, as shown in the figure.

2 Click the Project Assets button to open that panel, and locate Greenscreen.mov. Click once to select the clip, hold down the Shift key, and drag the clip toward the center of the Monitor panel.

3 Release the pointer and choose Place on Top and Apply Videomerge from the menu that appears.

Adobe Premiere Elements inserts Greenscreen.mov in the Video 2 track over Background.mp4, automatically detects the green background, and makes it transparent. The results are pretty much perfect, but let's look at Videomerge's configuration options in case any of your projects need a bit of work.

4 In the timeline, click Greenscreen.mov to select it, and then click the Applied Effects button to open that panel. If necessary, click Project Assets to close the Project Assets panel to make the entire Monitor panel visible.

5 In the Applied Effects panel, click the disclosure triangle to the left of the Videomerge effect to open the parameter settings.

6 If you're not achieving a clean effect and you see residue of greenscreen in the background video or the background video showing through the subject, *try any or all of the following:*

   • Reselect the background color. Select the Select Color check box, and then click the eyedropper (✐) to select it. The background behind the subject will reappear. Press Ctrl (Windows) or Command (Mac OS), and then click the background close to the subject's head. This tells Videomerge which color to eliminate, and pressing Ctrl (Windows) or Command (Mac OS) averages a 5x5-pixel block surrounding the pixel that you clicked to achieve a smoother result. If you're having problems around the edges, try clicking there, but the middle region of the clip is typically the most important.

   • Try cycling through the Presets, which are Soft, Normal, and Detailed.

   • Try adjusting the Tolerance slider in both directions.

7   If you're having trouble getting clean edges, try experimenting with one of the Garbage Mattes in the Keying folder in the Effects panel. Search for Garbage Matte in the Adobe Premiere Elements Help file for more information.

8   Repeat steps 13 and 14 from the previous exercise to apply a Fade Out effect to both clips.

9   Press the Home key to go to the start of your project, and then click the Play button to review your work. If the video doesn't play smoothly, click the Render button (Render) on the bottom right of the Monitor panel to render the clip.

10 If you want, save your project as **Videomerge_end.prel**.

● **Note:** If you're uncomfortable with the subject obscuring the launch of the Space Shuttle behind her, you could always use Motion controls to scale the frame to about 45 percent of its original size and move it to the bottom left.

Exploring on your own

Congratulations! Now you know how to apply video settings, change effects and settings, copy effects from one clip to another, create an image pan, animate an effect with keyframes, create a Picture-in-Picture effect, and composite one video over another with Videomerge. Here are some effects that you can experiment with on your own:

- Create a PiP effect using two or more clips on the same screen.

- Get a sense of the different effects available in Adobe Premiere Elements by choosing Help > Premiere Elements Help, or by pressing F1 to access the Help guide. The Applying Effects section includes a gallery of video effects.

- Experiment with the various effects presets located in the Presets folder in the Effects panel, including the Horizontal and Vertical image pans.

Review questions

1 What are curative effects, and when should you apply them?

2 What's the quickest way to apply identical effects and settings to multiple clips?

3 What is a keyframe, and what does it contain?

4 How do you modify keyframes once they've been added to a clip?

5 How do you apply the same effect to multiple clips on the timeline?

Review answers

1   Curative effects improve one or more aspects of a clip, such as exposure, backlighting, or excessive shakiness. You should apply curative effects to a clip before applying artistic and other effects.

2   There are two ways to copy effects from one clip to another. To copy a single effect from one clip to another, click the source clip in the timeline to select it, open the Applied Effects panel, right-click the effect, and choose Copy. Then click the target clip in the timeline, open the Applied Effects panel, right-click in the gray area beneath other effects, and choose Paste. To copy multiple effects from one clip to another or to multiple clips, right-click the source clip on the timeline and choose Copy. Then select the target clip or clips, right-click, and choose Paste Effects and Adjustments.

3   A keyframe contains the values for all the controls in an effect and applies those values to the clip at the specific time.

4   Once you have added keyframes to a clip, you can adjust them by clicking and dragging them along the connector line. If there are two keyframes, moving one keyframe farther away from the other extends the duration of the effect; moving a keyframe closer to another keyframe shortens the effect.

5   Select all target clips in the timeline and apply the effect to any single clip.

7 CREATING TRANSITIONS

Lesson overview

If you've followed the lessons in this book in order, you should now feel comfortable adding and deleting footage in your project, and trimming clips to improve the pacing of the movie you're producing. In this lesson, you'll work with a project in which the clips have already been sequenced and trimmed, and add nuance and dimension using transitions between the clips. You'll learn how to do the following:

- Apply video and audio transitions
- Preview transitions
- Customize transition settings
- Replace a transition
- Delete a transition
- Apply the default transition to multiple clips
- Create fade-ins and fade-outs
- Render transitions

 This lesson will take approximately one hour.

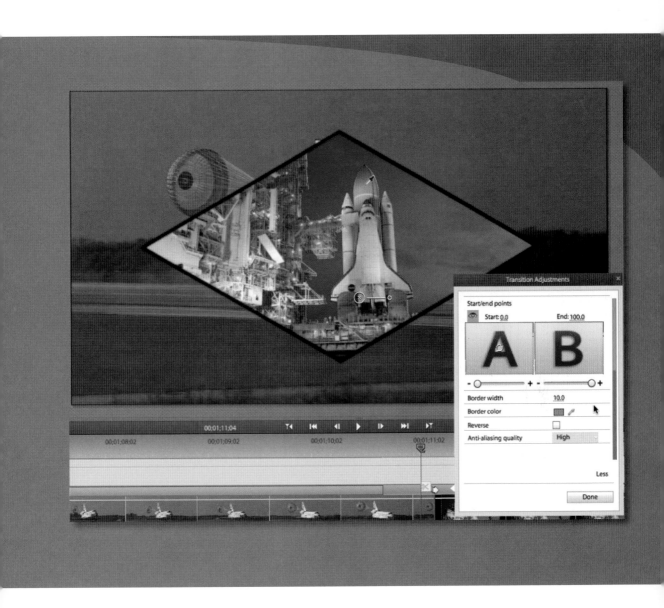

Customizing a transition.

Getting started

You'll modify scenes in this lesson's project by adding transitions in stages. But first you'll open the Lesson07 project and prepare your Adobe Premiere Elements workspace.

1   Make sure that you have correctly copied the Lesson07 folder from the DVD in the back of this book onto your computer's hard drive. See "Copying the Classroom in a Book files" in the "Getting Started" section at the start of this book.

2   Launch Adobe Premiere Elements. If it is already open, choose Help > Welcome Screen in the Adobe Premiere Elements menu to return to the Welcome screen.

3   In the Welcome screen, click Video Editor, select Existing Project, and click the Open folder.

4   In the Open Project dialog, navigate to the Lesson07 folder.

5   Within that folder, select the file Lesson07_Start_Win.prel (Windows) or Lesson07_Start_Mac.prel (Mac OS), and then click Open. If a dialog appears asking for the location of rendered files, click the Skip Previews button.

    Your project file opens.

6   Choose Window > Restore Workspace to ensure that you start the lesson in the default panel layout.

Viewing the completed movie before you start

To see what you'll be creating in this lesson, you can take a look at the completed movie. You'll have to be in Expert view to open the Project Assets panel to view the movie, so if you are not, click Expert (Expert) to enter that view.

1   On the upper-left side of the Adobe Premiere Elements interface, click the Project Assets button (Project Assets ▾) to open that panel. Locate the file Lesson07_Movie.mov, and then double-click it to open the video into the preview window.

2   Click the Play button (▶) to watch the video about powering the Space Shuttle, which you'll build in this lesson.

3   When you're done, close the preview window.

Working with transitions

Transitions phase out one clip while phasing in the next. The simplest form of a transition is the cut. A cut occurs when the last frame of one clip is followed by the first frame of the next. The cut is the most frequently used transition in video and film, and the one you'll use most of the time. However, you can also use other types of transitions to achieve effects between scenes.

Transitions

A transition can be as subtle as a cross-dissolve or as emphatic as a page turn or spinning pinwheel. You generally place transitions on a cut between two clips, creating a double-sided transition. However, you can also apply a transition to just the beginning or end of a clip, creating a single-sided transition, such as a fade to black.

When a transition shifts from one clip to the next, it overlaps frames from both clips. The overlapped frames can either be frames previously trimmed from the clips (frames just past the In or Out point at the cut), or existing frames repeated on either side of the cut. It's important to remember that when you trim a clip, you don't delete frames; instead, the resulting In and Out points frame a window over the original clip. A transition uses the trimmed frames to create the transition effect, or, if the clips don't have trimmed frames, the transition repeats frames.

—From Adobe Premiere Elements Help

Transitions in Quick and Expert views

Adobe Premiere Elements includes a wide range of transitions, such as 3D motion, dissolves, wipes, and zooms. To view the available transitions in the Transitions panel, click the Transitions button (◩ Transitions) on the Action bar on the bottom of the Adobe Premiere Elements interface to open the panel.

As you've seen with other collections of tools and effects, Quick view contains a smaller collection of the most commonly used transitions, whereas Expert view contains the whole kit and caboodle, organized by folders. Expert view also includes audio transitions, but Quick view doesn't. In Expert view, you can search for transitions by clicking the magnifying lens (🔍) on the upper right.

In both views you can see an animated preview of the transition by clicking the transition in the Transitions panel. Applying, replacing, deleting, and opening the customization window is slightly different in the two views, so I'll cover that for each view first. Then we'll circle back and look at the customization controls, which are identical in both views.

Quick view

Expert view

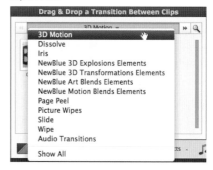

Working with transitions in Quick view

Let's start by reviewing the basics in Quick view. In both exercises, you'll insert a transition between the last video before the slide show, Video 12.mp4, and the first still image, Picture 1.jpg. You'll find it easier to follow along if you zoom into the timeline so that only the video clip and the first few pictures are showing.

If you're in Expert view, click the Quick button (Quick) at the top of the Monitor panel to enter Quick view.

● **Note:** You don't need to reposition the current-time indicator to place transitions between clips. However, it's often helpful to do so to locate the correct point in your project.

1   In the Monitor panel, click along the right edge of Video 12.mp4, moving your current-time indicator to that location.

2   In the Action bar, click Transitions (Transitions) to open the Transitions panel, click the Iris Diamond transition, and drag it to the intersection of Video 12.mp4 and Picture 1.jpg. When you hover the pointer over the intersection, Trim view appears in the Monitor panel, showing that you're at the intersection of those two clips. Note that the Transitions panel will close when you drag the transition from it; I've combined two screen shots in the figure so you can see the panel and the target.

3 Release the pointer. Adobe Premiere Elements opens the Transition Adjustments dialog.

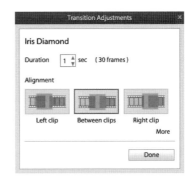

4 In the Transition Adjustments dialog, make sure that Duration is set to 1, and that the "Between clips" Alignment option is selected and outlined in blue. Then click Done. We'll explain these options and discuss additional configuration options in the "Viewing transition properties" section later in this lesson. Adobe Premiere Elements inserts the transition and an icon between the clips, showing its location.

5 Click the Render button (Render) to render the transition. Playback will start at the beginning of the clip, so you'll have to move toward the end of the project to see the transition you just added.

6 Press the spacebar to preview the transition. After the transition ends, press the spacebar to stop playback.

7 To replace a transition, repeat steps 2–4 with a different transition. That is, drag a different transition to the intersection between the two clips, release your pointer, and click Done in the Transition Adjustments dialog described in step 4. Adobe Premiere Elements will replace the first transition with the second. When you're done experimenting, make sure the Iris Diamond transition is in place between the two clips.

8 To access the Transition Adjustments dialog and reconfigure the transition settings, double-click the transition icon in the clip on the timeline.

9 To delete the transition, click the transition icon in the clip, making sure that it's outlined in blue and that neither clip involved in the transition is also outlined in blue. Press the Delete key, and Adobe Premiere Elements deletes the transition.

Working with transitions in Expert view

Let's move on to Expert view. To restore the project to its original pristine condition, either click Undo at the left end of the Action bar until the icon grays out or choose File > Revert in the Adobe Premiere Elements main menu and click Yes to discard your changes. Then click the Expert button (Expert) at the top of the Monitor panel to enter that view.

Again, you'll insert a transition between the final video clip before the slide show, Video 12.mp4, and the first still image, Picture 1.jpg. You'll find it easier to follow along if you zoom into the timeline so that only that video clip and the first few pictures are showing.

In addition to inserting, replacing, configuring, and replacing a transition, you'll also learn how to copy and paste a transition.

1   In the timelime, position the current-time indicator between Video 12.mp4 and Picture 1.jpg.

2   In the Action bar, choose Transitions (▨ Transitions) to open the Transitions panel, and click open the Iris folder. Click the Iris Diamond transition, and drag it to the intersection between Video 12.mp4 and Picture 1.jpg. Don't release the pointer.

Drag the pointer so that the transition box is only on Video 12.mp4; then center the box between the two clips and then only over Picture 1.jpg. Notice how the icon changes from the Between clips icon (🔁) to the Left clip and Right clip icons. This relates to the Alignment options in the Transition Adjustments dialog explained later in this lesson.

> ● **Note:** In the test software used while writing this lesson, where you dropped the transition did not affect the alignment shown in the Transition Adjustments dialog. For example, if you dropped the transition over Video 12.mp4 with the Left clip icon showing, the Transition Adjustments dialog might still default to the Between clips alignment option. This may be changed in the final version, but if it still functions this way, don't sweat it and just choose the preferred location in the Transition Adjustments dialog.

3 Release the pointer when it's centered between the two clips. Adobe Premiere Elements opens the Transition Adjustments dialog.

4 In the Transition Adjustments dialog, make sure that the Duration is set to 1 and that the Between clips Alignment option is selected and outlined in blue. Then click Done. We'll explain these options and discuss additional configuration options in the "Working with transitions in Expert view" section later in this lesson. Adobe Premiere Elements inserts the transition and an icon between the clips showing its location.

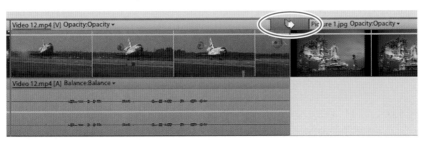

5 Click the Render button (█ Render █) to render the transition. Playback will start at the beginning of the clip, so you'll have to move toward the end of the project to see the transition you just added.

● **Note:** This is the perfect time to render only a specific Work Area, which you learned how to do in "Rendering a Work Area" in Lesson 6. The CliffsNotes version is as follows: Move the current-time indicator a few seconds before the transition, and press Alt+[(Windows) or Option+[(Mac OS) to set the start of the Work Area. Then move the current-time indicator a few seconds after the transition, and press Alt+] (Windows) or Option+] (Mac OS) to set the end of the Work Area. Then click the Render button and only the Work Area will render.

6 Drag the current-time indicator to a few moments before the transition on the timeline, and then press the spacebar to preview the transition. After the transition ends, press the spacebar to stop playback.

At this point, there are several ways you can change or refine your transition. None of them are necessary to complete the exercise, but I encourage you to try them all to get a feel for each function.

● **Note:** To restore the Work Area to the complete project, double-click the very top of the timescale at the top of the timeline and it will push the Work Area brackets to the start and end of the project.

- To replace a transition, repeat steps 2–4 with a different transition. That is, drag a different transition to the intersection between the two clips, release your pointer, and click Done in the Transition Adjustments dialog identified in step 4 (one second and Between clips). Adobe Premiere Elements will replace the first transition with the second. After trying this, make sure that the Iris Diamond transition is in place between the two clips.

- To access the Transition Adjustments dialog and reconfigure the transition settings, double-click the transition icon on the timeline.

- To delete a transition, click the transition icon in the clip, making sure that it's highlighted and that neither clip involved in the transition is also highlighted. Then right-click and choose Delete.

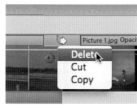

- To fine-tune transition duration, grab either edge and pull, though at times you may not be able to drag an edge. Adobe Premiere Elements will display a timecode box to let you know how much time you are adding or subtracting. For example, you can add 15 frames to the transition by dragging the left edge 15 frames.

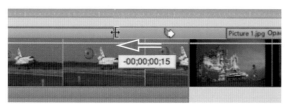

- To copy a transition, click the transition icon in the clip, making sure that it's highlighted and that neither clip involved in the transition is also highlighted. Then right-click and choose Copy, or press Ctrl+C (Windows) or Command+C (Mac OS).

- To paste the transition, move the current-time indicator between the target two clips and choose Edit > Paste in the Adobe Premiere Elements main menu, or press Ctrl+V (Windows) or Command+V (Mac OS).

Viewing transition properties

When you add a transition to a clip, the default length of the transition is determined by your preference settings, although you can change the length of transitions after applying them. Additionally, there are several other attributes of transitions that you can adjust, including the alignment of all transitions and border settings on some transitions.

In this exercise, you'll customize the Iris Diamond transition that you applied in the previous exercises. So if you changed or deleted that transition, drag it back between Video 12.mp4 and Picture 1.jpg. Let's do this in Expert view, so click the Expert button (Expert) at the top of the Monitor panel if necessary to switch to that view.

1   Drag the current-time indicator to the intersection of Video 12.mp4 and Picture 1.jpg, so the transition is showing in the Monitor panel.

2   Double-click the transition icon to open the Transition Adjustments dialog. Decision one is duration, which is how you override the default transition value set in your preferences. There are no hard and fast rules for duration, but here are some general recommendations:

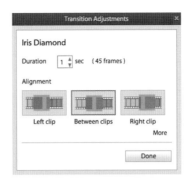

- One second is a good default for projects created for high-bandwidth computer or optical disc playback.

- If you're producing for streaming playback, one-second transitions can often create noticeable artifacting, so consider cutting the transition to a half second or shorter. Unfortunately, with the control available in the Transition Adjustments dialog when this lesson was written, you couldn't set transition duration shorter than one second.

   To set a transition shorter than one second, you can change the default transition duration in the Preferences dialog by choosing Edit > Preferences > General (Windows) or Adobe Premiere Elements 11 > Preferences > General (Mac OS). Or, in Expert view you can click and drag the edge of the transition to the desired duration. Be advised, however, that if you open the Transition Adjustments dialog after dragging the transition to a custom length, Adobe Premiere Elements will reset the duration to that selected in the Transition Adjustments dialog.

- If you want a noticeable transition between major sections or scenes in your production, consider a transition of 2–3 seconds.

   To set Duration, you can either click the number field to make it active, type the desired duration, and press Enter (Windows) or Return (Mac OS); or use the triangles to the right of the Duration field to increase or decrease the duration in whole seconds.

3   Set the transition Alignment. You have three options here:

- **Left clip**: Aligns the end of the transition to the end of the first clip.

- **Between clips**: Centers the transition over the cut.

- **Right clip**: Aligns the beginning of the transition to the beginning of the second clip.

I recommend using Between clips for most transitions. See "How transitions work—the deep dive," later in this lesson for more information on Alignment options.

4 On the bottom right of the Transition Adjustments dialog, hover your pointer over the text More to convert it to the More button (More), and then click the button to see more configuration options. Use the scroll bar on the right to view all the options.

5 At the top of the dialog (and not shown in the figure), click Play to play a preview of the transition. Click Stop to stop the preview.

6 To adjust the Start or End points of the transition, click and drag the sliders beneath these windows to the desired location. In most instances, you probably should just use the default values. Let's leave these at their default for this exercise.

7 Note that not all transitions have border configuration options, the ability to reverse the transition, or anti-aliasing options. This one does, so let's create and customize the transition border. Click the value for Border Width, type the number **10**, and then press Enter (Windows) or Return (Mac OS).

This creates a 10-pixel border on the edge of your transition. The default color of the border is black, but you can modify this as well.

8 You can modify the border color two ways: via the eyedropper or the Color Picker dialog. Let's use the former and then take a look at the latter. Click the eyedropper next to the Border color control and then click the goldish region at the top of the fuel tank. This changes the border to this color.

9 Just for fun, click the color swatch that just turned gold to open the Color Picker dialog. Here you can choose a color in multiple ways:

- Click the color slider in the middle to choose a general color, and then click to choose a specific color in the Color field.

- Type specific values in the Hue, Saturation, and Brightness settings (HSB); Hue, Saturation, and Lightness settings (HSL); Red, Green, and Blue settings (RGB); or YUV settings. Applying these latter settings is particularly useful when you're attempting to match colors from other design elements (like titles) because many other Adobe Premiere Elements color dialogs offer one or more of the settings. Jot down the numbers when you choose a color for your transitions so you can easily re-create the same color with your titles.

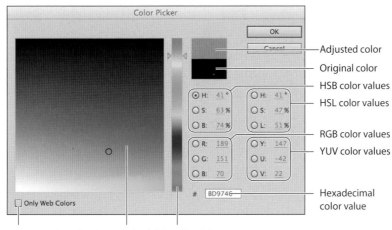

Displays only web colors   Color field   Color slider

10 Back in the Transition Adjustments dialog, if desired, select the Reverse check box. This reverses the transition so that rather than starting small and growing in size, the iris diamond starts large and shrinks in size. Typically, the default option (Reverse deselected) works best here.

11 The final option in the Transition Adjustments dialog is for Anti-Aliasing quality, which has four available settings: Off, Low, Medium, and High. Typically, if your transition has a border, you should choose High, which will smooth rough edges in some regions of the effect. Do so here.

12 Click Done to close the Transition Adjustments dialog.

13 Click the Render button (Render) to render the transition.

14 Drag your current-time indicator to a position before the transition, and then press the spacebar to play your modified transition. After the transition ends, press the spacebar to stop playback.

15 Choose File > Save As, name the file **Lesson07_Work.prel** in the Save Project dialog, and then click Save to save it in your Lesson07 folder.

Adding a single-sided transition to create a fade-in

Transitions do not necessarily need to be located between two clips. For example, you can quickly add a fade-in and fade-out to the beginning and end of your movie.

1   In Expert view, press the Home key (Windows) or Fn+Left arrow (Mac OS) to position the current-time indicator at the beginning of the first clip.

2   In the Action bar, choose Transitions () to open the Transitions panel, and click open the Dissolve folder. Drag the Dip to Black transition from the Transitions panel to the beginning of Video 1.mp4 on the Video 1 track.

3   In the Transition Adjustments dialog, make sure that the Duration is set to 1, and that the Right clip Alignment option is selected and outlined in blue. Then click Done.

4   Press the Home key to move the current-time indicator to the start of the project, and then press the spacebar to play the transition. The beginning of the transition starts at black and then fades into the video. After the transition ends, press the spacebar to stop playback.

5   To extend the duration of this transition by a half second, grab the right edge of the transition box, and drag it to the right until the text box next to the drag pointer indicates that you've added 00;00;00;15. Release the pointer.

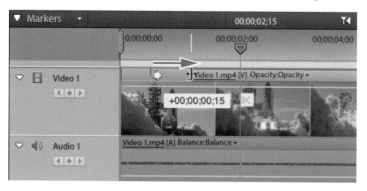

6   Save your project as **Lesson07_Work.prel**.

Applying the default transition to multiple clips

There's no rule that says you need to use transitions between all clips in your movies. However, rather than using cuts between clips, many producers insert very short cross-dissolve transitions between clips to smooth out any visual jarring between the clips. A feature in Adobe Premiere Elements makes this very simple to do. In this exercise, you'll start by changing the duration of the default video and audio transitions and then apply them to multiple clips simultaneously. You need to be in Expert view to complete this exercise.

1   Choose Edit > Preferences > General (Windows) or Adobe Premiere Elements 11 > Preferences > General (Mac OS) to open the Preferences panel.

2   Highlight the number in the Video Transition Default Duration box to make it active and type in **5**.

3   Highlight the number in the Audio Transition Default Duration box to make it active, and type in **.5**. Press Enter (Windows) or Return (Mac OS) to close the Preferences panel. Generally, you want your audio transitions to be slightly longer than the video transition so the progression from one clip to another will sound less abrupt.

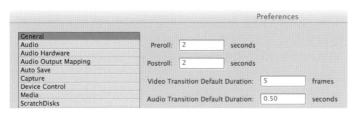

● **Note:** In the Preferences dialog, the Video Transition Default Duration is represented in frames and the Audio Transition Default Duration is represented in seconds. In a 30-frames-per-second video, that means that you selected a Video Transition Default Duration of ⅙ of a second and an Audio Transition Default Duration that's ½ of a second.

4   Now let's verify that the Cross Dissolve transition is the default video transition. Click the Transitions button in the Action bar to open the Transitions panel, and open the Dissolve folder. The Cross Dissolve transition has a yellow or dark gray box around it. If it doesn't, or to choose a different transition as the default, right-click the transition and choose Set Selected as Default Transition.

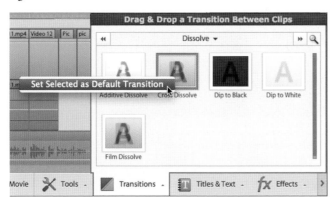

Working with audio transitions

The dominant audio in this project is the narration and the background music that you'll add in Lesson 9. Both run from start to finish with no breaks; so other than fading up from the start and fading out at the end, there are no transitions.

With some other projects where the primary audio follows the video, audio transitions can be as important as video. Fortunately, the workflow is almost identical to video transitions in Expert view: Open the Transitions panel, select the Audio Transitions folder, and choose one of the two audio transitions, Constant Gain or Constant Power. Most editors prefer Constant Power because it's smoother, whereas Constant Gain can sound abrupt. For that reason, Constant Power is the default audio transition, as indicated by the dark gray outline you see around it when you open the Audio Transitions folder.

You apply audio transitions the same way as video transitions by dragging them between two target clips. You'll see the same Transition Adjustments dialog, but you can adjust only Duration, because the Alignment controls are grayed out. Additionally, you can replace, switch, delete, and stretch audio transitions just as you can with video transitions, and even add them en masse to multiple clips, as you'll do in the "Applying the default transition to multiple clips" section.

5 Now let's verify that the Constant Power transition is the default audio transition. Open the Audio Transitions folder. If Constant Power isn't the default, right-click it and make it so.

6 Click the Fit to Visible Timeline icon (⬚) or press the Backslash (\) key to display the entire contents of the project in the timeline.

7 Drag to select Video 1.mp4 through Video 12.mp4 on the timeline. Don't select any of the photos or the audio on the Narration track.

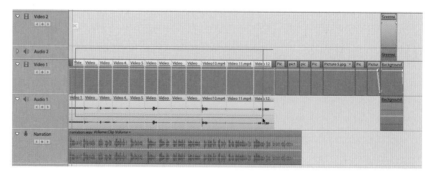

> **Tip:** Click OK if the "Insufficient media" error message appears. See "How transitions work—the deep dive," later in this lesson for an explanation of what this means.

8 In the Adobe Premiere Elements menu, choose Timeline > Apply Default Transition.

9 Adobe Premiere Elements applies the default transitions on the audio and video tracks between all selected clips. If you apply the default transition to clips with

existing transitions, Adobe Premiere Elements will replace the transitions but won't change the duration of the previously inserted transitions.

10 Click the Render button (⟨ Render ⟩) to render all of the transitions. If you previously selected a Work Area to render, double-click the very top of the timescale above the timeline to reset the Work Area to the whole project.

11 Drag the current-time indicator around the project and preview the transitions. This is definitely a subjective selection; if you don't like the look, don't use it. Note that you'll have a hard time hearing the audio transitions because the narration is the main element, not the audio in the clips.

Making transitions work in your movie

Now that you know the how of transitions, let's spend a bit of time discussing the "when" and "why." Although there are few absolutes about the art of transitions, your productions will benefit by incorporating these two factors into your creative decisions.

Recognize that you don't need to include a transition between every pair of clips in your movies. If you watch a Hollywood movie, for example, you'll see that noticeable transitions (that is, those longer than four or five frames) are seldom used between clips *within a scene* but are often used *between scenes.*

Why? Because the transition lets the viewer know that there's been a change in time or location. That is, if a scene jumped from a kitchen at night to the backyard the next day, simply jumping from scene to scene would confuse the viewer. You can imagine the viewer saying, "Hey, what happened here? One second they were in the kitchen drinking after-dinner milkshakes, and the next second they were playing dodgeball in the yard in sunlight." However, if the editor inserts a fade to black between the two scenes or adds some other noticeable transition, the viewer understands that a change of time or location has occurred.

Within the context of the Space Shuttle project, there are two distinct scenes: the videos and the slide show. Between these two scenes is a natural location for a noticeable transition; hence the Iris Diamond transition. Aesthetically, there are better choices for a movie, such as this one you're making in this project (you'll find lots of cool transitions in the NewBlue folders), but Iris Diamond served our purposes well in this lesson because it has all the available customization options.

You inserted the Dip to Black to fade from black at the start of the video and would have faded to black at the end if you didn't do it in Lesson 6 via Opacity keyframes. Virtually all edited home videos use these two effects, as do many business videos.

Within scenes, transitions are up for grabs. A very short transition between videos in a sequence works well because it smooths the flow, but many—if not most—producers use straight cuts. In slide shows, you should try more noticeable transitions because each slide is like a separate scene.

Of course, with family videos your goal is to produce smiles, not to win an Academy Award. If you want to use transitions as content rather than in their traditional role, feel free to add as many as you like, anywhere you'd like. Just be sure to consider the following rule: When you're using transitions, you should match the tone of the transition to the tone of the movie. In a fun, family video, like a trip to the aquarium or other vacation, you could use any transition that Adobe Premiere Elements offers—in some cases, the zanier the better. For this reason, highly noticeable transitions are used frequently in children's shows like *Barney & Friends* and *The Wiggles*.

On the other hand, when you're shooting a solemn event—say, a wedding or graduation—the tone is usually more serious. In these instances, you'd probably want to use only Cross Dissolves or the occasional Dip to Black transition to maintain that tone.

How transitions work—the deep dive

By now, you know enough to deploy transitions artfully in your projects, but you still may have some questions. For example, you may wonder why the "Insufficient media" error message appears at times or the significance of a transition containing "repeated frames."

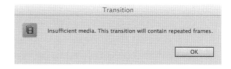

Or, you may notice that during some transitions, one side of the video looks static while the other is moving. As you may have suspected, this is the result of the "repeated frames" mentioned in the error message. So, we'll take a few moments to answer these questions, plus you'll learn some workarounds that involve the clip alignment controls that can fix the static frames.

How transitions should work

In Adobe Premiere Elements, you insert a transition at the intersecting point between two clips. Then you set a duration for that transition. For example, in the next figure, assume that the transition shown has a duration of two seconds. That means that in the first clip it precedes the transition point by one second and continues one second beyond it.

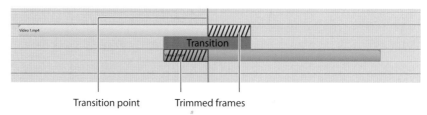

Transition point   Trimmed frames

Let's focus on the one second that the transition point continues *beyond* the intersecting point between the clips. Adobe Premiere Elements needs content to fill that time. If you've trimmed one second from the end of that video, Adobe Premiere Elements uses that, as the figure shows. However, if you haven't trimmed any frames, Adobe Premiere Elements is forced to use the last frame of the clip for the one second that extends beyond the intersecting point. This is when you get the "Insufficient media" error message and see static frames in your transition.

Let's see what the difference looks like in a real project. Following the directions (if necessary) from the "Getting started" section earlier, open the project Lesson07_Workshop_Win.prel (Windows) or Lesson07_Workshop_Mac.prel (Mac OS), which has a number of different transition examples on the timeline. Before starting, click the Render button (Render), or press Enter (Windows) or Return (Mac OS), to render all of the transitions.

The first two files have been trimmed at the transition location, but the second two haven't, which you can see in the titles over both clips (Trim and No Trim). Both have transitions applied to the center of the intersection (that's the "Center" title).

Drag the current-time indicator over the transition between the first two clips (Trim, Center). You'll notice that the second clip is moving during the entire transition. This is how your transitions look when you have sufficient trimmed footage to cover the duration of the transition.

For example, for the three-second transition used between these two clips, you would need 1.5 seconds trimmed from both clips for both clips to be fully in motion throughout the transition.

When you drag the current-time indicator over the transition between the second two clips (No Trim and Center), which starts around 00;00;18;00 into the project, you'll notice that the Shuttle doesn't start moving in the transition until the current-time indicator reaches the second clip. The reason is that there was no trimmed video to use during the transition, so Adobe Premiere Elements repeated the first frame of that video during the first half of the transition.

What does this mean? In general, unless you're an exceptionally good cameraperson, you'll be trimming most of your clips anyway, so you probably won't encounter this issue that often, if at all. If you do see one side of a transition frozen, however, there are some steps you can take.

First, recognize that most viewers won't notice the difference, particularly casual viewers. So unless you're a real perfectionist, just let it be. At least now you know the source of the problem.

Second, if you're a perfectionist, you should trim the clip that's causing the problem. Of course, you probably would have already done this to shorten the project as much as possible (being a perfectionist and all), so this probably won't be possible.

Third, if you have trimmed some frames, just not enough, trying shortening the transition duration to eliminate the freeze frames. For a two-second transition located between the two clips, you need 30 frames trimmed from each video. If you've trimmed only 15 frames from one of the clips, change the transition duration to one second.

Fourth, if one of the clips has trimmed frames and the other doesn't, try changing the location of the transition to eliminate the problem. The next two sets of clips in the Workshop project (starting around 00;00;34;00) show how this can help. In both sets, the first clip, Video 1.mp4, has been trimmed, whereas the second hasn't been trimmed.

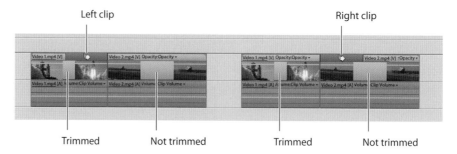

With the transition in the Left clip position (the third set of clips, starting around 00;00;34;00), there are no trimmed frames available from the second clip to use in the transition. If you drag the current-time indicator slowly over that transition, you'll see that the second clip doesn't start moving until you reach the second clip.

In the fourth set of clips, starting around 00;00;49;00, the transition is in the Right clip position. This means that it has frames from the trimmed first clip to use in the transition, so the first clip keeps moving throughout the transition and there is no freeze frame.

Exploring on your own

My compliments; that's another lesson well done! You've discovered how transitions can make your projects more professional-looking by adding continuity between clips. You've learned about placing, previewing, modifying, and rendering different transitions, as well as applying them en masse.

As you continue to edit with transitions, you'll get a better idea of how to use them to enhance the tone or style of your project. The best way to develop that style is by trying different transitions and discovering how they affect your movie. So here's your task list for further exploration.

- Experiment with different transitions; preview their animated icons in the Transitions panel. Remember that dragging a transition onto an existing transition will replace it.

- Get comfortable modifying the default parameters of your transitions. One by one select the transitions you've added and explore their settings in the Transition Adjustments dialog.

Review questions

1   Where are Video Transitions located, and what are two ways to locate specific transitions?

2   How do you modify transitions?

3   How can you extend the duration of a transition?

4   How can you apply a transition to multiple clips simultaneously?

Review answers

1   Video Transitions are located in the Transitions panel, which you can access in the Action bar. You can browse for individual transitions, which (in Expert view) are organized in categories and by transition type. Additionally, in Expert view, you can find a specific transition by typing its name or part of its name into the search field in the Transitions panel.

2   Double-click the transition icon in the timeline to open the Transition Adjustments dialog.

3   In Expert view, you can click and drag the transition to any length. In both views, you can double-click the transition icon in the timeline to open the Transition Adjustments dialog, and customize the duration there, but only using whole numbers.

4   You can use two techniques to apply transitions to multiple clips: One is to select multiple clips on the timeline and choose Timeline > Apply Default Transition. Adobe Premiere Elements will insert the default transition between all selected clips. You can also copy a previously applied transition, select multiple clips on the timeline, and then paste the transition onto any selected clip.

8 ADDING TITLES AND CREDITS

Lesson overview

In this lesson, you'll learn how to create original titles and rolling credits for a movie about powering the Space Shuttle. You'll be adding still titles and rolling titles, placing images, and using drawing tools. Specifically, you'll learn how to do the following:

- Add and stylize text

- Superimpose titles and graphics over video

- Use graphics elements like thought bubbles

- Create and customize rolling titles

- Use title templates

 This lesson will take approximately two hours.

Using a thought bubble in Adobe Premiere Elements.

Working with titles and title-editing mode

Within Adobe Premiere Elements, you can create custom graphics and titles. When you add a title over one of your video clips, it's also added to your Project Assets panel as a new clip. As such, it's treated much like any other clip in your project. It can be edited, moved, deleted, and have transitions and effects applied to it.

Adobe Premiere Elements allows you to create original titles using text, drawing tools, and imported graphics. However, to help you quickly and easily add high-quality titles to your project, Adobe Premiere Elements also provides a number of templates based on common themes, such as Sports, Travel, and Weddings.

By the way, in this lesson we substitute my daughter's final narration for the quick-and-dirty narration we used for timing purposes in previous lessons. Enjoy.

Getting started

You'll modify scenes in this lesson's project by adding titles and graphics to various clips in the project. But first you'll open the Lesson08 project and prepare your Adobe Premiere Elements workspace.

1   Make sure that you have correctly copied the Lesson08 folder from the DVD in the back of this book onto your computer's hard drive. See "Copying the Classroom in a Book files" in the "Getting Started" section at the start of this book.

2   Launch Adobe Premiere Elements. If it is already open, choose Help > Welcome Screen in the Adobe Premiere Elements menu to return to the Welcome screen.

3   In the Welcome screen, click Video Editor, select Existing Project, and click the Open folder.

4   In the Open Project dialog, navigate to the Lesson08 folder.

5   Within that folder, select the file Lesson08_Start_Win.prel (Windows) or Lesson08_Start_Mac.prel (Mac OS) and then click Open. If a dialog appears asking for the location of rendered files, click the Skip Previews button.

    Your project file opens.

6   Choose Window > Restore Workspace to ensure that you start the lesson in the default panel layout.

Viewing the completed movie before you start

To see what you'll be creating in this lesson, you can take a look at the completed movie. You'll have to be in Expert view to open the Project Assets panel to view the movie, so if you are not, click Expert (Expert) to enter that view.

1 On the upper-left side of the Adobe Premiere Elements interface, click the Project Assets button (Project Assets ▾) to open the Project Assets panel. Locate the file Lesson08_Movie.mov, and then double-click it to open the video in the preview window.

2 Click the Play button (▶) to watch the video about powering the Space Shuttle, which you'll build in this lesson.

3 When you're done, close the preview window.

Titles and text overview

Adding titles in Quick and Expert views is very similar, but let's discuss titles in general before learning that procedure. Adobe Premiere Elements contains a number of title templates that you can access by clicking the Titles & Text button (▦ Titles & Text ▾) in the Action bar to open the Titles & Text panel, which contains identical content in both Quick and Expert views. All content is separated into themed folders that match the categories that you will add as DVD menus in Lesson 10. Click the folder list box to view the categories, many of which contain multiple options.

Title templates are a great way to add a nice creative touch to your videos; after all, no one but you will know that you didn't create the professional-looking content from scratch. If you're creating a DVD from your video, you should review the available DVD themes while choosing your title templates.

You can then choose the matching title template and theme that you like best. Not surprisingly, Adobe Premiere Elements doesn't have either a title template or DVD theme for Space Shuttle videos, so you'll use titles from the General folder.

Adobe Premiere Elements offers two basic kinds of titles: full screen and overlay. A full-screen title has no video underneath, so it usually takes up the entire frame. In contrast, overlay titles are superimposed over a video or videos. You'll learn how to create both kinds of titles in this lesson and how to use thought bubbles, which are a graphic element that you complete using Adobe Premiere Elements' text tools.

Although you can create a title by choosing File > New > Title, it's simplest to just drag a title template where you want it; if you want a full-screen title, you drag it to the desired location on the video track (Quick view) or Video 1 (Expert view), making sure that the Insert icon (⊞) appears before you release your mouse. This tells Adobe Premiere Elements to push all content on the timeline to the right to fit the content that you just added. In Expert view, the operation is the same, except you drag the title to the start of the Video 1 track, assuming that's where the bulk of your video is.

In the figure, I've added the default title to the start of the project, which you'll do in Expert view in a moment. You can see the Insert icon, so all other content will be pushed back by the duration of the title. You set title duration in the Preferences dialog available by choosing Edit > Preferences > General (Windows) or Adobe Premiere Elements 11 > Preferences > General (Mac OS). Although titles aren't mentioned, Still Image Default Duration controls the length of titles as well as still images.

● **Note:** In my tests, changing the Still Image Default Duration preference took effect only after closing Adobe Premiere Elements and reopening it. It also affects only titles you created or images you import after you've changed the preference. It will not change the duration of any images in the project or titles created before you change the preference, whether they are in the Project Assets folder or deployed on the timeline.

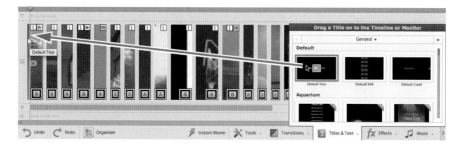

To create an overlay title, drag the title to the Title track in Quick view or any video track over your primary video track in Expert view. If you think you'll be switching between Quick and Expert views, you should place titles inserted in Expert view in the Video 3 track so they'll appear in the Title track in Quick view; otherwise, you won't be able to see them in Quick view. If you exclusively use Expert view, you can place titles in any video track.

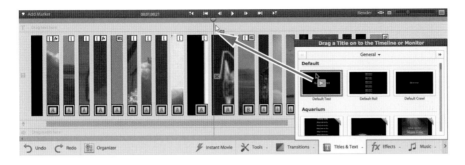

Interestingly, if you add an overlay title in Quick view over a clip that's shorter than the default title duration, Adobe Premiere Elements will cut off the title at the right edge of the clip. This is no biggie, because you can click and drag the edge of the clip to any duration. However, in Expert view, Adobe Premiere Elements will insert the title at its full duration with the edge of the title hanging over the next clip or— apropos of the project you've been building—hanging out over outer space if there is no following clip.

Once the title is added to your project, you edit it the same way in either view: Adobe Premiere Elements opens the title you just added in title-editing mode, which uses the Monitor panel as a WYSIWYG (what you see is what you get) editing tool. Because I've covered Quick view in this summary, I'll demonstrate the rest of the lesson in Expert view.

One final note: To exit title-editing mode, simply click anywhere in the timeline that's not the location of a title. Adobe Premiere Elements saves all changes automatically. To reenter title-editing mode, double-click any title.

Creating a simple full-screen title

If you were following along with the previous discussion by making the actual edits, congrats; that's a great way to learn, and much more fun than reading dry words on a page. To return to a clean slate, either click Undo (↺ Undo) until it grays out or reload Lesson08_Start_Win.prel (Windows) or Lesson08_Start_Mac.prel (Mac OS).

In this exercise, you'll add a title clip at the beginning of the movie, and then customize the title. Again, you'll be working in Expert view, so if you're not in that view, click Expert (Expert) at the top of the Monitor panel. If you want your project to look like the screen shots in the book, click the Zoom in icon (▣) on the right side of the Monitor panel twice, or press the equal key (=) twice. Also, press the Home key to make sure the current-time indicator is at the start of the project.

1 In the Action bar, click Titles & Text ( Titles & Text ▾) to open the Titles & Text panel. Make sure that the General category is selected.

2 Click and drag the Default Text title template to the beginning of the project. Pause for a moment while Adobe Premiere Elements pushes all other content to the right, and then release the pointer. Adobe Premiere Elements inserts the title at the start of the project and opens the title in title-editing mode with the text active. The text and drawing tools are visible in the Adjustments panel on the right with four tabs for Text, Style, Animation, and Shapes. You will visit all these tabs during your work in this lesson.

● **Note:** Let's sneak in a little fun while no one is watching. Click Undo to start over, and then drag the title back to the front of the clip, pressing the Ctrl key (Windows) or Command key (Mac OS). Note how the pointer changes to the Overlay icon (⬛). Release your pointer, and Adobe Premiere Elements inserts the title into the video clip, replacing the video to the full duration of the title. This is called an overlay edit, because the inserted content replaces, or overlays, the original content. You've been using "insert edits" throughout the book, because they're conceptually simpler and generally much more useful. I've been editing for close to 20 years and still use overlay edits very infrequently. One common use case, however, would be inserting a title into a clip as you just did. Now click Undo, and redo step 2 so that you insert the title at the front of the project. OK, it's time to get back to the program.

3 The Horizontal type tool should be selected by default. If it's not, click the Horizontal type tool button (T) in the Adjustments panel to select it now.

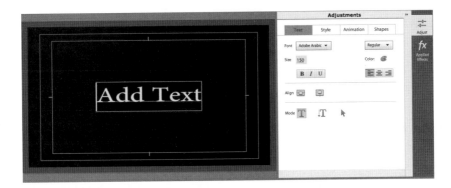

4   Click in the text box and drag your pointer over the default text to select it. Type the words **Powering the**, and then press the Enter (Windows) or Return (Mac OS) key to create a new line. Next, type the words **Space Shuttle**.

5   To reposition your text, click the Selection tool (⬉) and then click anywhere inside the text to select the text block. Drag to reposition the text so it appears centered in the upper third of the Monitor panel. Two white margins display in the title window. These are referred to as the title-safe and action-safe margins. Stay within the inner margin (title-safe) while repositioning your text. Don't worry about the exact position for now; you'll reposition the text later in this lesson.

Tip: You can add multiple text entries to a single title, or you can create multiple titles, each containing a unique text string.

6   Choose File > Save As. In the Save As dialog, name the file **Lesson08_Work. prel**, and then click Save to save it in your Lesson08 folder.

Adobe Premiere Elements treats basic titles, such as the one you just created, like still image files. After you've created a title, the application automatically adds an image file to your Project Assets panel.

Modifying text

After creating and adding a title to the project, you can change text or its appearance at any time, much as you would in a word processor or page layout program. In this exercise, you'll learn how to adjust the alignment of your type as well as its style, size, and color.

Changing text alignment, style, and size

OK, let's fine-tune the default title that you just inserted. You should be in the Text view of the Adjustments panel; if not, click Text (Text) on the top of the panel to enter that view.

1   To center the text within the text box, use the Selection tool (▶) to select the title text box, and then click the Center Text button (≡). You don't have to select the actual text, just the box. Note that you'll see only a minor change because the two lines are so even that they both look centered.

2   In the Monitor panel, choose the Horizontal type tool and drag it in the text box to select the first line of text. Click the Font list box and choose Adobe Garamond Pro from the list and Bold from the list box next to it. Choose another font and style if you don't have this font on your system.

3   With the first line of text still selected, to change the font size, *do the following*:

 •   Place the pointer over the number to the right of the Size descriptor. The pointer will change to a hand with two black arrows (🖐).

 •   Drag to change the Size value to 85. If you have difficulties getting a precise value by dragging, click the size value once, type **85** into the text field, and press Enter (Windows) or Return (Mac OS). Now that you've changed the size of the first line, you can see that the text is, in fact, centered.

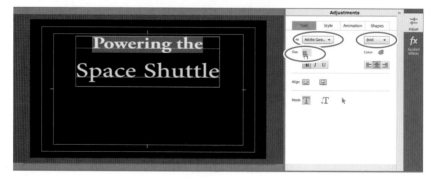

4   At the top of the Adjustments panel, click the Style tab (Style) to enter Style view. Scroll down until you can see the Lithos Gold Strokes 52 style, which is near the bottom. Then select the second line of text—the words "Space

Shuttle"—with the Horizontal Type tool, and choose Lithos Gold Strokes 52. This changes the style for the selected text.

5 At the top of the Adjustments panel, click the Text tab (Text) to enter that view. With the words "Space Shuttle" still selected, change the font size to 100, either by dragging the Size value to the right or by clicking the Size value once, typing **100** into the text field, and pressing Enter (Windows) or Return (Mac OS). This is probably not the font NASA would select, but hey, this is for a grade-school science project, and the style does have a vague *Jetsons*-like feel.

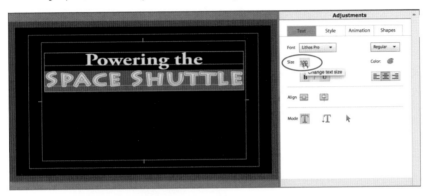

6 Choose File > Save to save your work.

Centering elements in the Monitor panel

At this point, your title probably isn't precisely centered horizontally within the frame. You can fix this manually, or you can let Adobe Premiere Elements do the work for you.

1 Using the Selection tool, click the text box to select the title.

2 Choose Text > Position > Horizontal Center. Or, right-click the text box, and then choose Position > Horizontal Center. Adobe Premiere Elements centers the text box horizontally within the frame.

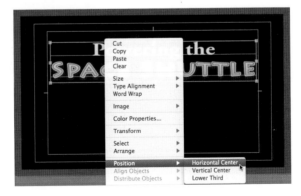

Depending on how you positioned the box earlier in this lesson, you might see little or no change.

3 Choose File > Save to save your work.

Title-safe and action-safe margins

The title-safe and action-safe margins visible in the Monitor panel when you're in title-editing mode designate a title's visible safe zones. These margins are visible by default, although you can turn them off as detailed here.

Safe zones are useful when you're producing DVDs or other video that will be viewed on a traditional TV set rather than on your computer. The reason is that when displaying video, most consumer TV sets cut off a portion of the outer edges of the picture, which is called *overscan*. The amount of overscan is not consistent across TVs, so to ensure that everything fits within the area that most TVs display, keep text within the title-safe margins and keep all other important elements within the action-safe margins.

If you're creating content for computer-screen viewing only, the title-safe and action-safe margins are irrelevant because computer screens display the entire image. You can place text as close to the edge as you'd like, and your viewer will still display it in full.

Safe Title margin

Safe Action margin

To turn title-safe and action-safe margins on or off, right-click inside the Monitor panel and choose View > Safe Title Margin or View > Safe Action Margin from the Monitor panel menu. The margin is visible if a check mark appears beside its name.

Changing the color of your type

As you've seen, changing the style and size of your type is easy. You can change all text within a text box equally by first selecting the text box using the Selection tool and then applying the change. Or, you can restrict the change to portions of the text by selecting them using the Horizontal Type tool. Now you'll change the color of the words "Powering the" to match the Space Shuttle text.

You should be in Text view for this exercise, so if you're not, click the Text tab (Text) near the top of the Adjustments panel to enter that view.

1   Select the Horizontal type tool (T), and then drag over the words "Powering the" to highlight the text.

Next, you'll change the gradient and color of the type. Note that any changes you make will apply to only the selected type.

2   Click the Color Properties button ( ) in Text view to open the Color Properties dialog.

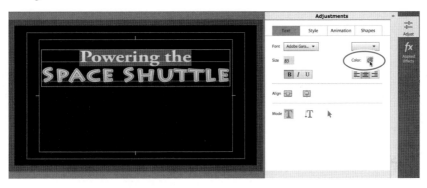

3   In the middle of the dialog, note the Gradient list box. Experiment with the different options in the list box, and notice how they change the appearance of the text. Choose the 4 Color Gradient. This means that the gradient is composed of the four colors in the boxes at the corners of the rectangle beneath the Gradient list box.

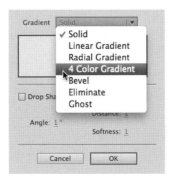

4 Click the box on the top left of the gradient rectangle to select it. Set the RGB values to R: **253**, G: **232**, and B: **73**. Note that after you enter the first value, you can switch to the next values by clicking the Tab key. Then click the box on the upper right and insert the same values: R: **253**, G: **232**, and B: **73**. Then, one at a time, click the two boxes on the bottom and set the values for both at R: **242**, G: **174**, and B: **54**.

> ▶ **Tip:** How did I know that these RGB values would work? I selected the Space Shuttle text, opened the Color Properties dialog, and copied down the RGB values used for that style (of course). If you want to maintain consistent colors among the various design elements in your project, isolate a single set of RGB values and use them consistently.

5 Click OK to close the Color Properties dialog. Use the Selection tool and click outside the text box in the Monitor panel to deselect the text and review your work.

6 Choose File > Save to save your work.

Adding an image to your title files

To add an extra element of depth and fun to your titles, you can import and insert images from any number of sources. For instance, you can use photos from your digital still camera as elements in your title file. In this exercise, you'll place a shot of the Space Shuttle in the lower half of the title image.

1 With the Monitor panel still in title-editing mode, right-click the Monitor panel, and then choose Image > Add Image.

The file Open dialog appears.

> ▶ **Tip:** If you have overlapping frames, you can change the stacking order by right-clicking on a selected frame and then choosing one of the Arrange commands from the context menu. To align multiple frames, select the frames you want to align, right-click, and then choose any of the Align Objects commands.

2 In the Open dialog, navigate to the Lesson08 folder. Within that folder, select the file marquee.psd, and then click Open (Windows) or Choose (Mac OS) to import the image into your title.

3 The image appears stacked in front of the text box in your title. Use the Selection tool to drag the placed image downward, making sure that the bottom

of the image stays above the action-safe area (if this were text, you'd have to make sure it was within the title-safe zone).

▶ **Tip:** How long should your titles appear onscreen? Long enough for your viewers to read them, of course. Want more specificity? The rule of thumb is that your title should be twice as long as it takes to read the title out loud. So start your timer, read the title twice, stop the timer, and that's your duration.

4   If you're unhappy with the size of the image you've inserted, drag any anchor point to resize the placed image. Hold down the Shift key while dragging to maintain the proportions of the image.

5   Let's make sure that the image is centered perfectly. Right-click the image, and choose Position > Horizontal Center.

6   Choose File > Save to save your work.

Applying fade-in and fade-out effects

Any transition that you use on video clips can also be added to title clips. In this exercise, you'll add a fade-in and fade-out effect to the title clip.

1   With the title still selected, click the Applied Effects button on the upper right of the Adobe Premiere Elements interface to open the Applied Effects panel.

2   Click the disclosure triangle next to Opacity to view the Opacity controls.

3   Under Opacity, click the Fade In button. The title image seems to disappear from the Monitor panel. Drag the current-time indicator in the timeline to the right to see the image fade in.

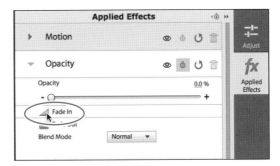

If you adjusted the default transition duration to five frames as detailed in Lesson 7, after five frames the clip's opacity reaches 100 percent and becomes fully visible again. Although five frames is an appropriate length for interscene dissolves, fade-ins should be one full second. Let's fix that (if necessary).

4   In the timeline, drag the second keyframe in the Video 2 track to the 00;00;01;00 mark. That extends the fade-in from five frames to one full second. Note that this step is easier if you're zoomed in to the timeline as shown in the figure.

5   Back in the Applied Effects panel, click the Fade Out button to fade out the title. If necessary, drag the third keyframe to the left to the 00;00;04;00 mark to extend the fade out to one second.

6   If the current-time indicator isn't at the start of the project, press Home to move it there. Then press the spacebar to play the title you just created. Press the spacebar to stop playback when you're finished.

7   Choose File > Save to save your work.

Animate a still title

Text animations are fun effects that are very easy to apply, although there's one prerequisite that prevented using animations with this project: Your titles can't have more than one line. If they have more than one line, the Apply button in the Animation panel never becomes active.

To apply an animation, you must be in title-editing mode; the easiest way to enter this mode is to double-click a title in the timeline. Then select the text element that you want to animate, and click the Animation tab (Animation) to enter that view in the Adjustments panel. You can preview any animation by hovering your pointer over the animation until the Play button appears and then clicking Play. Click Apply on the bottom of the Animation view to apply the selected animation to the selected text.

To remove an animation, choose the animated text, click the Animation tab to open that view, and click the Remove button on the bottom of the panel.

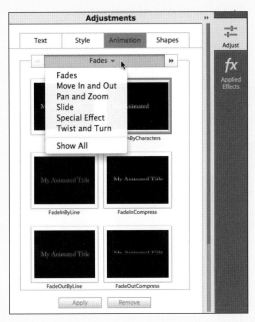

Superimposing a title over video clips

Now you know how to build a full-screen title. Next, you'll create an overlay title. In this exercise, you'll add an overlay title with pointers over Video 11.mp4, showing the viewer the location of the engines that are part of the Orbital Maneuvering System. The fun new skills you'll learn here are how to create a background for your title text so that it's readable over the background video and how to use shapes to highlight critical elements in your video content.

1   Move your current-time indicator to approximately 00;01;04;00, which should be about halfway through Video 11.mp4, assuming that you successfully added a five-second title to the start of the clip. If you skipped that task, move your current-time indicator to about five seconds to the left of the right edge of Video 11.mp4.

2   In the Action bar, click Titles & Text (Titles & Text) to open the Titles & Text panel. Make sure that the General category is selected.

Note: Because this title is on Video 2, not Video 3, you won't see it if you enter Quick view.

3   Click and drag the Default Text title template to the Video 2 track, right where it intersects with the current-time indicator, and release the pointer. Adobe Premiere Elements inserts the title and opens the title in title-editing mode.

4   Click in the text box and drag your pointer over the default text to select it. Type the words **Orbital Maneuvering**, and then press the Enter (Windows) or Return (Mac OS) key to create a new line. Next, type the words **System engines**. You can see right away that this text will be hard to read without some kind of a background. Let's get the text squared away, and then you'll create the background.

5   Drag the text you just added to select it. Click the Font list box, choose the Adobe Garamond Pro font, and change the font Size to **60**. Then click the Selection tool and position the text so that the top of the Shuttle's tail fin just touches the S in System, as shown in the figure.

6 Click elsewhere in the title to deselect the text that you just created.

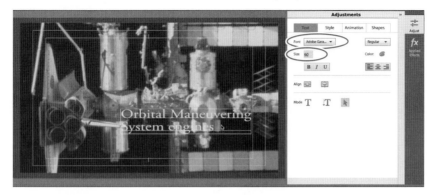

7 Now let's add a background. Click the Shapes tab (Shapes) to open that view. Select the Rectangle tool (▮); the cursor changes to a crosshair. Drag to create a rectangle over the text you just created. Don't worry about obscuring the text; in a moment, you'll position the rectangle behind the text.

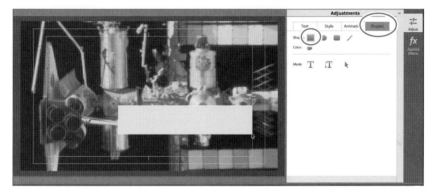

8 Click the Color Properties button (⬤) to open the Color Properties dialog. Set the color to black by clicking the large black color chip on the upper right of the Color Properties dialog. Click OK to apply the color to the rectangle you created, and close the Color Properties dialog.

9 Let's soften the black color by making the background slightly transparent. Right-click the rectangle, and choose Transform > Opacity. The Opacity panel opens. Type **60** into the Opacity % field, and click OK to close the panel.

10 Now you'll shift the new rectangle behind the text. Right-click the rectangle and choose Arrange > Send to Back to place your rectangle behind your white type. The white text is now clearly visible over the rectangle. If necessary, you can edit the size of the rectangle by clicking it to make it active and then dragging any edge to a new location. If necessary, you can also trim the right edge of the title so that it doesn't extend over to the next clip.

When you add multiple elements, such as text, squares, or circles, to a title, you create a stacking order. The most recent item added (in this case, the rectangle) is placed at the top of the stacking order. You can control the stacking order—as you did here—using the Arrange commands from the context menu or the Text menu.

11 Now let's add pointers to the actual engines that are described in the narration. Move the current-time indicator closer to the right edge of Video 11.mp4, say around 00;01;08;20. If you shift out of title-editing mode by clicking anywhere on the timeline that isn't a title, double-click the title to reenter it.

12 Click elsewhere in the title to deselect the box you just created. Then click the Line Tool (⁄) and draw a line from the text title to the top Orbital Maneuvering System engine. Click elsewhere in the title to deselect the line you just drew, and draw another from the text title to the bottom engine.

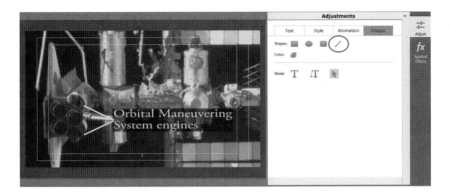

13 Following the instructions in the "Applying fade-in and fade-out effects" section, fade the title that you just created in and out. In this case, the fade-in and fade-out effect should be fairly short—say, about five frames. You want to soften its appearance and disappearance, not make it noticeable or memorable.

14 Move the current-time indicator a few moments before the title you just created. Then press the spacebar to view the title. Press the spacebar to stop playback when you're finished.

15 Choose File > Save to save your work.

Using graphics

Being the child of a book author is tough; you're frequently used to supply free content for a seemingly never-ending number of books and articles, which means being cute on call. Sure, your youth is chronicled in color for all to see, which is nice, but starting around the teenage years, apparently, you get a bit resentful. So, the quid pro quo I used to get my eldest to shoot the greenscreen video we're working with are the comments you'll be adding in this exercise.

Oh well, it's a great way to learn how to use some of the graphics elements included with Adobe Premiere Elements. Let's stay in Expert view because there are many more graphics elements to work with, although you can access a subset in Quick view.

1 Move the current-time indicator to the Greenscreen.mov clip, right after the fade in, which should be around 00;01;52;19. If that timecode doesn't match, don't sweat it; just move the current-time indicator immediately after the fade in in Greenscreen.mov.

2 On the far right of the Action bar, click Graphics (Graphics) to open the Graphics panel. Click the list box and choose the Thought and Speech Bubbles category.

3   Use the scroll bar on the right of the Graphics panel to scroll down to Speech Bubble 05-LEFT. Click and drag it to the Video 3 track right where it intersects the current-time indicator. Note that if you haven't used this graphic before, Adobe Premiere Elements may have to download it, which means you need to be connected to the Internet.

4   Double-click the graphic on the timeline to open it in title-editing mode.

5   Click the Text tab (Text) in the Adjustments panel (if necessary) to enter that view. Click the Selection tool (↖). Note that this graphic has two elements: the thought bubble graphic and the text.

You want to resize the graphic first, and then customize the text, resize it, and move it into the speech bubble. So start by clicking the speech bubble where there is no text—like close to any edge. Then grab the lower-left corner, press the Shift key to keep the adjustment proportional, and drag up and to the right.

6   Click in the text box and drag your pointer over the default text to select it. Type the words **My dad so**, and then press the Enter (Windows) or Return (Mac OS) key to create a new line. Next, type the words **made me**, create a new line, and type **do this** on the third line.

7   Your sizing and positioning will be different than what you see here, but to make the text fit and look like the finished product, the following steps were taken:

   • Change the font size to 43 in the Size field.

   • Center the text by clicking the Center text (≡) icon.

   • Move the text over the thought bubble.

Note: The thought bubble will always appear in the project where you first apply it, which is the typical use case for the vast majority of users. However, the thought bubble did not reliably reappear in subsequent projects created for later lessons from this project. For some reason, it doesn't seem to travel well to different projects in different folders, particularly on different systems. No sweat for you; it should not cause a problem, but don't be shocked if you don't see the thought bubble graphic in later projects, despite our best efforts.

8 Following the instructions in the "Applying fade-in and fade-out effects" section, fade the title that you just created in and out. In this case, the fade-in and fade-out effects should be fairly short—say, about five frames. You want to soften the appearance and disappearance of the thought bubble, not make it noticeable or memorable.

9 Move the current-time indicator a few moments before the title you just created. Then press the spacebar to view the title. Press the spacebar to stop playback when you're finished.

10 Choose File > Save to save your work.

OK, you're almost home. Let's add rolling credits and you'll be done.

Creating a rolling credit

The titles you have created to this point have been static, but Adobe Premiere Elements can create animated titles as well. There are two types of animated titles: rolls and crawls. A *rolling* credit is defined as text that moves vertically up the screen, like the end credits of a movie. A *crawl* is text that moves horizontally across the screen, like a news ticker. In this exercise, you'll create a rolling credit at the end of the project.

1 Press the End key to move to the end of the project.

2 In the Action bar, click Titles & Text (▣ Titles & Text ▾) to open the Titles & Text panel. Make sure that the General category is selected.

3 Click and drag the Default Roll title template to the Video 1 track, adjacent to Background.mp4.

4 Using the Horizontal Type tool, select the text Main Title at the top of the Monitor panel. In the Text Options area, click the Center Text (▤) icon to center the text. That way, whatever you type will continue to be centered. Make sure that the Main Title text is still selected, and type **Credits**.

5 Click the other text box, press Ctrl+A (Windows) or Command+A (Mac OS) to select all text, and then click the Center Text icon again to center the text.

6   In the second text box, press Ctrl+A (Windows) or Command+A (Mac OS) to
    select all text, and do the following:

- Type **All footage courtesy of NASA:** and press Enter (Windows) or Return
  (Mac OS) *twice*.

- Type **Narration: Eleanor Rose**, and press Enter (Windows) or Return (Mac
  OS) *twice*.

- Type **Greenscreen video: Elizabeth Whatley**, and press Enter (Windows)
  or Return (Mac OS) *nine* times.

- Type **The End**, and press Enter (Windows) or Return (Mac OS) *seven* times.

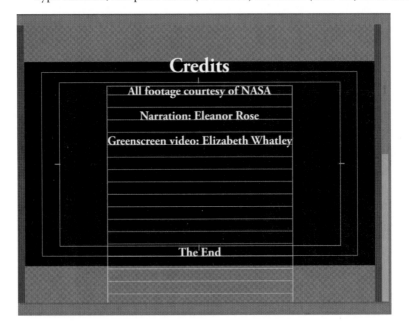

7   In the Adobe Premiere Elements main menu, choose Text > Roll/Crawl Options.
    Most of the options are self-explanatory; here are descriptions of the others
    from the Adobe Premiere Elements Help file:

- **Start Off Screen:** Specifies that the roll begins out of view and scrolls into
  view.

- **End Off Screen:** Specifies that the roll continues until the objects are out of
  view.

- **Preroll:** Specifies the number of frames that play before the roll begins.

- **Ease-In:** Specifies the number of frames through which the title rolls at a
  slowly increasing speed until the title reaches the playback speed.

- **Ease-Out:** Specifies the number of frames through which the title scrolls at
  a slowly decreasing speed until the roll completes.

- **Postroll:** Specifies the number of frames that play after the roll completes.

8 Let's set this up so that the credits start offscreen, quickly come into view, slow at the end, and then The End stays onscreen until the title fades out (which you'll do in the next exercise). To accomplish this, do the following:

- Select the Start Off Screen check box (if not already selected).

- Leave the End Off Screen check box deselected (or deselect it).

- Set Preroll and Ease-In at **0** to make the title appear as quickly as possible.

- Set Ease-Out at **80** so the title slows as The End is rising.

- Set Postroll at **60** so The End stays static before it fades out.

9 Click OK to close the Roll/Crawl Options dialog and apply your changes.

10 Place your current-time indicator just before the beginning of the rolling credits. Press the spacebar to play the rolling credits clip. If playback is too jerky, render the rolling credit title Work Area first.

When you play the clip, the text box with the credits will move—in the five-second default length of the title—from bottom to top across the monitor. This is a bit fast, so let's slow it down in the next exercise.

Changing the speed of a rolling title

When Adobe Premiere Elements creates a rolling title, it spreads the text evenly over the duration of the title. The only way to change the speed of a rolling title is to increase or decrease the length of the title clip. If you want the text to move more slowly across the screen, you need to increase the clip length. Let's do this here.

1 In the timeline, place your pointer over the right end of the rolling title you just created. When the pointer changes to a bracket pointing to the left (⇤), click and drag the clip to the right. Note that as you drag, a small context menu shows you how much time you are adding to the clip. Add about five seconds to the length of the clip, and then release the pointer.

2   Following the instructions in the "Applying fade-in and fade-out effects" section, fade the title that you just created in and out. In this case, the fade-in and fade-out effects should each be about five frames in duration.

3   Place your current-time indicator just before the beginning of the rolling credits. Press the spacebar to play the rolling credits clip. Notice how your titles are now moving more slowly on the monitor and how The End stays onscreen until it fades out at the end. Pretty sweet, eh?

4   You're done here, so save your project as **Lesson08_End.prel**.

Exploring on your own

To increase your skill and versatility with titles, experiment with the different templates Adobe Premiere Elements provides. Keep in mind that you can modify elements like the color of text and the position of graphics. Here are a few steps to follow as you discover what's available:

1   Replace the custom title you created with a title created from a template.

2   Explore the drawing tools available to you when you're in title-editing mode.

3   Create an animated title. Remember that you can animate only titles with one line of text.

4   Place different transitions between your title clips and your video clips to view the various effects you can achieve.

Congratulations; you have completed the lesson. You've learned how to create a simple still title with text and graphics. You changed the style, size, alignment, and color of text. You've positioned and aligned text and graphic frames in the Monitor panel, and you've used one of the Arrange commands to change the stacking order of overlapping frames. You applied fade-in and fade-out effects to your titles. You know how to create rolling credits and how to use and customize title templates. It's time for a well-earned break. But before you stop, review the questions and answers that complete this lesson.

Review questions

1 How do you create a new title?

2 How do you exit title-editing mode, and how can you reenter it to make adjustments to a title clip?

3 How do you change the color of title text?

4 How do you add a fade-in or fade-out effect to a superimposed title clip?

5 What is a rolling credit, and how do you speed it up or slow it down?

Review answers

1 The easiest way to create a new title is to drag a title template to the desired location. You can also choose Title > New Title > Default Still.

2 To exit title-editing mode, click anywhere in the timeline except on a title clip. To reenter title-editing mode, double-click any title on the timeline.

3 Double-click a title to enter title-editing mode in the Monitor panel. Select the text using the Horizontal Type tool. Then click the Color Properties button, and pick a new color in the Color Properties dialog.

4 Select the title, and then click the Applied Effects button to open that panel. Under Opacity in Properties, click the Fade In or Fade Out button.

5 A rolling credit is text that scrolls vertically across your screen. Duration on the timeline controls scrolling speed. To slow scrolling speed, click and drag the title to make it longer. To increase scrolling speed, click and drag the title to make it shorter.

9 WORKING WITH SOUND

Lesson overview

The sound you use has a big impact on your movies. Adobe Premiere Elements provides you with the tools to narrate clips while previewing them in real time; to create, add, and modify soundtracks; and to control the volume levels within clips. The project in this lesson helps you explore the basics of working with audio.

Specifically, you'll learn how to do the following:

- Create a custom-length background music track with SmartSound

- Add narration, and Normalize the volume of the narration

- Adjust volume and gain

- Use Smart Mix to automatically optimize the volume of your background music track and narration

- Adjust the volume of an audio track with and without keyframes

- Use the Audio Mixer

- Apply audio effects

 This lesson will take approximately 1.5 hours.

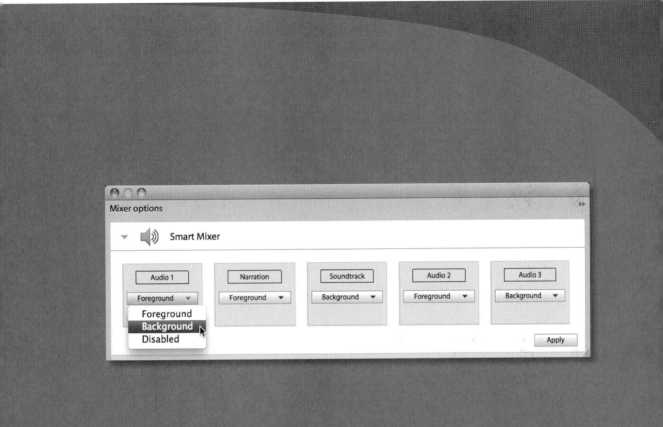

Applying SmartMix to your project.

Getting started

You'll modify this project by adding background music and narration, and by adjusting the loudness of the audio on several of the clips. But first you'll open the Lesson09 project and prepare your Adobe Premiere Elements workspace.

1   Make sure that you have correctly copied the Lesson09 folder from the DVD in the back of this book onto your computer's hard drive. See "Copying the Classroom in a Book files" in the "Getting Started" section at the start of this book.

2   Launch Adobe Premiere Elements. If it is already open, choose Help > Welcome Screen in the Adobe Premiere Elements menu to return to the Welcome screen.

3   In the Welcome screen, click Video Editor, select Existing Project, and click the Open folder.

4   In the Open Project dialog, navigate to the Lesson09 folder.

5   Within that folder, select the file Lesson09_Start_Win.prel (Windows) or Lesson09_Start_Mac.prel (Mac OS) and then click Open. If a dialog appears asking for the location of rendered files, click the Skip Previews button.

Your project file opens.

6   Choose Window > Restore Workspace to ensure that you start the lesson in the default panel layout.

Viewing the completed movie before you start

To see what you'll be creating in this lesson, you can take a look at the completed movie. You'll have to be in Expert view to open the Project Assets panel to watch the movie, so if you are not, click Expert (Expert) to enter that view.

1   On the upper-left side of the Adobe Premiere Elements interface, click the Project Assets button (Project Assets ▾) to open that panel. Locate the file Lesson09_ Movie.mov, and then double-click it to open the video into the preview window.

2   Click the Play button (▶▮) to watch the video about powering the Space Shuttle, which you'll build in this lesson.

3   When you're done, close the preview window.

Quick view or Expert view?

Although you can perform basic volume adjustments in Quick view, you'll have to work in Expert view for most other audio-related edits. For example, in Expert view, you can adjust audio volume, plus add keyframes to adjust volume over time. You also have access to Normalization and gain controls, plus a range of useful audio effects that you can't apply or configure in Quick view.

Probably the biggest advantage of working in Expert view is the ability to see your audio files as waveforms, which instantly conveys critical information about your audio files, like content and volume. You'll learn all about this in the "About waveforms" section later in this lesson. So, those serious about fine-tuning their audio should work in Expert view.

For those working in Quick view, to adjust volume, click the audio track, and then click Adjust (▦) on the upper right to open the Adjustments panel. Click the disclosure triangle to the left of the Volume adjustment to open the configuration screen, and then drag the clip volume adjustment to the right to increase volume or to the left to decrease volume. Or, click the numeric dB value (for decibels), type the desired adjustment, and press Enter (Windows) or Return (Mac OS).

Note that all adjustments increase or decrease the actual volume of the clip, so a dB level of 0.0 means no adjustment, not that the audio is set to 0.0 dB. You can increase audio to a maximum of +6 dB or drag the slider to −infinity (-∞), which brings the audio down to 0.0 dB. To go beyond this simple edit, you'll have to switch over to Expert view, which is the view you'll be using for the rest of the lesson.

Workflow overview

You've been working with a narration track for several lessons now, because many video-related edits were directed by timing in the audio. What you didn't know was that I adjusted the volume of the narration and several of the clips so you could hear the narration. In this lesson, you'll see what I did and learn how to do it.

Here's what you'll do during the bulk of this lesson. First, you'll add a background music track that adds flow to the project and helps maintain viewer interest through the slide show. Second, you'll add the Narration track and Normalize it.

This gives you four tracks of audio to work with: the audio captured with the video on the Audio 1 track, the audio captured with the greenscreen video on the Audio 2 track, the narration, and the background music. Once these tracks are on the timeline and optimized, you'll use Adobe Premiere Elements' SmartMix tool to automatically adjust the volume of all four tracks so they all play well together.

Creating background music with SmartSound

Adobe has partnered with SmartSound to provide you with a library of musical soundtracks to match your project, as well as easy access to a complete library of background music that you can purchase directly from SmartSound (www.smartsound.com). As you'll learn in this exercise, using SmartSound Express Track, you can quickly choose and create a custom-length soundtrack that matches the mood of your production. You can create SmartSound music tracks in either Quick or Expert views, but you'll be working in Expert view here.

1   Press the End key to move the current-time indicator to the end of the project. Note the timecode in the bottom left of the Monitor panel, which should be around 00;02;10;14. You'll use this duration in a later step to choose the duration of the background music track.

2   Press the Home key to return the current-time indicator to the start of the project.

3   On the right of the Action bar, click the Music button (🎵 Music ▾) to open the Music panel.

4   In the Music panel, hover your pointer over the text Use SmartSound, and it will convert to the Use SmartSound button. Click the button to start the SmartSound application. If this is the first time you're using SmartSound

Express Track, you may have to click through a license agreement, registration window, and search screen, and SmartSound may need to download and install some files. There's a scary looking Sonicfire Pro dialog that says "If you click Cancel, you will not be able to 'Send' your soundtrack back to Adobe Premiere using Sonicfire Pro." Do not click Cancel; this window will disappear in a moment. If you already clicked Cancel, close Sonicfire Pro 5 and start the exercise over.

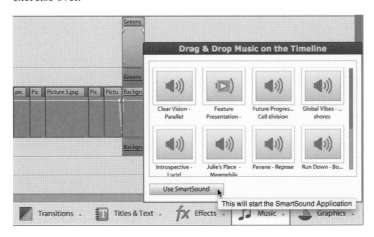

5   Adobe Premiere Elements opens SmartSound Express Track, which you'll use to find a background music track. In the column on the upper left, make sure only Owned Titles is selected, which limits the search to tracks that you actually own, including those that came free with Adobe Premiere Elements. For broader searches for your real projects, you can choose other sources to identify tracks and buy them from SmartSound. Once you choose your source, you can search by style and intensity to narrow your choices in the columns to the right.

6   In the Style list box, choose Corporate/Industrial.

7   In the Keyword list box, choose Futuristic. In this case, the keyword may not impact the tracks that appear in the Title window because you're searching through only the tracks on your computer. If you were searching in the SmartSound Store, which has a much wider selection, your keyword choice would further narrow the selection.

8   In the Title window that displays the tracks your search criteria returned, choose Future Progress, which is the track you'll add to this project (and perhaps the only available track). To preview the track, click the Play button (⊙) on the lower right of SmartSound Express Track. Then click the Pause button to stop preview; if the song finishes, Express Track will automatically switch to the next available track.

9   In the Length box, type **02;10;14**, which tells Express Track to produce a music file of this duration.

● **Note:** On Windows, you may see a big program named Sonicfire Pro looming behind SmartSound Express Track. If you follow the instructions in this exercise, the only time you'll need to interact with that program is to close it after you've added your track.

Note: If the Send button isn't active, it's because you selected a track that's not included with Adobe Premiere Elements. If you want to use that track, follow the prompts and purchase it from SmartSound. For this exercise, please use the Future Progress track.

Note: On the Mac, the application you work with is SmartSound Express Track as shown on the right. On Windows, the program is called Sonicfire Pro 5 - ET. Both work identically as shown in this chapter.

Note: You can't adjust the mix for all tracks, so the Mix button may be grayed out for some tracks that you choose to work with.

10 Note that each song has different variations and moods. You can experiment with these. I like the Frontier variation and the Atmosphere mood. For this exercise, choose these so your file is identical to the one used in this exercise.

11 Click the Mix button (Mix...) on the lower right to open the Customize Mix button, which lets you adjust the component instruments individually. While the audio is playing, drag the sliders for the Drums and Perc, Ostinato to about the – 4.8 dB level, approximately the same location as Bass. As you can hear, this adds these percussive elements back into the track. When you're finished, close the Customize Mix window.

Note: After completely previewing a track, Express Track automatically starts previewing the next track. If this happens, click Future Progress to return to this track, and be advised that you may have to reset the Variation and Mood of the Future Progress track, plus any mix adjustments. To prevent this from happening, click the Pause button to stop the preview before the end of the song.

12 Click the Send button. SmartSound saves the file, briefly displaying an export window, and inserts it into the Soundtrack track in the project starting at the location of the current-time indicator. If you can't see your Soundtrack track in the timeline, use the scroll bar on the right to scroll down and view it.

Note: SmartSound will create a WAV file on Windows and an AIFF file on the Mac. Both files should be named Future Progress - Frontier with either the .wav extension on Windows or .aiff on the Mac.

Note: You want the soundtrack file inserted at the start of the project. If this didn't happen, the reason is that the current-time indicator wasn't at that location when you clicked Send. All is not lost; just click on the file and drag it all the way to the left.

13 Choose File > Save As, name the file **Lesson09_Work.prel** in the Save As dialog, and then save it in your Lesson09 folder.

Narrating a clip

In this exercise, you're working with a narration that I supplied, but at some point you may want to create your own narration. Using your computer's microphone, you can narrate clips while previewing them in the timeline. Check the Adobe Premiere Elements Help files for a detailed procedure for narrating clips.

Adding narration

Now let's add the narration to the project.

1   Make sure that you are in Expert view.

2   Click the Project Assets button (Project Assets ▾) on the upper left to open the Project Assets panel.

3   Drag the narration.wav clip from the Project Assets panel and drop it onto the start of the Narration track in the timeline.

4   Press the spacebar to hear the voice-over added to the project.

Between the narration, background music, and ambient noise in the videos, you've got a royal audio mess on your hands. After learning a bit about waveforms, you'll fix that.

● **Note:** In the Project Assets panel in the next figure, I've used the Show/Hide toggles for video and still images to remove this content from sight in the panel. Audio is toggled to Show, which is why the only content showing in the panel are the two audio files.

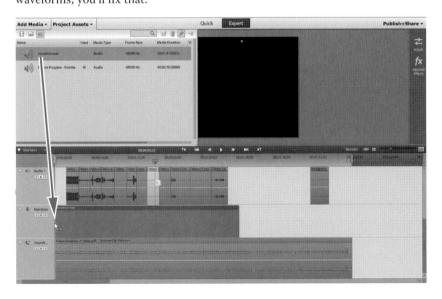

5   Choose File > Save to save your work.

About waveforms

When you're working with audio, it helps to view the waveforms and make the tracks as large as possible. To make your interface look like the next screen shot, do the following:

1   Hover your pointer over the dividing line between the timeline and the Monitor panel until it converts to a two-headed cursor. Then click and drag up to make the timeline taller.

2   In the Audio 1, Narration, and Soundtrack tracks, click the Collapse/Expand track disclosure triangle to the left of the track name to expand the track and show the waveform.

3   To increase the height of the individual audio tracks, hover your pointer over the dividing line between the tracks until it converts to a two-headed cursor. Then click and drag up to make the track taller. Note that this won't work until you expand the track as detailed in step 2.

4   If necessary, to see the track name in full, hover your pointer over the dividing line between the track descriptor and the timeline until it converts to a two-headed cursor. Then click and drag to the right to make the track descriptor larger.

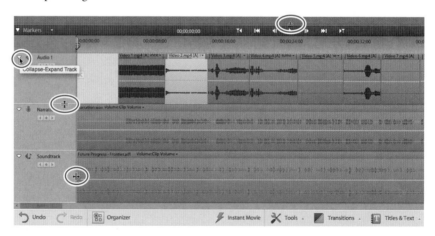

Now that you can see the waveforms, let's talk about what they are and what they tell you. Quite simply, a *waveform* is a graphic representation of the audio in the file. Each audio track in the project has two components—one on top and the other on the bottom. The reason is that all of these audio files are stereo and have left and right channels; the left channel is shown on the top and the right on the bottom. If the files were mono, you would see only one waveform for the entire track; if the files were recorded in 5.1 surround sound, you would see six.

The size of the graphics data in each channel represents volume. When volume is low, the bushy line representing the waveform narrowly surrounds the centerline or isn't visible at all. For example, in the Narration track, the first six seconds or so are flatlined, and then the waveform starts. This tells you that the first six seconds have no narration. If you play the project from the start to about ten seconds in, you'll hear what your eyes are telling you.

In the Audio 1 track, the Video 5.mp4 audio is very, very low, whereas the Video 1.mp4 audio is quite substantial. If you drag your current-time indicator over each track and play the project, you'll hear that Video 1.mp4 is quite loud and Video 5.mp4 has little audible volume.

How can you tell when the audio volume is acceptable? That depends on the track. For example, the audio in the Narration track should be much louder, because it's the most important audio in the project and it must be heard. However, the waveform is clustered around the centerline, which tells you that the audio is low. When the audio is sufficient, the tips of the audio waveforms approach the outer edges of the graph area but never touch for long. You'll fix this low audio in a moment with Normalization.

In contrast, the background music track is supposed to be in the background, so the fact that the waveforms there are concentrated in the center isn't as important. However, if this was the sole audio track associated with a project, you'd want the tips of the waveforms to be much closer to the edge.

Although not excessive within the context of a stand-alone audio file, the audio in Video 1.mp4 is also supposed to be in the background, lower than the narration and background music. So it's definitely too loud and must be adjusted, which you'll do using the SmartMix tool.

Adjusting audio volume

Adobe Premiere Elements offers multiple mechanisms for adjusting the loudness of a clip, but they all use one of two adjustments: volume and gain. Although there are some slight technical differences between volume and gain adjustment, they both accomplish the same thing: adjusting the loudness of your audio. But they use different toolsets that have implications discussed in this and the following section. Let's experiment with the two approaches on the Narration track, starting with volume adjustments.

In Lesson 6, you learned how to adjust clip opacity on the timeline by dragging the Opacity connector line upward and downward. You can adjust the volume of any audio clip the same way. Let's adjust the volume of the Narration track using this technique.

1 Let's preview the audio volume before making any adjustments. Move your current-time indicator over Video 5.mp4, right around 00;00;27;00. Press the spacebar to play the file. You can certainly hear the narration, but it could benefit from a volume boost. When you're ready, press the spacebar to stop playback.

2 In the Narration track, place your pointer over the yellow volume graph line on narration.wav at any location in the clip. The pointer changes to a double-arrow icon (⇕).

● **Note:** Adjusting the volume line doesn't change the waveform display. However, as you'll see in the next exercise, adjusting gain directly does change the waveform. Although adjusting the volume line is easier and more accessible than adjusting gain directly, if you overboost volume, you can produce distortion without being able to view the clipping in the waveform.

3 Click and drag the volume graph upward to the limit, which should be about 6.02 dB, and then release it.

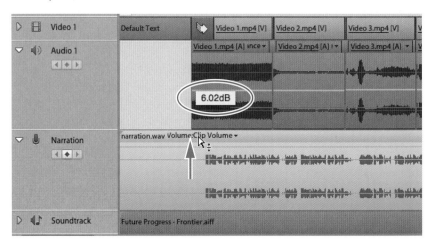

4 Shift the current-time indicator back to the start of Video 5.mp4, and press the spacebar to play the movie. The loudness of the narration clip has increased substantially.

A few notes on volume adjustments

Volume adjustments are keyframeable, which means you can vary volume over the duration of the clip. With gain, which you'll explore in the next exercise, all adjustments are for the entire clip.

Because volume is keyframeable, it's the mechanism used by Adobe Premiere Elements in the SmartMix tool, which varies clip volume over time. You can also use keyframes to fade in the volume of a clip at the start and to fade it out at the end.

Adjusting loudness via volume adjustments does have some negatives, however. First, volume adjustments don't change the waveform, so you're flying blind in terms of whether volume is sufficient or if you've boosted volume too much and caused distortion. This is the reason you're limited to an increase of 6 dB, which may not be enough for some audio files. Second, you can adjust the volume of only one clip at a time; with gain controls, you can adjust multiple clips simultaneously.

Third, with volume adjustments, there's no concept of Normalization, a magical adjustment that ensures that the audio is as loud as possible without causing distortion. More on this in the next exercise.

Adjusting audio gain and normalization

Now let's experiment with adjusting audio gain.

1   Press Undo on the lower left (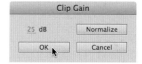) to undo the volume adjustment you made in the previous exercise.

2   Right-click narration.wav in the Narration track and choose Audio Gain. Adobe Premiere Elements opens the Clip Gain dialog.

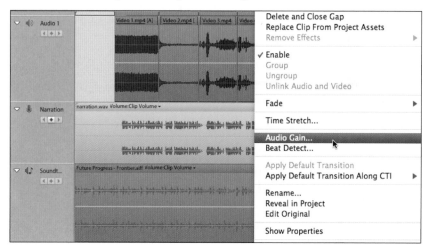

3   Click the Gain level text box to make it active, and type **25**. Or, click on the number and drag it to the right to about the same level.

4   Click OK to apply the gain adjustment and close the Clip Gain dialog.

The waveform expands dramatically, and much of the waveform is flattened against the top and bottom of the track. This is called *clipping*, and in moderate-to-extreme cases, clipping will distort your audio. If you preview the video now, you'll hear that distortion (but turn down the volume on your computer first, because this video will be very loud).

On occasion, manual volume adjustments can cause distortion if you boost the levels too high. When you use the Gain control, you get a visual indicator of clip volume and know when you've overcooked your audio.

5   Click Undo to undo this adjustment.

6   Right-click narration.wav again, choose Audio Gain to open the Clip Gain dialog, and click the Normalize button. Adobe Premiere Elements closes the dialog.

This time the waveform expands out with little or no clipping (some areas may look clipped, but if you zoom into the timeline to examine the waveform more closely, you'll see that they aren't). The reason is that Normalization boosts clip volume as much as possible without introducing distortion into the clip. By definition, Normalization can't cause clipping. This makes the Normalization filter a superior option for volume adjustments, because other adjustments can distort your audio and don't show you when they do. When you adjust gain, either manually or via Normalization, Adobe Premiere Elements updates the waveform, so you can see if you've boosted volume to the point where it might cause distortion.

7 Choose File > Save to save your work.

● **Note:** To see how many decibels Normalization boosted the gain, right click narration.wav and choose Audio Gain again to open the Clip Gain dialog. You'll see that Adobe Premiere Elements boosted audio volume by 10 dB.

Volume, gain, or Normalize?

So, now you know the pros and cons of volume and gain adjustments. Which should you use? Although there are no hard-and-fast rules, here are some suggested workflows.

Normalize when increasing loudness

When you're adjusting clip volume upward, use Normalization to avoid distortion. The only problem with Normalization comes when you have a single long clip with extreme low and high volumes. Let's say you were shooting a wedding and didn't get close enough (or mic the bride, groom, or officiant) to capture the vows at sufficient volume. As a result, the levels are very low when the bride and groom are speaking. However, when the crowd starts applauding, the levels are quite high.

If you apply Normalization to this clip, Adobe Premiere Elements won't boost the volume of the applause beyond the point of causing distortion, which often means that it won't boost the volume of the vows at all. Your best option in this case is to split the clip into low- and high-volume regions—vows in one and applause in another—and apply Normalization separately or only to the vows audio.

Of course, you can apply both functions—normalization, which is a form of gain, and volume adjustments—to the same clip. So if you need to fade a clip in and out, Normalize first to achieve optimal levels and then fade in and out via volume controls.

Normalize when decreasing loudness on multiple clips

If your project has multiple clips that are too loud, you can adjust them all en masse via the gain control. Just select all the clips, right-click, and choose Audio Gain to open the Clip Gain dialog. Insert the desired gain adjustment and click OK. Adobe Premiere Elements lowers the gain of all clips by the adjustment value.

Adjusting volume for fades and SmartMix

As mentioned earlier, gain adjustments aren't keyframeable. For this reason, Adobe Premiere Elements uses volume adjustments for fade ins and outs, and for SmartMix.

OK, now that you've boosted narration volume to the ideal level, let's adjust the volume of the entire project with SmartMix.

Adjusting project volume with Smart Mix

Just to set the stage, you now have four audio tracks: the audio included with the NASA videos on Audio 1 track, the greenscreen audio on Audio 2 track, the background music from SmartSound, and the Normalized narration. Intuitively, when present, the narration takes precedence and needs to be heard over the other two tracks. Let's use SmartMix to do just that.

Note that I boosted narration volume first because SmartMix never increases volume: It works by adjusting the volume of background tracks downward. So if any clip needs to be louder, fix that before using SmartMix.

1 Press the Backslash (\) key to show the entire project. Adjust the interface so you can see all four audio tracks.

2 Press the Home key to move the current-time indicator to the start of the project.

3 In the center of the Action bar, click the Tools button (✕ Tools) to open the Tools panel. Drag the scroll bar on the right down until you see the SmartMix button.

4 Click SmartMix to open the Smart Mixer.

5 Here's where you tell Adobe Premiere Elements which audio tracks to place in the foreground and which to place in the background. Adobe Premiere Elements assumes that Audio 1—the audio shot with the video—should be in the foreground—which, in many instances, it should be. However, here it should not, so click the Audio 1 list box and choose Background. Make sure that Narration is set to Foreground, Soundtrack is set to Background, and Audio 2

Note: At times, the SmartMixer opens in a truncated window that shows only a portion of the first audio track. If this happens, click and drag the lower-right edge to the right until it looks like the figure.

is set to Foreground. Then click Apply. Adobe Premiere Elements analyzes all audio tracks and applies the SmartMix.

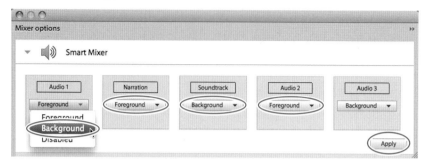

● **Note:** In some instances, for one reason or another, SmartMix may not be effective for one track but will be quite effective on the other tracks. In this case, choose Disabled for the track that's not working well, run SmartMix for the other tracks, and adjust the excluded track via volume or gain controls.

6 Adobe Premiere Elements prioritizes the Narration and Audio 2 tracks by reducing the volume of the Soundtrack and Audio 1 tracks with keyframes in the Soundtrack and some files on Audio 1.

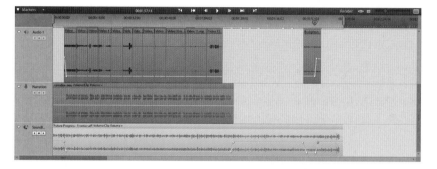

● **Note:** While I was writing this book, SmartMix worked as shown in the figure on Windows computers. On Macs, SmartMix did not make the second adjustment to the Soundtrack beneath the greenscreen clip or to Background.mp4. Adobe is aware of the problem, but I'm not sure if it was fixed by the final release. If it doesn't work on your Mac, either let it go or add the keyframes and adjust volume manually. You'll learn how to add keyframes in the next exercise.

7 Press the spacebar to play the first few moments of the video through to about 20 seconds in. Overall, the audio is much better, but the background music is too low in the areas where SmartMix reduced the volume—you simply can't hear it. Let's fix that.

8 In the Soundtrack track of the timeline, place your pointer over the yellow volume graph line on Future Progress – Frontier in the first dip inserted by SmartMix. The pointer changes to a double-arrow icon (⬍).

9   Click and drag the volume graph upward until the text box accompanying the edit reads around –8 dB. If it's tough to achieve that precise value, anywhere in the vicinity is fine.

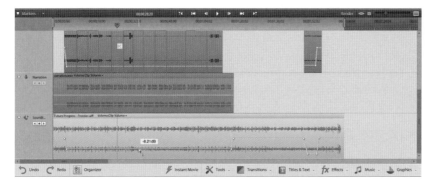

10 Press the spacebar to replay the first few moments of the video. You want the soundtrack to be audible but not get in the way. Does the –8 dB value work for you? If not, find a level that does.

11 When you've found the perfect level for the soundtrack, raise the volume of the second dip in the soundtrack on the right, which starts at about 01;52;06 into the project.

12 Choose File > Save to save your work.

Raising and lowering volume with keyframes

You learned about working with keyframes in video in Lesson 6 in a section titled (appropriately enough) "Working with keyframes." Audio keyframes operate identically to the video-related keyframes discussed in that lesson. To refresh your memory, a keyframe is a point in the timeline where you specify a value for a specific property—in this case, audio volume. When you set two keyframes, Adobe Premiere Elements interpolates the value of that property over all frames between the two keyframes. As you saw in the previous exercise, Adobe Premiere Elements uses keyframes in the SmartMix function to vary volume over time.

For some properties, including opacity for video and volume for audio, you can create keyframes in the timeline by pressing the Ctrl (Windows) or Command (Mac OS) key and then clicking the associated graph with your pointer. Next, you drag the keyframe upward or downward to adjust its value, or to the left or right to adjust its location. To delete keyframes in the timeline, you click to select them, right-click, and then choose Delete.

This exercise will review these procedures. Specifically, in this exercise, you'll add keyframes to fade in the volume of the soundtrack at the beginning of your movie.

1   Drag the current-time indicator near the start of the project, around the 00;00;01;00 mark.

2 Click to select the Future Progress – Frontier clip in the timeline's Soundtrack.

3 Click Zoom in (=) until you can see the 00;00;01;00 timecode in the timeline and spacing looks like the following figure.

4 With the current-time indicator at the 00;00;01;00 mark, position the pointer over the orange volume graph of the Future Progress – Frontier clip at the current-time indicator. The pointer needs to change to a white arrow with double arrows ($\leftrightarrow$), not the Trim Out tool ($\blacksquare$). Press the Ctrl (Windows) or Command (Mac OS) key, and the pointer changes to the Insert Keyframe pointer ($\blacktriangleright_+$). Click the volume graph to add a keyframe at the 00;00;01;00 mark.

5 Press the Home key to move the current-time indicator to the beginning of the movie. If necessary, use the Zoom slider to zoom in for more detail.

6 Using the procedure detailed in step 4, create another keyframe at the 00;00;00;00 mark.

7 Drag the new keyframe all the way down to create the start of the fade in. The text box should display –oo dB to resemble the mathematical symbol –∞ for negative infinity.

8 To hear this change, press the Home key, and then press the spacebar to play. You'll hear the soundtrack fade in over the first second of the production rather than starting at full strength.

9 Save your project as **Lesson09_Work.prel**.

● **Note:** You can easily fade your audio in and out by right-clicking any audio track and choosing Fade > Fade In Audio or Fade Out Audio, whichever applies. This inserts the selected effect using the duration selected as the default for audio transitions.

Working with the Audio Mixer

If, for some reason, SmartMix doesn't produce the result you want, you have an alternative: Adobe Premiere Elements' Audio Mixer. Using the Audio Mixer, you can adjust the volume and balance of the different audio tracks as the audio plays, so you can make sure your audience hears what you want it to hear. For example, you can lower the volume for the soundtrack during the narration and increase it again during the slide show at the end of the project when the narration is complete.

Let's start fresh by reloading Lesson09_Start_Win.prel (Windows) or Lesson09_Start_Mac.prel (Mac OS) and then the narration and background music clips.

1 In the Adobe Premiere Elements main menu, choose File > Open Project. Navigate to your Lesson09 folder and select the project file Lesson09_Start_Win.prel (Windows) or Lesson09_Start_Mac.prel (Mac OS). Click the Open (Windows) or Choose (Mac OS) button to open your project.

2 Press the Home key to move the current-time indicator to the start of the clip.

3 Click the Project Assets button to open that panel. Then drag the narration.wav clip from the Project Assets panel and drop it onto the start of the Narration track in the timeline.

4 Let's Normalize the audio volume in narration.wav. Right-click narration.wav and choose Audio Gain to open the Clip Gain dialog. Then click the Normalize button.

5 Now let's add the background music track, which SmartSound should have added in a Sonicfire Pro subfolder in the Lesson09 folder. Choose File > Add Media from > Files and Folders, click open the Lesson09/Sonicfire Pro folder, select the file Future Progress-Frontier, and click Open (Windows) or Import (Mac OS).

6 Drag the Future Progress-Frontier clip from the Project Assets panel and drop it onto the Soundtrack track in the timeline at the start of the movie.

7 If it isn't there already, press the Home key to place the current-time indicator at the beginning of the movie. Press the spacebar to begin playing your video. You should hear the same familiar mess that you started with.

8 When you're finished previewing the movie, press the spacebar and then press the Home key again to set the current-time indicator right at the beginning of the video, which is where you want to start mixing audio.

● **Note:** At times, the Audio Mixer opens in a truncated window that shows only a portion of the first audio track. If this happens, click and drag the lower-right edge to the right until it looks like the figure.

9 In the center of the Action bar, click the Tools button (✕ Tools ▾) to open the Tools panel. Click Audio Mixer to open the Audio Mixer.

10 Your Audio Mixer panel shows five audio tracks, but only the first four—Audio 1, Narration, Soundtrack, and Audio 2—contain audio. You can ignore Audio 3.

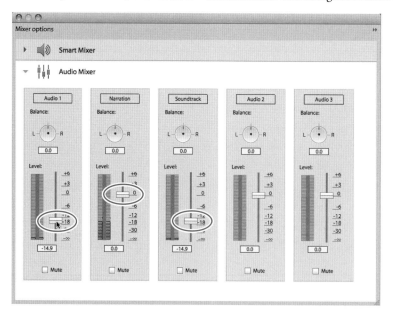

11 Press the spacebar to begin playback.

12 Grab the levels handles for Audio 1, Narration, and Soundtrack, and adjust them as desired while the video plays. Good luck. Note that all adjustments made via the Audio Mixer will be reflected as keyframes on the audio track but will become visible only after you stop playback.

13 When you're done making adjustments, press the spacebar to stop playback and then close the Mixer options window.

Edit to the beat of your favorite song

You can use Adobe Premiere Elements' Beat Detect tool to automatically add markers at the beats of your musical soundtrack. Beat detection makes it easy to synchronize slide shows or video edits to your music.

1 Add an audio clip or a video clip that includes audio to the Soundtrack track.

2 Right-click the audio track and choose Beat Detect. The Beat Detect Settings dialog opens.

3 In the Beat Detect Settings dialog, specify the settings as desired and click OK (in most instances, the default settings should be fine).

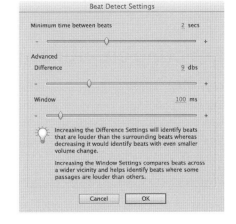

4 Adobe Premiere Elements opens a Beats track beneath the timescale with markers corresponding to the beats in the soundtrack. To "edit to the beat," make sure that your cuts from shot to shot or picture to picture occur at a marker.

Working with sound effects

In most projects, the primary audio-related variable that you'll adjust is volume, and you've explored a number of techniques to accomplish that here. In addition, Adobe Premiere Elements has multiple audio effects that you can use to further enhance your projects, including controlling the volumes and frequencies of the different channels in your audio

files, detecting and removing tape noise, eliminating background noise, and adding the reverberation of sounds to give ambience and warmth to the audio clip. If you have any audio clips with excessive background noise, or hiss or hum, you should give these effects a try.

You can find the audio effects in the Effects panel by choosing Audio Effects in the Effect Type list box, but only in Expert view. You apply audio effects by dragging them onto the target audio clip. You can then configure them in the Applied Effects panel. If any of the effects look particularly interesting, you can search Adobe Premiere Elements Help for more details.

Exploring on your own

Great news: You've finished another lesson and learned the basics of working with sound. Specifically, you learned to create a custom-length soundtrack with SmartSound, add narration to your projects, use SmartMix to adjust audio gain directly, and create and adjust keyframes.

But you're not finished yet. The best way to master the audio tools in Adobe Premiere Elements is to continue to explore them. Try the following:

- Experiment with different songs available in SmartSound. Think of some upcoming projects (birthdays, holidays, vacations), and try to find the appropriate tracks for those videos.

- Experiment with various audio effects, such as Delay and Channel Volume. A description of the audio effects in Adobe Premiere Elements can be found in the "Audio Effects" section of Adobe Premiere Elements Help.

- As you did for the fade in of the soundtrack, create a fade out for the soundtrack at the end of your project.

Review questions

1 What is a waveform, and why are waveforms so important?

2 What is SmartMix, and when should you use it?

3 What is the Audio Mixer, and how do you access it?

4 How would you change the volume of a clip over time using keyframes?

5 What is Normalization, and how is it different from adjusting audio volume directly?

Review answers

1 Waveforms are graphical representations of audio in a file. They're important because they instantly reveal details about the clip's content and volume that direct many loudness adjustments.

2 SmartMix is a feature that lets you identify which audio track(s) you want in the foreground and which ones you want in the background. It automatically adjusts the volume of the background clips to ensure that the foreground clip—usually speech or narration—is clearly audible. You should use SmartMix whenever you're trying to mix two or more audio tracks, especially when one contains narration or other dialogue and the other contains ambient noise and/or background music.

3 Using the Audio Mixer, you can easily adjust the audio balance and volume for different tracks in your project. You can refine the settings while listening to audio tracks and viewing video tracks. Each track in the Audio Mixer corresponds to an audio track in the timeline and is named accordingly. You can access the Audio Mixer by clicking Tools in the Action bar.

4 Each clip in the Adobe Premiere Elements timeline has a yellow volume graph that controls the keyframes of the clip. To add keyframes, Ctrl-click (Windows) or Command-click (Mac OS) the line. You must have at least two keyframes with different values to automatically change the volume level of an audio clip. You can also use the Audio Mixer to set keyframes to change the volume of your audio clip over time.

5 Normalization boosts the audio volume of all samples of an audio clip the same amount, stopping when further volume increases would produce distortion in the loudest sections of the clip. When you boost volume manually, you run the risk of causing distortion.

10 CREATING MENUS

Lesson overview

In this lesson, you'll create a menu for a movie to be recorded on a DVD, Blu-ray, or AVCHD disc, or to a web DVD. You can follow along with most of this lesson, even if your system does not have a disc recorder, although it will be helpful if it does. You'll learn how to add menu markers that allow your viewers direct access to scenes in your movies and how to create and customize disc menus. You'll also learn how to preview a menu and then burn a disc for playback on a standard DVD or Blu-ray Disc player. Specifically, you'll learn how to do the following:

- Add menu markers to your movie
- Create an auto-play disc
- Use templates to create disc menus
- Customize the look of the menus
- Preview a disc menu
- Record a DVD, Blu-ray, or AVCHD disc
- Create and upload a web DVD

You can create menus for your optical disc or web DVD projects in either Quick or Expert view. I have a strong feeling that most readers who have made it this far are now comfortable in Expert view, so you'll work in that view in this lesson.

 This lesson will take approximately two hours.

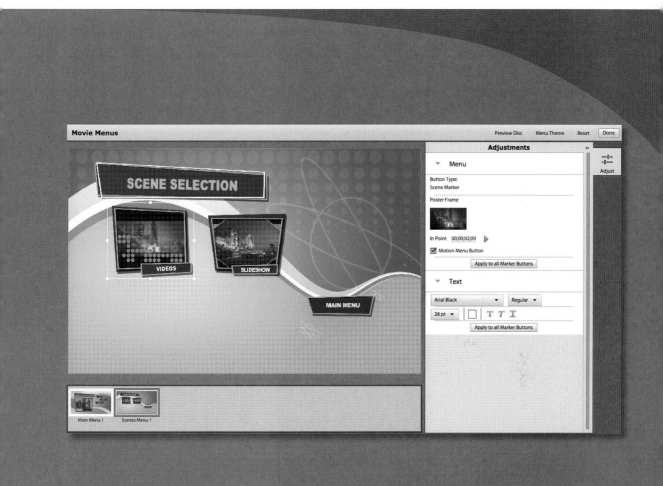

Creating a DVD with menus.

Getting started

Note: If you purchased the downloadable version of Adobe Premiere Elements, using the menus demonstrated in this chapter will involve a download that could be lengthy depending upon the speed of your Internet connection. For example, on a connection with about 10 Mbps download speed, the required components downloaded in about five minutes. If possible, start running the first exercise to download these materials in advance of the time you actually intend to start the exercise. That way, the materials that you need will already be downloaded. If you can't, we apologize in advance for any delays.

To begin, launch Adobe Premiere Elements, open the Lesson10 project, and review a final version of that project.

1 Before you begin, make sure that you have correctly copied the Lesson10 folder from the DVD in the back of this book onto your computer's hard drive. See "Copying the Classroom in a Book files" in the "Getting Started" section at the beginning of this book.

2 Launch Adobe Premiere Elements. If it is already open, choose Help > Welcome Screen in the Adobe Premiere Elements menu to return to the Welcome screen.

3 In the Welcome screen, click Video Editor, select Existing Project, and click the Open folder.

4 In the Open Project dialog, navigate to the Lesson10 folder you copied to your hard drive, select the file Lesson10_End_Win.prel (Windows) or Lesson10_End_Mac.prel (Mac OS), and then click Open. If a dialog appears asking for the location of rendered files, click the Skip Previews button.

A finished version of the project file you will create in this lesson opens. You may review it now or at any point during the lesson to get a sense of what your project should look like.

5 In the Action bar at the bottom of the Adobe Premiere Elements interface, click Tools (✕ Tools ▾) to open the Tools panel. Click Movie Menu to open Menu Theme panel.

6 At the top of the Menu Theme panel, click the drop down list and choose General to open that folder, and click to choose the Fun theme. Then, on the bottom right of the panel, click Continue. If the template isn't installed on your system, Adobe Premiere Elements will auto-

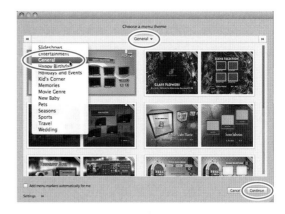

matically download it. As noted in the margin, download time will depend upon your Internet connection speed, but should take no more than 5–10 minutes. Once the menu downloads, Premiere Elements will enter the Disc Layout workspace.

7 On the upper right of that workspace, click Preview Disc (Preview Disc) to open the Preview Disc window.

The Preview Disc window allows you to view and test your menus as they will appear when played on an optical disc or web DVD.

8   In the Preview Disc window, click the Scene Selection button in the main menu to switch to the Scene Selection menu. Click either button to begin playing the selection. As with chapters in a Hollywood DVD, these are links to scenes on the timeline that you'll create in the first exercise.

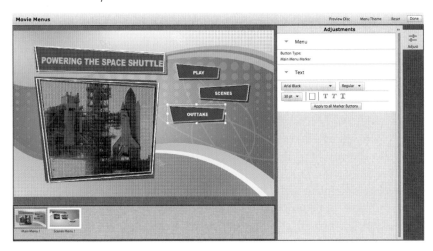

9   Press the spacebar to stop playback, and then close the Preview Disc window by clicking the Exit button ( ) in the lower-right corner of the window.

10 After reviewing the finished file, choose File > Open Project and select the file Lesson10_Start_Win.prel (Windows) or Lesson10_Start_Mac.prel (Mac OS). Click No when the dialog asks if you want to save changes to Lesson10_End_Win.prel (Windows) or Lesson10_End_Mac.prel (Mac OS). If a dialog appears asking for the location of rendered files, click the Skip Previews button.

11 Choose Window > Restore Workspace to ensure that you start the lesson in the default layout.

Understanding DVD, Blu-ray, and AVCHD discs, plus web DVDs

DVD is a generic term that encompasses a few different formats. The format you'll work with in Adobe Premiere Elements is commonly referred to as DVD-Video. In terms of disc content and playability, this is the same type of DVD that you can purchase or rent and play on a DVD player connected to your TV set or on a computer fitted with the appropriate drive. Adobe Premiere Elements can burn single-layer (4.7 GB) and dual-layer (8.5 GB) DVD media.

A Blu-ray Disc—often abbreviated as BD—is an optical disc format that can store 25 GB on a single-layer disc or 50 GB on a dual-layer disc. It gets its name from the blue-violet laser a Blu-ray player uses to read it (as opposed to the red laser used by CD and DVD players and drives).

An AVCHD disc is a traditional DVD that contains HD video in AVCHD format but not the menus you can create for standard DVDs or standard Blu-ray Discs. AVCHD discs are playable on Blu-ray players and some computers but not traditional DVD players. The key benefit of the AVCHD disc is that it enables you to burn HD content to inexpensive DVD media without purchasing a Blu-ray Disc recorder, which makes it a wonderfully convenient way to affordably view and share your HD content on Blu-ray players.

To make a DVD, Blu-ray, or AVCHD disc in Adobe Premiere Elements, you must have a compatible DVD or Blu-ray Disc burner. It's important to note that although your system may have a DVD or Blu-ray Disc player, it may not be a recordable drive, also known as a DVD or Blu-ray Disc writer or burner. A computer drive that's described as DVD-ROM or BD-ROM will play only DVDs or Blu-ray Discs, not record them. (But a BD-ROM/DVD-R/CD-R drive will play Blu-ray Discs, play and record DVDs, and play and record CDs.) Check your computer's system specifications to see which drive (if any) you have. Drives capable of recording DVDs and Blu-ray Discs are also available as external hardware. Often, such external recordable drives are connected through your system's IEEE 1394 port, although some drives connect through the USB port.

Note that the process of authoring your projects or creating menus and menu markers is identical for Blu-ray Discs and DVDs. You'll designate which type of disc to record just before you burn the disc in the final exercise of this lesson.

In contrast to the other disc-based options discussed previously, a web DVD is a collection of files that you upload to a website to display your content online—complete with the menus and interactivity available for disc-based output. As you'll learn in the section "Creating web DVDs," you create the files using a separate option in the Publish+Share panel, and then upload them to a website for hosting. In previous versions of Adobe Premiere Elements, you had the option to host the files on Photoshop.com, but that service has been discontinued.

Physical media

The type of disc onto which you'll record your video is important. You should be aware of two basic formats: recordable (DVD-R and DVD+R for DVD and AVCHD discs, BD-R for Blu-ray Discs) and rewritable (DVD-RW and DVD+RW for DVDs and AVCHD discs, BD-RE for Blu-ray Discs). Recordable discs are single-use discs; once you record data onto a recordable disc, you cannot erase the data. Rewritable discs can be used multiple times, much like the floppy disks of old.

Also available are dual-layer DVD-Recordable discs (DVD-R DL and DVD+R DL) that offer 8.5 GB of storage space instead of the 4.7 GB of standard DVD-R, DVD+R, DVD-RW, and DVD+RW discs. Dual-layer BD-R discs, featuring 50 GB of storage space, are also available.

So which format should you choose? The first thing to note is that DVD-R and DVD+R discs are 100 percent interchangeable. Any drive that records one will record the other, and the same players and drives that play one will almost certainly play the other, at least with single-layer media. It's the same with DVD-RW and DVD+RW. In the very early days of DVD, there was a meaningful distinction between the – and + formats, but it's been irrelevant for more than a decade now.

Compatibility is one of the major issues with recordable disc formats. On the DVD side, many older DVD players may not recognize some rewritable discs created on a newer DVD burner, for example. Compatibility is also more of a concern with dual-layer media than with single-layer discs. Another issue is that, as of this writing, the media for recordable discs is less expensive than the media for rewritable discs (usually much less than $1 per disc). However, if you make a mistake with a recordable disc, you must use another disc, whereas with a rewritable disc you can erase the content and use the disc again. For this reason, I suggest using rewritable discs for making your test discs and then using recordable discs for final or extra copies.

On the Blu-ray Disc side, playback compatibility is at least a minor issue with all media. But because the BD-R and BD-RE formats were developed at the same time, BD-RE discs are just as likely to play in a given player as their BD-R counterparts. That said, BD-R discs have come down in price to well under a dollar in quantities of 25+, whereas BD-RE discs remain quite a bit more expensive, so you'll probably find BD-R discs more cost-effective, even though they can't be erased and reused. Dual- or Double-Layer BD-R Discs sell online for under $2 per disc.

Manually adding scene markers

When you're watching a DVD or Blu-ray Disc movie, you normally have the option to jump to the beginning of the next chapter by clicking a button on the remote control. To specify the start of chapters or sections in your project, you must add scene markers.

● **Note:** This project is only about two minutes long due to necessary limitations on the file size. Most projects would likely be longer, but the basic principles remain the same.

1   Scroll through the entire movie in the timeline. This project consists of two main sections, the videos and the slide show. You will place scene markers at the beginning of each section so your viewers can access these sections more easily during playback. You'll start by adding the marker for the videos.

2 Click anywhere in the timeline, and then press the Home key to move the current-time indicator to the start of the movie. Then press the Page Down key to move to the start of Video 1.mp4.

3 On the top left of the timeline, click the Markers drop-down list box (▼ Markers ▼), and choose Menu Marker > Set Menu Marker. The Menu Marker panel opens.

● **Note:** When you click the Add Marker button in Quick view, the Menu Marker dialog opens automatically (you don't have to choose Menu Marker). The reason is that the other two marker-related options available in Expert view, TimeLine Markers and Beat Markers, are not available in Quick view, so the only kind of marker you can create in Quick view is a Menu Marker.

4 You'll work more with this panel later in this lesson; for now, just click OK to close the panel.

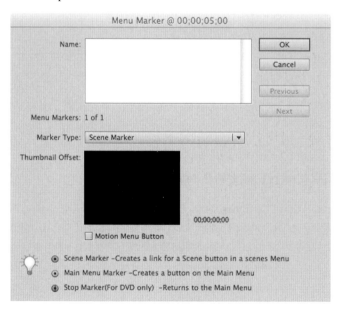

5 Notice the green scene marker icon added on the time ruler.

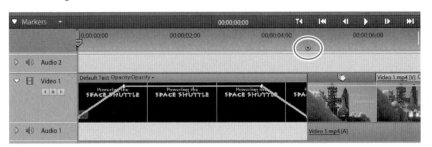

Note: You may have to move the current-time indicator and zoom into the video project to better see the green scene marker. For example, in the figure, the current-time indicator is at the start of the project.

6 At the top of the Monitor panel, click the Quick button to switch to Quick view. Notice that the marker looks identical in this view.

7 Click the Expert button at the top of the Monitor panel to return to that view.

8 Drag the current-time indicator to the start of the slide show, which should be around 00;01;16;08.

9 Right-click the time ruler at the current-time indicator and choose Set Menu Marker. Click OK to close the Menu Marker panel.

You should now have two markers in your project, one for each section of this short movie.

Creating an auto-play disc

Most professional DVDs and Blu-ray Discs have menus to help viewers navigate through the disc content. You will work with menus shortly, but there is a quick and easy way to produce a disc without menus: creating an auto-play disc. An auto-play disc is similar to videotape: When you place the disc into a player, it will begin playing automatically. There is no navigation, although viewers can jump from scene to scene—defined by the markers you just added—using a remote control.

Auto-play discs are convenient for short projects that don't require a menu or as a mechanism for sharing unfinished projects for review. For most longer or finished projects, you'll probably prefer to create a menu.

As you'll see, the procedure for creating an auto-play disc is simple: Just burn the disc without applying a menu. Here are the steps.

1   On the extreme upper right of the Adobe Premiere Elements interface, click Publish+Share (Publish+Share ▾), and choose Disc.

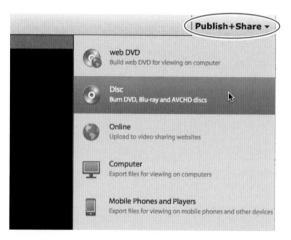

2   Adobe Premiere Elements opens the Missing Disc Menu dialog. To burn an auto-play disc, click No.

3 The Disc Burning panel opens. We cover the options in this panel near the end of this chapter in the section "Burning DVD, Blu-ray, and AVCHD discs." To actually burn a disc now, jump ahead to that section. To continue on to the next exercise, click the Back button, and then click anywhere in the Monitor panel to close the Publish+Share panel.

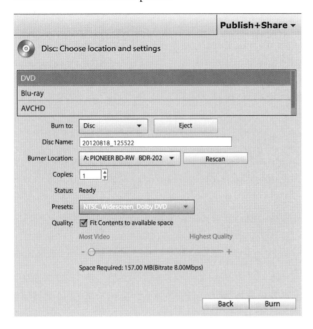

Note: There's no need to preview before burning an auto-play disc, but if you'd like to, add a menu as detailed in "Creating a disc with menus" section. Then, above the Adjustments panel on the upper right, click Reset to remove the menu. This will remove the menu so you can burn an auto-play disc and allow you to preview as well. Use this same procedure to create a disc with automatically generated scene markers. When you're ready to burn the disc, follow the same procedure detailed in this exercise.

4 Choose File > Save As and save this project file to your Lesson10 folder as **Lesson10_Work.prel**.

Automatically generating scene markers

Manually placing markers in the timeline, as you did in the first exercise in this lesson, gives you ultimate control over the placement of your markers. For long videos, however, you may not want to place all the markers by hand. To make the process of placing markers easy, Adobe Premiere Elements can create markers automatically based on several configurable parameters.

1 Choose File > Save As and save the **Lesson10_Work.prel** project file in your Lesson10 folder as **Lesson10_Markers.prel**. You'll return to **Lesson10_Work.prel** after you finish exploring the automatic generation of scene markers.

2 In the Action bar at the bottom of the Adobe Premiere Elements interface, click Tools (✗ Tools) to open the Tools panel. Click Movie Menu to open the Menu Theme panel.

3 In the lower-left corner of the Menu Theme panel, click Settings (Settings ») to expose the scene marker options.

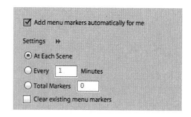

4 The "Add menu markers automatically for me" check box is selected by default. To automatically create menu markers, click the "Add menu markers automatically for me" check box to select it if it's not already selected. Then choose one of the following three options:

- Click the At Each Scene radio button to place a marker at the start of each video clip in your project. Leave this option selected for now.

- Click the Every *X* Minutes radio button and enter the duration in minutes to insert a marker at the designated interval in the project. Do not select this option for this exercise.

- Click the Total Markers radio button and enter the number of markers in the designated field. Adobe Premiere Elements will insert the designated number of markers at even intervals in the project. Do not select this option for this exercise.

5 The "Clear existing menu markers" check box will delete any existing markers. Select this to remove the markers you created manually earlier.

6 At the top of the Menu Theme panel, click the folder list box and choose General. Then click the Fun theme.

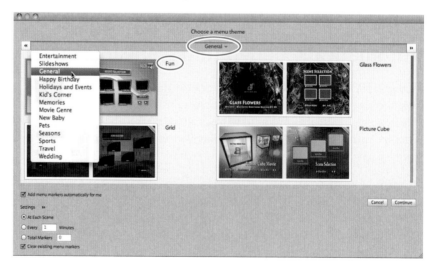

7 On the bottom right of the Menu Theme panel, click Continue. If you haven't downloaded the Fun theme previously, Adobe Premiere Elements will download it now, so you must be connected to the Internet. After downloading is complete, Adobe Premiere Elements will apply the theme, add the automatic menu markers at the start of each video clip, and enter the Disc Layout workspace.

8 On the upper right of the Disc Layout workspace, click Preview Disc (Preview Disc) to open the Preview Disc panel.

9 In the Preview Disc window, click the Play button (▶) to begin playing your project. Once the first video clip begins playing, click the Next Scene button (▶❙) repeatedly and notice how the video jumps from scene to scene.

10 Click the Exit button (⊠ EXIT) on the bottom right of the Preview Disc window to close it.

11 On the upper right of the Movie Menu workspace, click Menu Theme (Menu Theme) to reopen that panel. Click Settings to expose the automatic marker settings.

12 Click the "Add menu markers automatically for me" checkbox (if not already selected), then click the Total Markers option, type **4** into the number field, and select the "Clear existing menu markers" check box. Then click Continue.

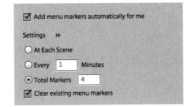

Four markers are now evenly spread out across the timeline.

Using the Total Markers option may be preferable to creating a marker for every clip to reduce the number of scenes in your movie.

13 Choose File > Save to save Lesson10_Markers.prel. Then choose File > Open Recent Project > Lesson10_Work.prel to return to the project file from the previous exercise.

Creating a disc with menus

Building an auto-play disc as you did in the previous exercise is the quickest way to go from an Adobe Premiere Elements project to an optical disc you can watch in your living room. However, auto-play discs lack the ability to jump directly to different scenes, as well as other navigational features that most users expect when watching a DVD, Blu-ray Disc, or AVCHD disc. You can quickly create such navigation menus in Adobe Premiere Elements using a variety of templates designed for this purpose.

1 In the Action bar at the bottom of the Adobe Premiere Elements interface, click Tools (✕ Tools) to open the Tools panel. Click Movie Menu to open the Menu Theme panel.

2   At the top of the Menu Theme panel, click the folder list box and choose General. Then click the Fun theme. Note that Adobe Premiere Elements ships with many distinctive menu templates—predesigned and customizable menus that come in a variety of themes and styles. The Fun theme is topical, and once you finish customizing it, it will look and sound entirely appropriate. For your own projects, you should be able to find a template with a theme that matches your content, particularly for family-related events.

3   On the bottom left of the Menu Theme panel, make sure the "Add menu markers automatically" check box is not selected. You want to use the markers that you manually created in a previous exercise.

4   On the bottom right of the Menu Theme panel, click Continue. If you haven't downloaded the Fun theme previously, Adobe Premiere Elements will download it now, so you must be connected to the Internet. After downloading the theme, Adobe Premiere Elements will apply the theme and enter the Disc Layout workspace.

Each template contains a main menu and a Scene Selection menu. The main menu is the first screen that the viewer sees when the disc is played. The Scene Selection menu is a secondary panel accessed when the viewer clicks the Scenes button in the Main menu (or the equivalent of that button in other templates).

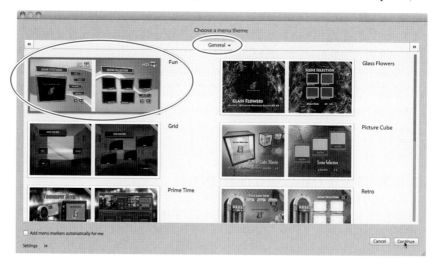

● **Note:** To replace a template after you've selected it, click the Menu Theme button on the far upper right of the Disc Layout workspace to reopen the Menu Theme panel. Choose a different theme in that panel and click Continue; Adobe Premiere Elements will replace the existing theme with the newly selected theme. Be sure to recheck your Menu Marker settings when you're changing themes because Adobe Premiere Elements seems to select the "Add menu markers automatically" check box each time you open the Menu Theme panel.

5 At the bottom left of the Disc Layout workspace, click to select Main Menu 1 if it's not already selected. You see three text objects in the WYSIWYG preview area: Movie Title Here, Play, and Scenes. The first is a simple text title that you'll customize to match the project.

The second two are button links that your viewers will use to access the content in the project, clicking Play to start the video playing from the start and Scenes to access the Scene Selection menu. The text in both is fine so you'll leave them alone.

6 When you're producing an optical disc, safe zones for titles can be important, so let's make sure your safe zones are showing. If they're not, right-click in the WYSIWYG (What You See Is What You Get) preview area and choose Show Safe Margins.

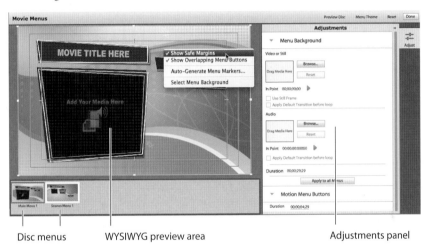

Disc menus   WYSIWYG preview area   Adjustments panel

7 Let's customize the movie title. In the preview area of the Disc Layout workspace, click the Movie Title Here text once. A thin, white rectangle appears around the button indicating that it is selected.

8 Double-click the Movie Title Here text to open the Change Text dialog. If the Movie Title Here text is not already highlighted, select it now, and then type **Powering the Space Shuttle**. Click OK to close the Change Text dialog and to apply the change.

9 Let's make the text smaller. Back in the preview window, click the text to make it active, and then on the right in the Adjustments panel, click the Font drop-down list box and choose 48 pt. It's still a bit snug against the background graphic. You'll fix that in a moment. Note that you can also change the font, font color, and other attributes, which you'll do to some button text later in the lesson.

10 On the extreme upper right of the Disc Layout workspace, click the Preview Disc (Preview Disc) button to preview the main menu. Place your pointer over the Play and Scenes buttons, but don't click them yet. Notice the three circles that appear over each button as the pointer passes over the text. This rollover effect is part of the menu template and shows viewers which button they're selecting. Click the Play button and the movie begins to play.

● **Note:** Rollover effects like the circles in this example vary from template to template. Sometimes they are a symbol of some kind and sometimes a color change. However, there will always be some visual cue as to which button is about to be selected.

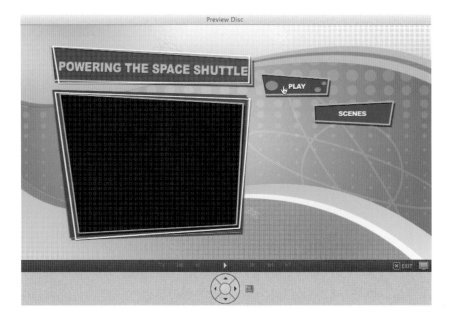

11 As the movie is playing, you can use the DVD-remote-like controls below the preview window to control playback. To return to the main menu of your project during your testing, click the Main Menu button (▣) at the bottom of the Preview Disc window.

12 Click the Exit button (▣ EXIT) on the bottom right of the Preview Disc window to close it.

13 Choose File > Save to save your project file.

OK, so you've changed the text in the title and resized it to fit within the text background. Next, you'll customize the Scene Marker buttons, and then you'll insert a video into the drop zone in the main menu and add a soundtrack to the main menu.

Modifying Scene Marker buttons

One of the benefits of optical discs and web DVDs is the ability to jump quickly to specific scenes in a movie. For each scene marker you add in the timeline, Adobe Premiere Elements automatically generates a Scene Marker button on the Scenes menu. If you have more scene markers than scenes on a Scenes menu, Adobe Premiere Elements creates additional Scenes menu pages and navigational buttons to jump back and forth between the pages.

If the template that you selected has image thumbnails on the Scenes menu, as the menu you're working with does, Adobe Premiere Elements automatically assigns an image thumbnail to it. You can customize the appearance of a Scene Marker button by providing a name for the label and changing the image thumbnail used to identify the scene.

Changing button labels and image thumbnails

Let's begin by opening the Scenes menu.

1 Click the Scenes Menu 1 thumbnail in the lower-left corner of the Disc Layout workspace to view the Scenes menu.

Adobe Premiere Elements has generated the two Scene Marker buttons and their image thumbnails based on the scene markers you added in the first exercise. By default, Adobe Premiere Elements named the Scene Marker buttons Scene One and Scene Two, although this will vary according to the template. You'll customize these for your content shortly.

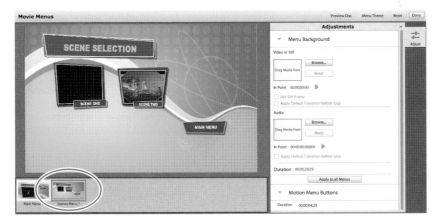

In addition, by default, the thumbnail in the Scene Marker button is the first frame of the clip the button links to. This doesn't work well for the first thumbnail, because it's obscured by a fade from black, so viewers can't easily discern the content of the scene. You'll fix that in a moment.

2 In the Disc Layout workspace, double-click the Scene One button to open the Menu Marker panel for the first marker. In the Name field, type **Videos**.

3 In the Thumbnail Offset section, notice that the timecode is set to 00:00;00;00. Place your pointer over the timecode, drag to the right to about 00;00;02;00, and then release the pointer to freeze the movie at that location. Or, click the time counter and enter the timecode directly. Click OK, and Adobe Premiere Elements updates the button name and image thumbnail in the Scene Selection menu.

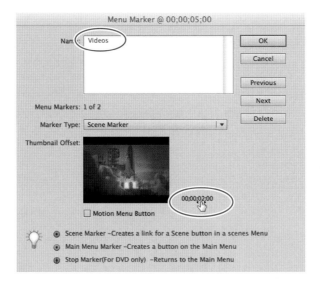

Note: You opened the Menu Marker dialog briefly when you were creating markers on the timeline in the first exercise. Had you customized the name field then, Adobe Premiere Elements would have used the name that you entered, not the default name. If you know the button name you want to use when you create the menu marker on the timeline, it's more efficient to enter it then. Just keep it short.

Next, you'll change the name of the remaining button.

4 Double-click the second button, Scene Two, to open the Menu Marker window. Type **Slideshow** into the name field and click OK. (You'll leave this image thumbnail on the default frame.) Adobe Premiere Elements updates the button name in the Scene Selection menu.

5 When you're finished, click the Preview Disc button on the upper right to open the Preview Disc window. Click the Scenes button to navigate to the Scene Selection menu. Notice that Adobe Premiere Elements has updated the button names and thumbnails.

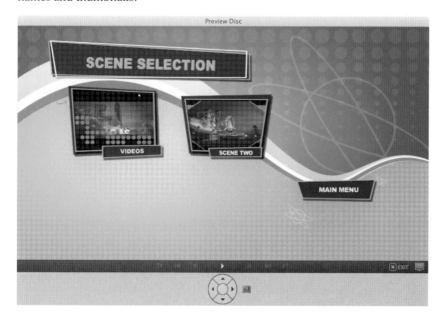

6 At the bottom of the Preview Disc window you can see a group of navigation buttons, which simulate the controls on a DVD remote control. Click any of the arrows to advance through the Scene Menu buttons, and click the center circle (the Enter button) to play that scene. Adobe Premiere Elements automatically controls the navigation of all menu buttons, so you should preview all scenes on the disc to ensure that you placed your markers where you want them. When you're done, click the Exit button (![EXIT]) to close the Preview Disc window.

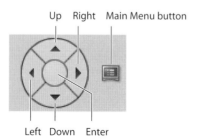

7 Choose File > Save to save your project file.

Working with submenus

Before you start customizing menu appearance, you should be aware of some other navigation and button placement options. For example, on the DVDs of many Hollywood movies, you'll find a link on the main menu to bonus or outtake clips sections accessed via submenus. Adobe Premiere Elements lets you create a sub-menu button on your main menu by adding a special menu marker.

In addition, by default, once a viewer starts watching any portion of the movie, the video will continue on to the end, even if there are intervening scene markers. In the project you've been working on, this isn't a problem, but with other projects, you may want to stop playback after a scene completes and return the viewer to the menu. You can accomplish this by using the stop marker discussed here.

In this exercise, you'll add a stop marker to your project and a button on the main menu linking to a bonus video clip.

1   In the lower-left corner of the Disc Layout workspace, click to select Main Menu 1. Currently, two buttons are in this menu: the Play and Scenes buttons.

2   Click in the timescale above the timeline to select the timeline. Press the End key to move the current-time indicator to the end of the last clip.

You will now add a special marker to the end of your movie.

3   Right-click the time ruler at the current-time indicator and choose Set Menu Marker. The Menu Marker panel opens.

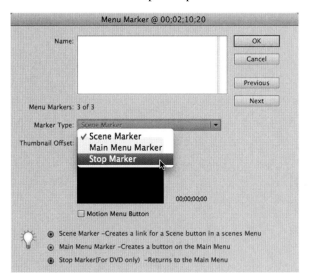

4   Choose Stop Marker from the Marker Type menu. When a stop marker is reached during playback, the viewer will return to the main menu.

5   Click OK to add the stop marker. In the timeline, stop markers are colored red to help you differentiate them from the green scene markers and the blue main menu markers. You will learn more about main menu markers later in this lesson.

Next, you'll add an additional clip named Outtake.mp4 to the end of the timeline. This clip will be a bonus clip that users can access from the main menu but is not part of the main movie. You can't do this from the Disc Layout workspace, so you'll have to exit that first.

6   In the upper-right corner of the Disc Layout workspace, click Done (Done) to close that workspace and return to the main Adobe Premiere Elements workspace. Use the slider bar on the bottom and zoom controls to configure your interface like the next figure so you can see the end of the project and have room to drag a file onto the Video 1 track.

7   In the upper-left corner of the Adobe Premiere Elements interface, click Project Assets (Project Assets) to open that panel, and drag the slider on the right down to locate Outtake.mp4 (which is actually a pretty cool shot of the Space Station). Then drag the Outtake.mp4 clip into the Video 1 track after the credit title sequence at the end of your timeline. Be sure to place the clip a few seconds after the last clip, leaving a gap between the clips.

8 Press the Page Down key to advance the current-time indicator to the beginning of the added Outtake.mp4 clip, and then right-click and choose Set Menu Marker to open the Menu Marker dialog.

9 In the Menu Marker dialog, choose Main Menu Marker from the Marker Type menu. In the name field, type **Outtake**, and then click OK to close the Menu Marker dialog.

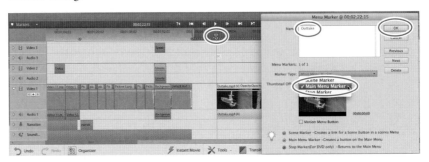

Adobe Premiere Elements adds a button named Outtake to Main Menu 1 in the Disc Layout workspace.

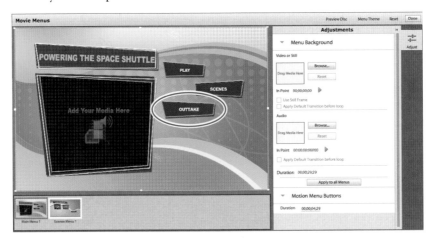

10 Let's return to the Disc Layout workspace. In the Action bar at the bottom of the Adobe Premiere Elements interface, click Tools (✗ Tools ·) to open the Tools panel. Click Movie Menu to enter the Disc Layout workspace.

11 Click the Preview Disc button, and then click the Outtake button to play that video. When the clip has finished playing, the main menu appears. If you play the main movie from start to finish, the video will stop after the credits because of the stop marker you added, and you will not see the Outtake.mp4 clip.

12 Close the Preview Disc window.

13 Choose File > Save to save your project file.

Three types of menu markers

There are three types of menu markers that you can apply in Adobe Premiere Elements. Each one appears and functions differently within the interface and your projects, as described here:

- **Scene markers (◉):** Adding a scene marker to your timeline automatically adds a Scenes button to the Scenes menu of your disc. Scenes menus are secondary to the main menu. A Scenes button on the main menu will link to the Scenes menu.

- **Main menu markers (◉):** Adding a main menu marker to your timeline automatically adds a button to the main menu of your disc. Most templates have space for either three or four buttons on the first menu page. The Play button and the Scenes button are present by default. This will leave you with space for one or two more buttons, depending on the template you've chosen. If you add more main menu markers to your movie, Adobe Premiere Elements will create a secondary main menu.

- **Stop markers (◉):** Adding a stop marker to your timeline forces Adobe Premiere Elements to stop playback of your timeline and return the viewer to the main menu. Use stop markers to control the viewer's flow through the movie. For example, if you want the viewer to return to the main menu after each scene, insert a stop marker at the end of each scene. You can also use stop markers to add bonus or deleted scenes after the main movie, linking to this content using either scene or main menu markers.

Customizing menus with video, still images, and audio

You can customize your menus in Adobe Premiere Elements by adding a still image, video, or audio to the menu. You can also combine multiple items, such as a still photo and an audio clip. Alternatively, you can add a video clip and replace the audio track with a separate audio clip.

Although Adobe Premiere Elements allows you to customize a disc menu, keep in mind that changes made will not be saved back to the template; they apply only to the current project.

Adding a still image or video clip to your menu

When you're adding visual content to a menu, you'll use the same procedure regardless of whether it's a still image or a video clip. In this exercise, you'll insert a video clip into a menu. By default, when you insert a video, the audio plays with the video as well, although you can change this by inserting a separate audio file, as you'll do later.

Note: You'd follow this same procedure to select a still image or video either to fit into the drop zone or to use as a full-screen background image.

Follow this procedure to add a video clip to your menu.

1   In the lower-left corner of the Disc Layout workspace, click to select Main Menu 1 and then click anywhere on the menu background to open those controls in the Adjustment panel.

2   In the Adjustments panel, in the Menu Background box, click the Browse button, navigate to the Lesson10 folder, and choose Menu.mp4. Click Open to close the dialog and insert the clip into the menu.

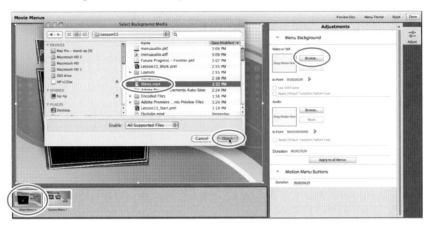

● **Note:** In the pre-release versions of software that I used while writing this book, I had issues with the Space Shuttle not being centered in the drop zone playback window. If Menu.mp4 is positioned off-center, try using Menu1.mp4, which is also in the Lesson10 folder.

3   Note the options available in the Menu Background box in the Adjustments panel. Specifically, you can do the following:

   •   Play the video by clicking the green Play triangle (▷).

   •   Choose an In point for the video to start, either by dragging the time counter or by typing in the timecode for the desired starting point.

   •   After choosing an In point, you can select the Use Still Frame check box to use the current frame as the background or within the drop zone.

   •   Apply the default transition to the video clip before the menu starts to loop by selecting the "Apply Default Transition before loop" check box. Note that the maximum duration for video menus is 30 seconds, and that the menu will loop indefinitely after that time.

   For this exercise, leave the options at their default settings, and click Preview Disc to preview the menu. If it looks a bit jerky, don't sweat; it will look much smoother once it is rendered for your optical disc or web DVD.

4   Choose File > Save to save your project file.

When you add a video to a menu with a drop zone, as you just did, the video plays within that drop zone. When you add a video to a menu without a drop zone, the video plays in the background of the menu. Sometimes this works out well; sometimes it doesn't. For example, if you follow the same procedure to add a video clip in the background of Scenes Menu 1, you'll see that the video is almost totally obscured by graphics that you can't delete or replace.

Accordingly, to create a menu with your own full-screen still image or video in the background, choose a template without a drop zone or other graphic content that will obscure a video or still image. Check out the Faux Widescreen template in the General folder as an example.

If you opt to customize a menu with a full-screen background image or video, you can use the Apply to all Menus button on the Menu Background Adjustments panel to apply the background to all menus. You can also insert a different still image or video clip as a background in each menu, or simply use the background image included with the menu template.

Adding an audio clip to the background

Let's substitute a separate audio clip for the audio included with the Menu.mp4 video clip. Use this same procedure to add audio to any menu template, whether it is modified with a custom video or image background or used as is.

1   Click Main Menu 1 in the Disc Layout workspace to open the Adjustments panel.

2   Click the Browse button in the audio section, select the Menuaudio.aiff clip in the Lesson10 folder, and then click Open.

3   If you want to add a fade out so the audio loops nicely, select the "Apply Default Transition before loop" check box.

4   In the Disc Layout workspace, click the Preview Disc button. You can see the video and hear the audio track you selected for the main menu background.

    If the Audio controls are not showing, click the menu background in the Disc Layout workspace to reveal them.

5   Close the preview window.

6   If you want to remove the audio portion from the menu background, click the Reset button next to the speaker icon in the Audio section of the Adjustments panel (but for the purposes of this task, don't actually do this).

7   To insert the same video and audio file combination as background for your other menu, click the Apply to All Menus button in the Adjustments panel. Don't do this in this case, because the video will be obscured by the graphic in the Scene Selection menu.

8   Save your project.

Animating buttons

If the menu template that you select uses thumbnail scene buttons, you can elect to animate the buttons. With an animated button, a designated duration of video from the linked scene will play within the thumbnail while the menu displays. The main menu for this project does not include any buttons with image thumbnails. However, the Scenes menu does have image thumbnails. Let's animate these thumbnails.

1   In the lower-left corner of the Disc Layout workspace, select the Scenes Menu 1 thumbnail.

2   Click the Videos button to select it. Currently, this button displays a still frame extracted from the video clip at the 00;00;02;00 mark.

3   In the Adjustments panel, in the Menu box, scroll down if necessary to see all of the Poster Frame section, and then select the Motion Menu Button check box. Click the Apply to all Marker Buttons button to animate all Marker buttons.

● **Note:** You can't set the Out point or the end of clips in the Adjustments panel, but you can set all your motion menu buttons to be the same duration, as explained in the following steps.

4   If you want to change the In point of the video clip and play a different segment in the animated thumbnail, drag the time counter (which currently reads 00;00;02;00) to the desired spot.

5   Now let's set the duration of the motion menu buttons. To access that control, click an empty area of your background menu. This deselects the current scene button, and the Adjustments panel switches to the Menu Background properties. Scroll down to the bottom of the Adjustments panel, if necessary, to locate the Motion Menu Buttons box. If necessary, click the disclosure triangle to reveal the Duration control.

6   Note that the default duration for the Motion Menu Buttons is 00;00;04;29, which is the length of Video 1.mp4, the first clip after the scene marker. You can shorten this duration but not lengthen it. Note that the default duration will be as long as the first clip after the scene marker, up to 00;00;29;29, or just under 30 seconds.

7   Click the Preview Disc button in the Disc Layout workspace. In the main menu, click the Scenes button to access the Scene Selection menu. Both buttons should now be animated, which is definitely a bad idea for the Videos button, because the first video is so short. If you decide to use animated buttons, make sure the footage in the video works in the context of the motion menu and isn't just plain irritating.

8   Close the Preview Disc window.

9 If you want to pick a different In point for your thumbnail video, select the Motion Menu Button option and choose a suitable In point for the other scene button. If you didn't click the Apply to all Marker Buttons button in step 3, you must individually activate scene buttons to animate them. All animated buttons share the same duration.

10 Let's deselect Motion Menu Buttons for this project by clicking each button and deselecting the Motion Menu Button check box for each.

11 Save your project.

Customizing button size, location, and text attributes

Beyond adding still images, video, and audio to your menu, you can also change the size, appearance, and location of buttons and text on your menus. In this exercise, you'll make changes to your menu appearance and buttons.

1 Make sure you're in the Disc Layout workspace; if not, click Tools (✘ Tools ▾) in the Action bar at the bottom of the Adobe Premiere Elements interface, and select Movie Menu to enter the Disc Layout workspace.

2 Under Disc Menus in the Disc Layout workspace, click the Main Menu 1 thumbnail to make sure the main menu is loaded.

3 The background behind the text Powering the Space Shuttle is a bit small and the text looks cramped. Let's fix that. Click the background shape behind the text (not the text itself) and an eight-point bounding box opens. Place your pointer on the lower-right corner, and then drag it just a smidge to the right until the edge touches the Play button.

● **Note:** Scaling text boxes in this manner can be tricky because the width and height do not scale proportionally. Text can easily become distorted.

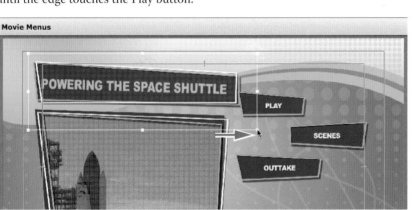

4 Click the text box Powering the Space Shuttle to make it active, and then drag it a bit to the right to center it within the newly enlarged background.

5   Click the Play button and drag that to the right to move it away from the Powering the Space Shuttle background. If you're feeling particularly persnickety, click and drag the Outtake button to the right to match.

6   Save your project.

● **Note:** All buttons and titles within Adobe Premiere Elements templates are designed to fall within the title-safe zone. If you plan to resize or move buttons or text on the menu, you should enable Show Safe Margins in the Disc Layout workspace by right-clicking the menu and choosing Show Safe Margins.

Overlapping buttons

Buttons on a disc menu should not overlap each other. If two or more buttons overlap, there is potential for confusion. Someone who is using a pointer to navigate and click the menu may not be able to access the correct button if another one is overlapping it. This can easily happen if button text is too long or if two buttons are placed too close to each other.

In some instances, you can fix overlapping buttons by shortening the button name or simply by moving the buttons to create more space between them. By default, overlapping buttons in Adobe Premiere Elements are outlined in red in the Disc Layout workspace. You can turn this feature on or off by right-clicking in the Disc Layout workspace and choosing Show Overlapping Menu Buttons from the menu.

Changing menu button text properties

The Adjustments panel lets you modify the font, size, color, and style of your menu buttons, and you can automatically apply changes made to one button to similar buttons. You can modify the text attributes of five types of objects: Menu Titles, which are text-only objects that aren't linked to clips or movies; Play buttons, which link to the beginning of your main movie; Scene Marker buttons, which link to the Scenes menu; Marker buttons, which directly link to a menu marker on the timeline; and Navigational buttons, such as the link back to the main menu in the Scenes menu.

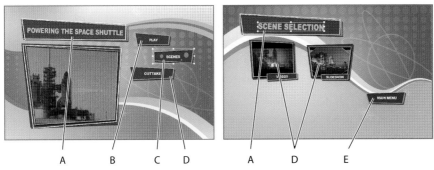

A   B   C   D   A   D   E

A. Text. B. Play button. C. Scenes button. D. Scene Marker button. E. Navigational button.

You need to know about these different designations because anytime you change a single item (say a Marker button), you can apply the same change to all items (all Marker buttons). However, this won't affect other button or text types (like Play or Navigational buttons). So if you wanted to change all text and buttons to the same color, you'd have to change all five categories to effect the change. Let's take a look.

1 Under Disc Menus in the Disc Layout workspace, click the Scenes Menu 1 thumbnail.

2 Click the Videos button. The Adjustments panel updates automatically and shows that this is a Scene Marker button. The Text subsection allows you to change the properties of the text.

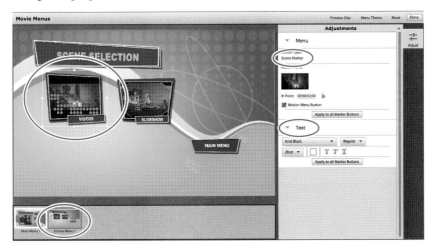

3 In the Text subsection, click the font menu, and note that you can change the font of this or any text in the menu. The Arial Black font looks fine here, so let's leave that selected.

4 Let's make the text a bit larger. Click the Change Text Size drop-down list beneath the font selector and choose 30 pt.

5 Next, let's change the color of the text to match the orange that was used in the opening title back in Lesson 8. To begin, click the white Change Text Color button next to the Text Size menu to open the Color Picker dialog. To select a color freestyle, click once in the color slider in the general range of the color that you're targeting, and then fine-tune your setting in the color field.

You can skip all that and directly enter the RGB colors, which are R: **242**, G: **174**, and B: **54**. Note that you can use the Tab key to move from value to value. Then click OK to apply the color.

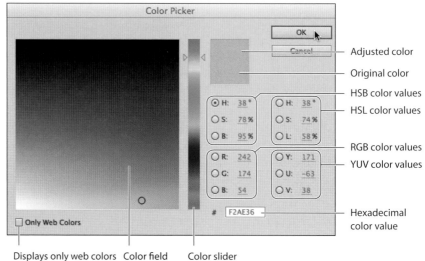

Displays only web colors Color field Color slider

Notice that the other Scene Marker button retained its original formatting. Normally, changes affect only the selected object. But Adobe Premiere Elements also gives you the option to change the text attributes of all buttons of the same type simultaneously.

6 In the Text subsection of the Adjustments panel, click the Apply to all Marker Buttons button. This applies the same text attributes to both Scene Marker buttons.

7   Under Disc Menus in the Disc Layout workspace, click the Main Menu 1 thumbnail. Notice that the Outtakes marker has also changed in its appearance. The reason is that the Marker Button category encompasses both Scene Marker and Main Menu Marker buttons. To fix this, you could change the Outtake button back to 30 pt white, or change the Play and Scenes buttons to match the new look.

8   Choose File > Save As and save this project file to your Lesson10 folder as **Lesson10_End.prel**.

Creating web DVDs

Web DVDs create the DVD experience within a web page, complete with menus, links, and high-quality video. If you have your own website or FTP access to some-one else's, you can create files to upload and present from there, and invite friends and family to watch it. This lesson will take you through the file-creation and upload workflows.

1   In the upper-right corner of the Disc Layout workspace, click Done to close the Disc Layout workspace and return to the main Adobe Premiere Elements workspace.

2   Save your current project. It's always a good idea to save your Adobe Premiere Elements project file before rendering your project.

3   In the upper-right corner of the main Adobe Premiere Elements workspace, click Publish+Share, and then click web DVD.

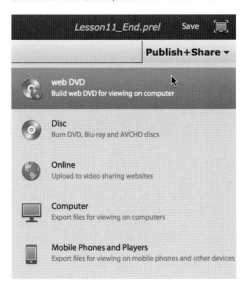

4 In the "web DVD: Choose location and settings" workspace, your only option is Save to folder on Computer.

Note: You can create SD web DVDs from HD content, but you shouldn't try to create HD web DVDs from SD content, because the video will likely look pixelated and/or blurry.

5 Choose the appropriate preset in the Presets list box. In this case, you have three choices: HD NTSC, SD High Quality NTSC, and SD Medium Quality NTSC. When you're choosing, try to select the quality level that best matches the connection speed of your intended viewers. Although HD provides the best overall quality, only viewers with fast connection speeds will be able to play the videos without stopping. SD High Quality NTSC is the best-quality, highest-bandwidth option in SD mode, and SD Medium Quality NTSC will create an experience that can be viewed most smoothly by the broadest range of viewers but will have the lowest frame quality.

● **Note:** After you choose a preset, Adobe Premiere Elements will display its parameters below the Presets list box. The HD NTSC preset uses a frame size of 1280x720 at 29.97 frames per second and will produce a presentation with a total size of 62.42 MB.

6 Type **Powering_The_Space_Shuttle** in the Project Name field.

7 Click the Browse button, and save the presentation in the Lesson10 folder.

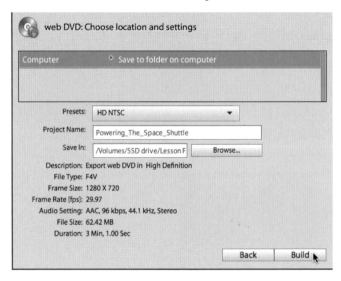

8 Click Build to continue. Adobe Premiere Elements will render the menus and content, and when complete, will display a Build Completed message with a clickable link to the content just saved to your hard drive. Click the link to display the web DVD in your browser.

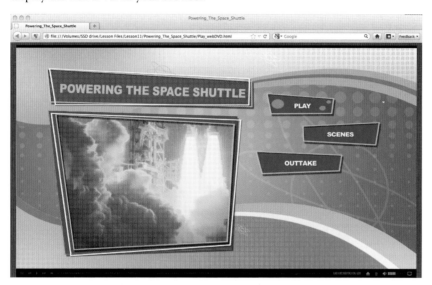

● **Note:** Rendering time will relate to the speed of your computer, but could take 5–10 minutes or longer. Check the Build in Progress screen to gauge time to completion.

9 Click open Windows Explorer (Windows) or File Manager (Mac OS), and navigate to the Powering_The_Space_Shuttle subfolder in the Lesson10 folder. Here you'll find the files that Adobe Premiere Elements just created. To make this presentation available on a website, you have to upload all of the files to a website and send your viewers a link to the Play_web DVD.html file. To do this, you need FTP access to a website and an FTP upload utility like Filezilla, which is free and available on Windows and Macintosh platforms.

▼ 📁 Powering_The_Space_Shuttle	Today, 9:32 AM	--	Folder
SCENE_MENU_1_over.png	Today, 9:32 AM	25 KB	Portable Network Graphics image
SCENE_MENU_1_down.png	Today, 9:32 AM	25 KB	Portable Network Graphics image
Play_webDVD.html	Today, 9:32 AM	4 KB	HTML Document
AuthoredContent.xml	Today, 9:32 AM	4 KB	XML Project Document
MAIN_MENU_1_over.png	Today, 9:32 AM	12 KB	Portable Network Graphics image
MAIN_MENU_1_down.png	Today, 9:32 AM	12 KB	Portable Network Graphics image
thumbnail.png	Today, 9:32 AM	360 KB	Portable Network Graphics image
Movie5.f4v	Today, 9:32 AM	9.5 MB	Flash video
Movie4.f4v	Today, 9:31 AM	2.7 MB	Flash video
Movie3.f4v	Today, 9:31 AM	12.7 MB	Flash video
Movie2.f4v	Today, 9:30 AM	17.3 MB	Flash video
Movie1.f4v	Today, 9:30 AM	995 KB	Flash video
SCENE_MENU_1.f4v	Today, 9:30 AM	6.2 MB	Flash video
MAIN_MENU_1.f4v	Today, 9:27 AM	6.4 MB	Flash video
flashdvd.swf	Jul 18, 2012 9:17 AM	127 KB	Shockwave Flash Movie

10 Here's a screen of Filezilla uploading the web DVD files to the PRE10 folder on my website at www.doceo.com. I created the PRE10 folder to reduce clutter on the root content directory on my website, but that's not essential. To play the web DVD, go to www.doceo.com/PRE11/Play_webDVD.html. I used the HD preset, so after clicking the link, wait a few moments for the necessary bits to download to your computer.

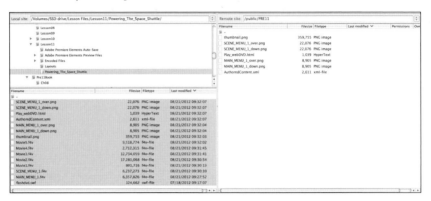

11 Click Done to close the web DVD window and return to Adobe Premiere Elements.

Burning DVD, Blu-ray, and AVCHD discs

After you've previewed your disc and have checked the menus and button names, you're ready to record the project to a DVD, AVCHD, or Blu-ray Disc. As noted at the beginning of this lesson, you must have a DVD recorder to produce a DVD or AVCHD disc, or a Blu-ray Disc writer to record a Blu-ray Disc.

When you're making any of these discs, Adobe Premiere Elements converts your video and audio files into a compressed format. Briefly, compression shrinks your original video and audio files to fit them on a disc. For example, a 60-minute video in AVCHD, DSLR, DV, or HDV format requires approximately 13 GB of hard disk space. However, a DVD-Video holds only 4.7 GB of space. So how do you fit a 13 GB video onto a 4.7 GB disc? Through compression!

Compressing video can take a long time, particularly if you're working from HD source material, so you should allow quite a bit of time for this process. For example, 60 minutes of video may take 4–6 hours to compress and record onto a DVD, and compressing and recording video onto a Blu-ray Disc can take even longer. For this reason, it may be a good idea to initiate the disc-burning process (which begins with compressing the video) at a time when you don't need your computer.

To maintain maximum quality, Adobe Premiere Elements compresses a movie only as much as is necessary to fit it on the disc. The shorter your movie, the less compression required, and the higher the quality of the video on the disc.

1   Save your current project. It's always a good idea to save your Adobe Premiere Elements project file before burning a disc.

2   In the upper-right corner of the main Adobe Premiere Elements workspace, click Publish+Share, and then select Disc.

3   Choose DVD at the top of the Disc: Choose location and settings panel. Encoding parameters for Blu-ray and AVCHD discs are covered in the sidebar, "Choosing Blu-ray and AVCHD disc quality options."

4   In the Burn to: drop-down list, choose Disc. If you don't have a disc recorder on your editing workstation, you can burn the project to a 4.7 or 8.5 GB folder, copy that folder to another computer with a recorder, and burn the content to disc there using another program.

5   In the Disc Name field, type **Space_Shuttle**. Software playing DVDs or Blu-ray Discs on a personal computer may display this disc name.

● **Note:** With AVCHD and Blu-ray Discs, you may be able to play content from a USB drive by plugging the drive into the USB port of a Blu-ray player. To create these files, burn your content to a folder and copy the content to the USB drive.

● **Note:** This exercise ends with the burning of a DVD. If you don't want to create a DVD, follow the steps of the exercise only up to the point of writing the disc. If you will be creating a DVD, I suggest using a DVD-RW or DVD+RW (rewritable) disc, if you have one available, so that you can reuse the disc later.

6 Select the desired DVD or Blu-ray Disc burner from the Burner Location menu. If you don't have a compatible disc burner connected to your computer, the Burner Location menu is disabled and the Status line reads "No burner detected."

7 If you want to create a DVD, AVCHD, or Blu-ray Disc, ensure that you've inserted a compatible blank or rewritable disc in the disc burner. If you insert a disc after you start this process, click Rescan to have Adobe Premiere Elements recheck all connected burners for valid media.

8 Next to Copies, select the number of discs you want to burn during this session. For this exercise, choose 1. When you select multiple copies, Adobe Premiere Elements prompts you to insert another disc after the writing of each disc is completed until all the discs you specified have been burned.

9 From the Presets menu, select the NTSC_Widescreen_Dolby DVD option. Adobe Premiere Elements is also capable of burning a project to the PAL standard (used in Europe, parts of Africa, South America, the Middle East, Australia, New Zealand, some Pacific Islands, and certain Asian countries) in normal or widescreen format.

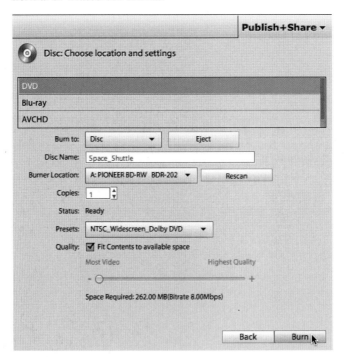

10 Select the "Fit Contents to available space" check box to ensure that Adobe Premiere Elements maximizes the quality of your video based on disc capacity.

11 If you want to burn a disc at this point, click the Burn button. If you don't want to burn a disc, click the Back button.

Choosing Blu-ray and AVCHD disc quality options

When you're burning to a Blu-ray or AVCHD disc, you have multiple resolution and video standard options. If you're producing your video for playback in the United States or Japan, choose NTSC; otherwise, choose PAL.

When you're choosing a target resolution, use the native resolution of your source footage. For example, HDV has a native resolution of 1440x1080, so if you recorded in HDV, you should produce your disc at that resolution. If you're shooting in AVCHD, you may be recording in native 1920x1080, so use that resolution for your disc. If you're not sure what resolution you're recording in, check the documentation that came with your camcorder. Ditto if you're shooting with a DSLR or other capture device.

Quality:	✓ H.264 1440x1080i NTSC Dolby
	H.264 1440x1080i PAL Dolby
	H.264 1920x1080i NTSC Dolby
	H.264 1920x1080i PAL Dolby

Congratulations! You've successfully completed this lesson. You learned how to manually and automatically add scene markers to your movie, create an auto-play disc, and—by applying a menu template—create a disc with menus. You added a submenu for an outtake clip and learned about stop and main menu markers. You customized the disc menus by changing text attributes, background images, button labels, and image thumbnails. You added sound and video clips to the menu background, and activated (and then deactivated) motion menu buttons. You created a web DVD to upload to the web and share with the world, and you learned how to burn your movie onto a DVD, Blu-ray, or AVCHD disc.

Review questions

1   What is an auto-play disc? What is one advantage and one disadvantage of creating such a disc?

2   How do you identify separate scenes for use in your disc menu?

3   What is a submenu, and how would you add one to your disc menu?

4   Which menu button text properties can you change, and how do you modify these properties?

5   Which type of menu template should you choose if you want to insert a still image or video file as a full-screen background for your disc menus?

6   What is a web DVD, and when should you use one?

7   What are the key benefits of burning an AVCHD disc?

Review answers

1   An auto-play disc allows you to create a DVD or Blu-ray Disc quickly from the main movie of your project. The advantage of an auto-play disc is that it can be quickly and easily created; the disadvantage is that it doesn't have a menu for navigation during playback.

2   Separate scenes can be defined by placing a scene marker on a specific frame in the timeline. You set scene markers in the timeline using the Add Menu Marker button.

3   A submenu is a button on your main disc menu that points to a specific section of your project, such as a credit sequence or a bonus clip. You create submenus by adding a main menu marker to your timeline.

4   You can change the font, size, color, and style of your text buttons. You change the properties of your text in the Adjustments panel for objects selected in the Disc Layout workspace.

5   You should choose a template that does not include a drop zone. If you insert a still image or video into a menu template with a drop zone, Adobe Premiere Elements will display that content within the drop zone.

6   A web DVD presents a DVD-like experience on the web, complete with menus, themes, and high-quality video. Use web DVDs to share your productions with friends and family without having to burn and send them a physical DVD.

7   The key benefit of an AVCHD disc is the ability to record HD video onto a standard DVD-Recordable or rewritable disc using a standard DVD recorder. The resulting disc will play only on a Blu-ray player.

11 SHARING MOVIES

Lesson overview

In this lesson, you'll learn how to send your completed video project to your digital media site or device of choice—for example, to YouTube or an iPad. You'll also learn the different ways you can export movies to view online or on a personal computer. Specifically, you'll learn how to do the following:

- Upload a video file to YouTube

- Export a video file for subsequent viewing from a hard drive

- Export a video file for viewing on an iPad

- Export a single frame as a still image

- Create a custom preset to save and reuse your favorite encoding parameters

Sharing movies works identically in Quick and Expert views, so you can choose the view you're most comfortable with to work through this lesson.

Just a final note: Adobe can supplement the list of presets and their configuration options dynamically online. So don't be surprised if the screens that you see when you perform these exercises have more presets and perhaps even different configuration options than are shown on these pages.

 This lesson will take approximately 1.5 hours.

Grabbing a frame of the video via the
Freeze Frame tool.

Sharing and exporting video

Apart from creating web DVDs, DVDs, or Blu-ray Discs, you can export and share movies, still images, and audio in a variety of file types for the web, computer playback, mobile devices, and even videotape. The Publish+Share panel is your starting point for exporting your finished project. Here you choose your target and configuration options.

Selecting any of the options opens a view in the panel that provides output-specific options and settings. The panel simplifies sharing and exporting by providing presets of the most commonly used formats and settings. With some presets, if you want to specify unique settings for any format, you can click Advanced options and make changes. Other formats, particularly those targeted at video sharing websites (online) and devices (mobile phones and players), may be locked down to ensure that your file conforms to the requirements of the target service or device.

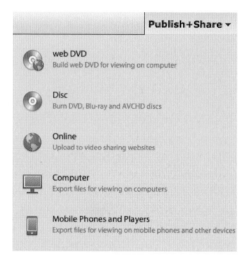

The first step for all sharing is choosing your desired target. The exercises in this lesson walk you through examples of the available targets in the Publish+Share panel.

Getting started

To begin, you'll launch Adobe Premiere Elements and open the project used for this lesson.

1   Make sure that you have correctly copied the Lesson11 folder from the DVD in the back of this book onto your computer's hard drive. See "Copying the Classroom in a Book files" in the "Getting Started" section at the start of this book.

2   Launch Adobe Premiere Elements. If it is already open, choose Help > Welcome Screen in the Adobe Premiere Elements menu to return to the Welcome screen.

3   In the Welcome screen, click Video Editor, select Existing Project, and then click the Open folder.

4 In the Open Project dialog, navigate to the Lesson11 folder you copied to your hard drive.

5 Within that folder, select the file Lesson11_Start_Win.prel (Windows) or Lesson11_Start_Mac.prel (Mac OS) and then click Open.

Your project file opens.

6 Choose Window > Restore Workspace to ensure that you start the lesson in the default panel layout.

Viewing the completed movie for the first exercise

To see what you'll be exporting in this lesson, press the spacebar to play the completed movie. If the movie looks familiar, that's because it's the project you finished back in Lesson 9 after adding a soundtrack and narration. Now it's time to share the fruits of your hard work with the world!

Rather than duplicating the project file and content from Lesson 9 to Lesson 11, I inserted the rendered file that you just played onto the timeline, because it simulates the Lesson 9 project completely and saves a few hundred megabytes on the DVD that accompanies this book. The experience will be *the same* as if you were working with the original content and project file.

Still, if you want to work with the original assets, you can load the Lesson09_Work.prel file that you created in Lesson 9 or load Lesson09_Start_Win.prel (Windows) or Lesson09_Start_Mac.prel (Mac OS) if you didn't work through that lesson. Obviously, those projects would be in the Lesson09 folder, not the Lesson11 folder. In your shoes, I would simply use the project file you currently have loaded, but feel free to work with the original content if that's your preference.

Uploading to YouTube

Adobe Premiere Elements provides presets for three online destinations—Facebook, Vimeo, and YouTube. The workflow is very similar for all of them: A simple wizard guides your efforts. In this exercise, you'll work through uploading to YouTube. It's faster if you already have an account with YouTube, but if not, you can sign up as part of the process. Follow these steps to upload your project to YouTube.

1 In the upper-right corner of the main Adobe Premiere Elements workspace, click Publish+Share (Publish+Share ▾), and then click Online. If this is your first time clicking this option, it may take Adobe Premiere Elements some time to download the presets.

2 Choose Upload video to YouTube.

Note: If you shot in 720p resolution with your AVCHD or DSLR camera, I recommend that you try uploading using both Flash Video for YouTube (widescreen) and High Definition Video for YouTube 1920x1080, and retaining the video that looks the best. Then again, by the time you work through this exercise, there might be a 720p output preset.

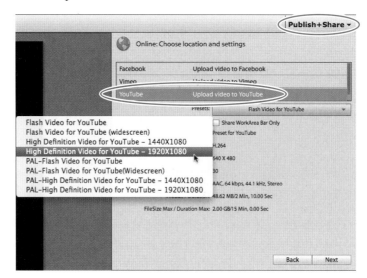

3 Choose the Flash Video for YouTube (Widescreen) preset. For your own projects, use Flash Video for YouTube for standard definition (SD) 4:3 projects and Flash Video for YouTube (widescreen) for (SD) 16:9 projects. To upload high-definition (HD) video to YouTube, choose the preset that matches your source footage, which will be High Definition Video for YouTube (1440x1080) for HDV and AVCHD camcorders that don't have the "FullHD" seal emblazoned on the side, and High Definition Video for YouTube 1920x1080 for most "FullHD" AVCHD camcorders and most DSLR cameras.

4 If desired, click the Share WorkArea Bar Only check box to upload only the Work Area bar. It's not shown in the figure because it's hidden behind the Preset drop-down list box, but you'll see it after selecting your preset.

5 Click Next.

6 Enter your YouTube username and password. If this is your first time uploading to YouTube, click Sign Up Now and register. Once you have a username and password, enter it on this screen.

7 Click Next.

8 Enter the required information about your project: Title, Description, Tags, and Category as shown in the figure on the right, and then click Next.

9 Choose whether you want to allow the public to view your project or to keep it private, and then click Share. Adobe Premiere Elements renders the project and starts uploading to YouTube. Status messages advise you of the progress during each step.

10 When the upload is complete, the URL appears in the Publish+Share panel. You can choose View My Shared Video to open YouTube and watch your video, or choose Send an E-mail to alert friends to your new posting.

11 Click Back to return to the Publish+Share panel.

Sharing on your personal computer

In the previous exercise, you exported an Adobe Premiere Elements project to YouTube. In this exercise, you'll export your project as a stand-alone video file to play on your own system, upload to a website, email to friends or family, or archive on DVD or an external hard drive.

As you'll see in a moment, Adobe Premiere Elements lets you output in multiple formats for all these activities. Each file format comes with its own set of presets available on the Presets menu. You can also customize a preset and save it for later reuse, which you'll do in this lesson.

See the sidebar "Choosing output formats" for more information on which preset to choose. In this exercise, you'll customize a preset and output a file using the QuickTime format.

1 In the upper-right corner of the main Adobe Premiere Elements workspace, click Publish+Share (Publish+Share ▾), and then click Computer.

2 In the list at the top of Share view, scroll down if necessary, and choose QuickTime.

3 In the Presets list box, choose NTSC DV 16:9. After you complete the lesson, the custom preset that you create will be available via this list box.

4 Enter **Lesson11_SharePC** in the File Name field, and then click Browse to select the Lesson11 folder as the "Save in" folder.

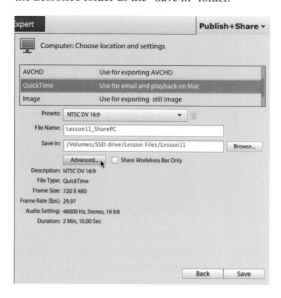

5 Click the Advanced button (Advanced...) below the "Save in" text box. Adobe Premiere Elements opens the Export Settings dialog.

The NTSC DV 16:9 preset is great if you want to edit the file further in a Mac-based program, but the files are too large to easily email to friends and family. You'll create a custom preset that creates more compact files.

6 To start, click the Video Codec list box and choose the H.264 codec.

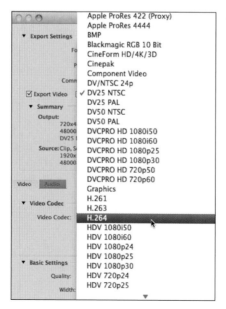

7 In the Basic Settings box, if a link icon appears in the box to the right of the Width and Height values, click the box to remove it, and then click and insert **640** in the Width text box and **360** in the Height text box. Then make the following selections to set the other parameters of your preset:

- Leave the Frame Rate at 29.97.

- Click the Field Type list box, and choose Progressive.

- Click the Aspect list box and choose Square Pixels (1.0).

● **Note:** Note the circled box in the figure next to Width and Height. When a link (⊟) appears in the box, Adobe Premiere Elements links the width and height to maintain the aspect ratio of the source footage. Most of the time, that's the right decision. But sometimes you'll want to change the aspect ratio, and if the link appears, Adobe Premiere Elements will automatically adjust the values in the height and width fields to maintain the aspect ratio, preventing you from entering the desired values. In these cases, simply click the link to disable this option. The box should not be selected when you're using the preset that you selected, but if it is, click the box to deselect it.

8 Scroll down in the Export Settings dialog and click the disclosure triangle next to Advanced Settings (if necessary) to reveal those controls. Leave all settings deselected.

9 Click the disclosure triangle next to Bitrate Settings (if necessary) to reveal that control. Select the "Limit data rate to" check box, click the text field, and type **3000**.

10 Click the Audio tab in the Export Settings dialog to open the Audio controls. In the Audio Codec list box, choose AAC, and conform the other settings to those shown in the figure on the right.

11 Click OK to close the Export Settings dialog; the Choose Name dialog opens. Type the title **H.264 640x360 3 Mbps preset** into the name field, and click OK to close the dialog.

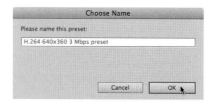

12 Back in the Publish+Share panel, note that Adobe Premiere Elements inserted the preset that you just created into the Presets list box, meaning that you'll produce the file using the parameters that you just selected. The next time you click that list box, the new preset will be available with the other custom presets.

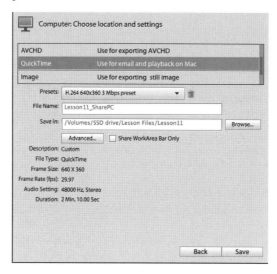

13 If desired, select the Share WorkArea Bar Only check box.

14 To start exporting your movie, click Save.

Adobe Premiere Elements begins rendering the video and displays a progress bar and an estimated time to complete the rendering process. Click Cancel at anytime to stop the exporting process. Otherwise, you'll see a Save Complete! message when the rendering is complete.

15 Click Back to return to the Publish+Share panel. To play the movie, open Windows Explorer (Windows) or File Manager (Mac OS), navigate to the file you just created, and double-click it. The default player for the MOV format, typically the QuickTime Player, should open and play the file.

Choosing output formats

The output format you choose is often dictated by how you plan to distribute your video, whether you're exporting it for user playback or further editing in other systems, or what kinds of computers your target audience will use to play it. Here's a rundown of the output formats available in Adobe Premiere Elements, how compatible they are with various playback environments, and where they're typically used:

- **Adobe Flash Video:** Adobe Flash Video is a very high-quality format that's used by the majority of sites on the Internet for playback via the ubiquitous Adobe Flash Player. Use this format if you're producing files to be distributed from a website. However, for playback from hard drives outside of the browser environment, the FLV files produced by this format require a stand-alone player that many viewers don't have. Accordingly, the format is not appropriate for creating files to view on other computers outside the browser environment, whether by email, file transfer protocol (FTP), or via a Universal Serial Bus (USB) drive.

- **MPEG:** MPEG is a widely supported playback format, although it is used almost exclusively for desktop or disc-based playback rather than for streaming. Use MPEG to create files for inserting into Blu-ray or DVD projects produced in other programs. For most casual hard drive-based playback, however, either QuickTime or Windows Media offers better quality at lower data rates, making each a better option for files shared via email or FTP.

- **AVCHD:** AVCHD is a high-definition format that you can burn to a DVD to play on a Blu-ray player (as you learned in Lesson 10). AVCHD is also a good choice for archiving a high-quality version of your edited video for long-term storage or for playing back on a computer that has software that can play AVCHD files. Although very high quality, AVCHD is not a good medium for sharing video files because the files are quite large and difficult to transfer.

- **AVI (Windows only—not available on the Mac version of Adobe Premiere Elements):** Use DV presets to archive standard-definition (SD) productions or to produce SD files for further editing in other programs. But note that DV AVI files are too large for casually distributing via email or FTP, and although many Mac OS programs can import AVI files, QuickTime is a better choice when you're planning to edit your projects further on the Mac platform. You can also access other AVI codecs via the Advanced button in the preset, but again, QuickTime is generally a better choice for distributing files because of near universal compatibility on both Windows and Macintosh computers.

- **Windows Media (Windows only—not available on the Mac version of Adobe Premiere Elements):** Windows Media files—whether distributed via a website, email, or FTP—can be played by virtually all Windows computers via the Windows Media Player. Quality is good at low bitrates, making Windows Media a good choice for producing files to be distributed via email to other Windows users. However, Macintosh compatibility may be a problem because Microsoft hasn't released a Windows Media Player for OS X, forcing users to download a third-party solution from Flip4Mac. When you're producing files for viewing on Macintosh computers, use the QuickTime format.

(continues on next page)

Choosing output formats *(continued)*

- **QuickTime:** QuickTime is the best choice for files intended for viewing on both Macintosh and Windows computers, whether distributed via the web, email, or other technique. All presets use the H.264 codec, which offers very good quality but can take a long time to render.

- **Image:** Use Image to export images from your project.

- **Audio:** Use Audio to export audio from your project.

When you're producing a file for uploading to a website like Yahoo Video or Blip.tv, check the required file specifications published by each site before producing your file. Typically, a QuickTime file using the H.264 codec offers the best blend of high quality at modest data rates and near universal compatibility.

Exporting to mobile phones and players

Adobe Premiere Elements also includes an option for producing files for mobile phones and players, such as the Apple iPod, iPad, and iPhone, and the Sony PlayStation Portable. Note that most of these devices have very specific and inflexible file and format requirements, so you shouldn't change any parameters in the Export Settings window, because you may produce a file that's unplayable on the target device.

In this exercise, you'll learn how to create a file for an iPad; if you're producing a file for a different device, just choose that device and preset in the appropriate steps.

1 In the upper-right corner of the main Adobe Premiere Elements workspace, click Publish+Share (Publish+Share), and then select Mobile Phones and Players.

2 In the list at the top of the Publish+Share panel, choose Apple iPod, iPad and iPhone.

3 In the Presets list box, choose a preset that matches your target device, aspect ratio (widescreen or standard), and desired output quality. Note that high-quality files produced for an iPad may not load on older iPhones or iPods. For the purposes of this exercise, choose Apple iPad Widescreen High Quality.

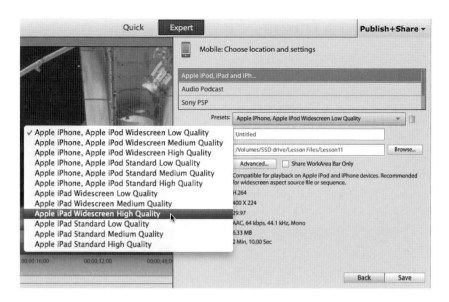

4 Next to File Name, enter **Lesson11_iPad**, and then click Browse to select your Lesson11 folder as the Save in folder.

5 If desired, select the Share WorkArea Bar Only check box.

6 To start exporting your movie, click Save.

Adobe Premiere Elements starts rendering the video and displays a progress bar and an estimated time to complete each phase of the rendering process. Click Cancel at anytime to stop the exporting process. Otherwise, you will see a Save Complete! message when the rendering is complete.

7 Click Back to return to the Publish+Share panel.

After producing the file, transfer it to your device in the appropriate manner. For example, use iTunes to upload the file to your iPod or iPhone.

● **Note:** If you produce your movies using video captured from DV or HDV tape, you may want to archive your project back to tape. For instruction regarding this process, search the Adobe Premiere Elements Help file for Sharing to Videotape.

Exporting a frame of video as a still image

Occasionally, you may want to grab frames from your video footage to email to friends and family, include in a slide show, or use for other purposes. In this exercise, you'll learn to export and save a frame from the project.

1 In the timeline, drag the current-time indicator to timecode 00;00;36;21, or click the current timecode box at the lower left of the Monitor panel, type **3621**, and press Enter (Windows) or Return (Mac OS).

2 In the Action bar on the bottom of the Adobe Premiere Elements interface, click Tools ( ), and then select Freeze Frame.

3 In the Freeze Frame dialog, click Export to create a separate still image, which is what you want to do here. Note the Insert in Movie option, which you would use to insert the frame into the movie if that's why you were grabbing the image. If you have Adobe Photoshop Elements installed, you can also select the check box to edit the captured frame in Adobe Photoshop Elements if you choose the Insert in Movie option.

4   In the Export Frame dialog, locate the Lesson11 folder and name your file **shuttle.bmp**. Click Save to save the still image to your hard drive and then close the Freeze Frame dialog.

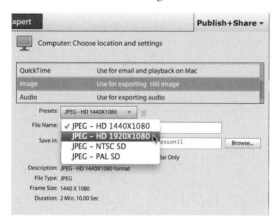

▶ **Tip:** The snapshot export function is very quick and easy but outputs only BMP files at the resolution of your current project. For more control over export size and formats, click Publish+Share, click Computer, and then choose Image, which exposes multiple presets that you can customize by clicking the Advanced button.

Congratulations! You've completed the penultimate lesson in this book! You've learned how to export your finished movies to YouTube, create compatible files for playback on iPads and other mobile devices, and compress movies in various formats for distribution via email and FTP and playback on Windows and Macintosh computers. And you've also learned how to grab still images from your video and export them in the format of your choice. On to Lesson 12, where you'll learn how to fine-tune and enhance those images in Adobe's companion program for still-image editing, Photoshop Elements.

Review questions

1 What's the best format to use for creating files to view on Windows computers or to share with other viewers with Windows computers?

2 Why shouldn't you change any encoding parameters for files produced for iPods or other devices?

3 What's the easiest way to write a project to an analog tape format, such as VHS?

4 What's the easiest way to upload your movie to a website, such as YouTube or Facebook?

5 When might you want to export a file into AVCHD format?

Review answers

1   Windows Media is the best format for Windows because it combines small file size with high quality. Although virtually all computers can play MPEG-1 or MPEG-2 files, the files are usually too large for easy transport. QuickTime files may pose a problem because not all Windows computers support QuickTime (but most do), and Adobe Flash Video files with a .flv extension require a stand-alone player, which not all computers have installed.

2   Devices have very specific playback requirements, and if you change a file parameter and deviate from these requirements, the file may not load or play on the target device.

3   Connect a VHS recorder to your DV camcorder via composite or S-Video connectors plus audio while writing your project to DV tape. Most DV camcorders will display the recorded signal out the analog ports while recording, which you can record on the VHS deck by pressing the Record button on the deck.

4   Open the Publish+Share panel, and then click the Online button. Choose YouTube, Facebook, or Vimeo, and then follow the instructions for your selected destination site to render and upload your movie.

5   You might want to export a file into AVCHD format for subsequent burning to a Blu-ray Disc or as a high-quality archive of the project.

12 WORKING WITH ADOBE PHOTOSHOP ELEMENTS

Lesson overview

Adobe Photoshop Elements and Adobe Premiere Elements are designed to work together and let you seamlessly combine digital photography and video editing. You can spice up your video projects with title images created in Adobe Photoshop Elements, or select images in the Elements Organizer and send them to Adobe Premiere Elements to create a slide show.

To work on the following exercises, you must have Adobe Photoshop Elements installed on your system. In this lesson, you will learn several techniques for using Adobe Photoshop Elements together with Adobe Premiere Elements. Specifically, you'll learn how to do the following:

- Add single and multiple images from the Elements Organizer to an Adobe Premiere Elements project

- Create a Photoshop file optimized for video

- Edit a Photoshop image from within Adobe Premiere Elements

 This lesson will take approximately one hour.

A cool text title created in Adobe Photoshop Elements
for use in Adobe Premiere Elements.

Viewing the completed movie before you start

To see what you'll be creating, let's take a look at the completed movie.

1   Before you begin, make sure that you have correctly copied the Lesson12 folder from the DVD in the back of this book onto your computer's hard drive. See "Copying the Classroom in a Book files" in the "Getting Started" section at the start of this book.

2   Navigate to the Lesson12 folder, and double-click Lesson12_Movie.mov to play the movie in your default application for watching QuickTime files.

Getting started

You'll now open Adobe Photoshop Elements 11 and import the files needed for the Lesson12 project. Then you'll create an Adobe Premiere Elements project from images, much like you created a video project using videos back in Lesson 1. Let's review that procedure quickly in this exercise.

Briefly, if you have a project open in Adobe Premiere Elements when you use this technique, the Organizer will add the selected files to the current project at the end of the current timeline. If no project is open, the Organizer will create a new project, which is the workflow you'll follow in this exercise. Accordingly, if you have a project open in Adobe Premiere Elements, please close it (after saving if necessary) before starting this exercise.

To sort images in the Organizer, Adobe Photoshop Elements uses the date and time information embedded in the image file by the digital camera. In the Organizer menu, choosing to show the newest files first by selecting Sort By: Newest enables you to create a slide show in chronological order when transferring the photos to Adobe Premiere Elements.

1   Launch Adobe Photoshop Elements. If it is already open, click Help > Welcome screen in the Adobe Photoshop Elements menu to open the Welcome screen.

2   In the Welcome screen, click the Organizer button to open the Elements Organizer.

3   If you've previously used Adobe Photoshop Elements, your Organizer may be displaying the photos in your current catalog. If this is the first time you've launched Adobe Photoshop Elements, you may receive a message asking if you want to designate a location to look for your image files. Click No to close the dialog.

4   Choose File > Get Photos and Videos > From Files and Folders. Navigate to your Lesson12 folder and select—but do not open—the Images subfolder. Then click Get Media. Adobe Photoshop Elements imports the photos.

5   If a message appears telling you that only the newly imported files will appear, click OK. In the Organizer, you should see seven images from the Space Shuttle project. Thumbnail images are small versions of the full-size photos. You'll be working with the full-size photos later in this lesson.

6 Take these steps to make sure your Organizer looks the same as the figure:

- In the Organizer menu, choose View > Media Types. Make sure Photos, Video, and Audio are all selected.

- Choose View > Details, View > File Names, and View > Grid Lines to show these elements.

- In the Sort By list box on top of the Organizer's media browser, make sure Newest is selected.

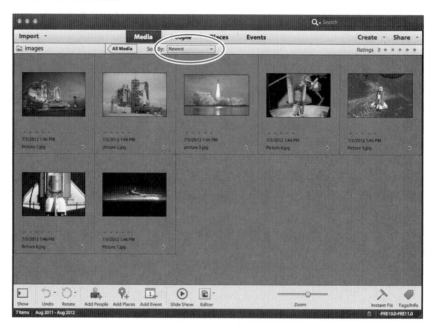

7 Press and hold the Ctrl (Windows) or Command (Mac OS) key, and then in the Photo Browser click the first six images to select them (Picture 1.jpg–Picture 6.jpg). The Organizer highlights the gray area around the thumbnail to indicate a selected image.

8 In the Tools panel on the bottom of the Organizer, click the down triangle next to the Editor icon, and choose Video Editor. A dialog will appear informing you that the files will be inserted at the end of your timeline and that the Adobe Premiere Elements defaults will be used. Click OK. If Adobe Premiere Elements is not already open, it will launch automatically.

An Adobe Premiere Elements project is created, and the images you selected in Adobe Photoshop Elements are now visible in the timeline. The first image is displayed in the Monitor panel. If desired, click the backslash key (\) to spread the images over the open timeline.

● **Note:** Although you might assume that the total length of the slide show is equal to the number of images multiplied by the default duration for still images, it's actually less than that. The reason is that Adobe Premiere Elements inserts the transition effect between the images by overlapping the clips by the default length of the transition effect. Note that you can change the default still image duration and transition duration in the Adobe Premiere Elements Preferences panel. See the section "Working with project preferences" in Lesson 2 for more details.

9 Select all scenes in the timeline and choose Clip > Group to place the entire group onto one target that can be moved as a single clip. Then choose Clip > Ungroup to treat each still image as its own scene in the timeline.

10 Press the spacebar to play your project. Adobe Premiere Elements uses the default duration of five seconds for each still image and applies a cross-dissolve as the default transition between each clip.

11 Return to the Organizer by clicking the Organizer button on the lower left of the Adobe Premiere Elements interface or by holding down the Alt (Windows) or Command (Mac OS) key and pressing Tab until you see the icon for the Elements Organizer. Release the Alt (Windows) or Command (Mac OS) key. The Elements Organizer opens.

● **Note:** Because
you're sending only
a single image from
Adobe Photoshop
Elements to Adobe
Premiere Elements, no
transition has been
placed on the image. In
this case, if you wanted
to add a transition, you
would have to do so
manually, but do not
add one at this time.
See Lesson 7 for more
information about
adding transitions.

12 Click to select only one image, the one named Picture 7.jpg, and then choose
Edit > Edit with Premiere Elements Editor in the Organizer menu. Click OK to
close the Edit with Premiere Elements dialog if it appears. Click No in the Smart
Fix dialog and do not fix the quality problems. Your open application should
switch to Adobe Premiere Elements, and the image will be placed at the end of
your timeline.

13 Choose File > Save As and save this project file in your Lesson12 folder as
Lesson12_Work.prel.

Creating a new Photoshop file optimized for video

The first part of this lesson focused on importing image files from the Organizer
into Adobe Premiere Elements. In this exercise, you'll create a new still image and
modify it in Adobe Photoshop Elements, and then use it in your Adobe Premiere
Elements project.

1 Make sure you're in Adobe Photoshop Elements. Choose File > New > Blank
File. In the New file dialog, type **Title**. Then click the Preset list box and choose
Film & Video.

2 Click the Size list box and choose HDTV 1080p, which matches the resolution
of the project you should have open in Adobe Premiere Elements. If you're
working on a different project, choose the size that matches the resolution of
your Adobe Premiere Elements project. If you don't know or have forgotten
the resolution of the project, click Edit > Project Settings > General in Adobe
Premiere Elements to view your project settings.

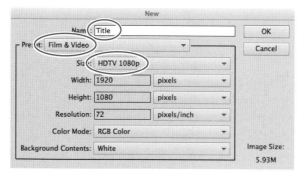

3 Click OK to create the file.

4 Now let's save the file in the Lesson12 folder. Choose File > Save As, and in
the Save As dialog, check to make sure that you named the file **Title.psd**; then
navigate to your Lesson12 folder and click Save.

Customizing a title in Adobe Photoshop Elements

Now you have your Photoshop file. Next, you'll add the background that you captured in the previous lesson, customize the background, and then add some text.

1   On the top of the Editor, make sure Expert (**Expert**) is selected.

2   If necessary, in the top menu, choose View > Guides to hide the title and action safe guides, which you don't need because you're not producing a DVD with this project or otherwise producing a file that will be viewed on a television set.

3   In Adobe Photoshop Elements, choose File > Open. The Open dialog opens. Navigate to the Lesson12 folder on your hard drive, choose shuttle.bmp, and click Open to load the image into Adobe Photoshop Elements.

4   In the Adobe Photoshop Elements menu, choose Select > All to select the image, and then choose Edit > Copy to copy the image to the clipboard.

5   Click Title.psd to make it active, and choose Edit > Paste to paste the copied shuttle.bmp image into Title.psd. If you see an error message about the background of the image being locked, click OK to enable the paste.

6   You may need to adjust the size of the pasted image to fit Title.psd, which you accomplish by clicking and dragging any of the eight small squares on the edges and sides of the bounding box. Position the image so that it fills the white area. Then click the Commit Current Operation check mark on the lower right to set the adjustment.

7 On the bottom right of the Adobe Photoshop Elements interface, click Effects (🖼) to open that panel. On the upper right of the Adobe Photoshop Elements interface, click Filters, and select Sketch in the drop-down list.

8 Drag the Halftone Pattern effect onto Title.psd and release. Adobe Photoshop Elements applies the effect to the image.

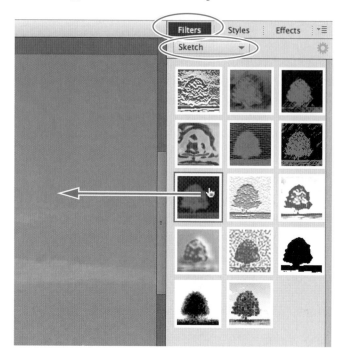

9 Let's add a text title to Title.psd. Click the Horizontal Type Text (T) tool in the Draw section of the Tools panel on the extreme left.

10 In the Text tool options bar, choose the Lithos Pro style at 72 pt, center the text alignment, and leave the color of the text black. If you don't have that font on your system, choose a different font that delivers the same *je ne sais quoi*.

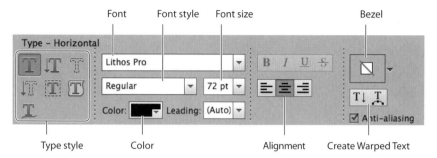

11 Click the image to the right of the shuttle and type **Powering The** (two carriage returns) **Space** (carriage return) **Shuttle**.

12 Highlight the words Space Shuttle and change the font size to 130 pt. Note that you'll have to type in **130** because the largest size in the drop-down list is 72 pt.

13 Click the Move tool (✛) in the toolbox to return to the selection arrow. Position the text to approximately where it's shown in the figure (if necessary). Now let's make the text more legible. To do this, right-click the text box and choose Edit Layer Style. The Style Settings dialog opens.

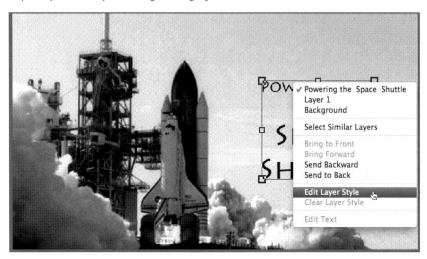

14 Let's make several adjustments in the Style Settings dialog:

- Click the Drop Shadow box to add a drop shadow.

- Add a stroke by selecting the Stroke check box.

- Click the color chip next to the stroke controls to open the Select stroke color dialog. In the RGB values, type R: **242**, G: **174**, B: **54**, which is the orange color you used when creating the opening title. Then click OK to close the Select stroke color dialog.

- Click OK to close the Style Settings dialog.

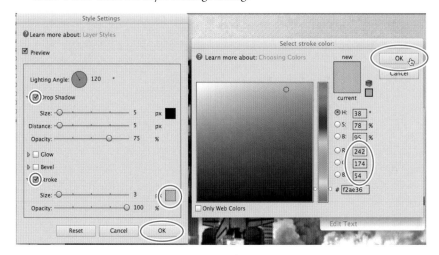

The text is much more legible and distinctive. Now let's warp the text.

15 Double-click the text box to select all text, and then click the Create Warped Text icon on the Type Tools panel.

16 In the Warp Text dialog, click the Style drop-down list and choose Inflate. Make sure that Bend is set to +50. Then Click OK to close the dialog.

17 OK, that's enough for now. Choose File > Save to save Title.psd.

18 Switch to Adobe Premiere Elements by holding down the Alt (Windows) or Command (Mac OS) key and pressing Tab until you see the icon for Adobe Premiere Elements. Release the Alt (Windows) or Command (Mac OS) key and Adobe Premiere Elements opens.

19 Now let's import the file into Adobe Premiere Elements. Make sure that you're in Expert view. Then click the Add Media button and choose Files and folders. The Add Media dialog opens. Navigate to the Lesson12 folder, click to select Title.psd, and click Open (Windows) or Import (Mac OS). Adobe Premiere Elements imports the file and displays it in the Project Assets panel, although you may need to drag the slider on the right down to see the imported file.

20 Drag Title.psd from the Project Assets panel to the beginning of the movie, waiting for about two seconds for the other images to shift to the right. Then release the pointer. If Adobe Premiere Elements opens the Smart Fix dialog, click No.

Adobe Premiere Elements inserts Title.psd at the start of the movie and shifts all other content to the right.

21 Save your work.

Editing a Photoshop image in Adobe Photoshop Elements

You can edit an Adobe Photoshop Elements image (or any image for that matter) while you're working in Adobe Premiere Elements by using the Edit in Photoshop Elements command. Once you save your image, changes you make to the image in Adobe Photoshop Elements will be updated in Adobe Premiere Elements, even if the clip is already placed in your timeline. That orange isn't working for me; let's go all gray.

1 Right-click the Title.psd clip in the timeline and choose Edit in Adobe Photoshop Elements. The Title.psd file opens in Adobe Photoshop Elements.

2 If necessary, click the Move tool (✛) in the toolbox to choose the selection arrow. Then right-click the text box and choose Edit Layer Style.

3 In the Style Settings dialog, click the color chip next to the stroke controls to open the Select stroke color dialog. Change the RGB values to R: **240**, G: **240**, B: **240**. Then click OK to close the Select stroke color dialog, and click OK again to close the Style Settings dialog.

4 Choose File > Save As. Click the file Title.psd in the Lesson12 folder. In the Save As dialog, deselect the Save in Version Set with Original check box. Click Save and then click OK (Windows) or Replace (Mac OS) to overwrite Title.psd. Then switch to Adobe Premiere Elements.

The changes made to the Title.psd file in Adobe Photoshop Elements have automatically been updated in the Adobe Premiere Elements project. This is very useful because it eliminates the need to re-import an image file every time a change is made.

5 Click the top of the timeline to select it, and then press the Home key to place the current-time indicator at the beginning of the timeline. Press the spacebar to play your project. When you're finished reviewing, save your work.

Congratulations! You've finished the lesson on working with Adobe Photoshop Elements. You've discovered how to get photos from the Organizer to Adobe Premiere Elements and how to enhance them using Adobe Photoshop Elements. You've also learned how to create a title in Adobe Photoshop Elements for use in Adobe Premiere Elements.

This is the last lesson in this book. We hope that you have gained confidence in using Adobe Premiere Elements 11, developed some new skills, and increased your knowledge of the product and the many creative things you can accomplish with it.

But this book is just the beginning. You can learn more by studying the Adobe Premiere Elements 11 Help system that is built into the application. Simply choose Help > Adobe Premiere Elements Help and browse or use the search functionality to find what you need. Also, don't forget to look for tutorials, tips, and expert advice on the Adobe Systems website at www.adobe.com.

Review questions

1 What's the best way to make sure that an image you create in Adobe Photoshop Elements matches the video that you'll be adding it to?

2 How can you edit an image included in an Adobe Premiere Elements project in Adobe Photoshop Elements?

3 What are the advantages of creating your titles and editing your images in Adobe Photoshop Elements compared to Adobe Premiere Elements?

Review answers

1 Make sure that you create the file using the same dimensions as your video project.

2 Right-click the image in the Adobe Premiere Elements timeline and choose Edit in Adobe Photoshop Elements.

3 Adobe Photoshop Elements has many more still image effects and several more advanced text-related adjustments than Adobe Premiere Elements.

INDEX

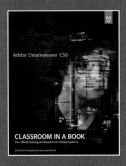

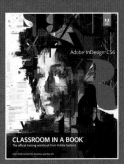